Leaders and Supe in Child Care Programs

D0825717

Early Childhood Education
providing lessons for life

www.EarlyChildEd.delmar.cengage.com

Leaders and Supervisors in Child Care Programs

Dorothy June Sciarra, Ed.D.
University of Cincinnati

Anne G. Dorsey, M.Ed.
University of Cincinnati

DELMAR
CENGAGE Learning™

Australia • Brazil • Japan • Korea • Mexico • Singapore • Spain • United Kingdom • United States

Leaders and Supervisors in Child Care Programs
Dorothy June Sciarra, Anne G. Dorsey

Business Unit Director: Susan L. Simpfenderfer

Executive Editor: Marlene McHugh Pratt

Acquisitions Editor: Erin O'Connor Traylor

Developmental Editor: Melissa Riveglia

Editorial Assistant: Alexis Ferraro

Executive Production Manager:
  Wendy A. Troeger

Production Editor: J. P. Henkel

Technology Project Manager: James Considine

Executive Marketing Manager: Donna J. Lewis

Channel Manager: Nigar Hale

Cover Design: Judi Orozco

© 2002 Delmar, Cengage Learning

ALL RIGHTS RESERVED. No part of this work covered by the copyright herein may be reproduced, transmitted, stored or used in any form or by any means graphic, electronic, or mechanical, including but not limited to photocopying, recording, scanning, digitizing, taping, Web distribution, information networks, or information storage and retrieval systems, except as permitted under Section 107 or 108 of the 1976 United States Copyright Act, without the prior written permission of the publisher.

For product information and technology assistance, contact us at
Cengage Learning Customer & Sales Support, 1-800-354-9706

For permission to use material from this text or product,
submit all requests online at **www.cengage.com/permissions**
Further permissions questions can be emailed to
permissionrequest@cengage.com

Library of Congress Control Number: 2001028011

ISBN-13: 978-0-7668-2577-2

ISBN-10: 0-7668-2577-9

Delmar
Executive Woods
5 Maxwell Drive
Clifton Park, NY 12065
USA

Cengage Learning is a leading provider of customized learning solutions with office locations around the globe, including Singapore, the United Kingdom, Australia, Mexico, Brazil, and Japan. Locate your local office at **www.cengage.com/global**

Cengage Learning products are represented in Canada by Nelson Education, Ltd.

To learn more about Delmar, visit **www.cengage.com/delmar**

Purchase any of our products at your local college store or at our preferred online store **www.cengagebrain.com**

Notice to the Reader

Publisher does not warrant or guarantee any of the products described herein or perform any independent analysis in connection with any of the product information contained herein. Publisher does not assume, and expressly disclaims, any obligation to obtain and include information other than that provided to it by the manufacturer. The reader is expressly warned to consider and adopt all safety precautions that might be indicated by the activities described herein and to avoid all potential hazards. By following the instructions contained herein, the reader willingly assumes all risks in connection with such instructions. The publisher makes no representations or warranties of any kind, including but not limited to, the warranties of fitness for particular purpose or merchantability, nor are any such representations implied with respect to the material set forth herein, and the publisher takes no responsibility with respect to such material. The publisher shall not be liable for any special, consequential, or exemplary damages resulting, in whole or part, from the readers' use of, or reliance upon, this material.

Printed in the United States of America
10 11 12 13 16 15 14 13 12

CONTENTS

SECTION III   THE LEADER IN ACTION — 185

Chapter 7   The Leader as a Change Agent — 187

Chapter 8   **The Leader As a Professional**   **209**

Preface

This book is about leadership and supervision in the field of child care and early childhood education. Although there are over a thousand books on the subject of leadership and many on supervision, few address leaders who work in programs for young children.

Several groups will find this book valuable:

- students in an associate or baccalaureate degree program in child care or early childhood education
- students in masters degree programs who are seeking a directorship credential
- students enrolled in distance learning programs
- individuals who are currently managers or leaders in programs for young children and their families
- board members who may have limited knowledge of the professional field and who are interested in providing compatible support to directors.

Some faculty may choose to use this book as a companion to the basic administration text, *Developing and Administering a Child Care Center, 4th edition,* also by Sciarra and Dorsey. Such usage provides new descriptive material on leadership and detailed coverage of the entire supervisory process. Both of these areas and their subtopics are of particular interest in the profession today.

The book is divided into three sections. Section I, Describing the Leader, provides background on leadership and the roles leaders assume. Each of the two chapters brings principles from business and applies them specifically to the business of child care. In Section II, Supervision 101, four chapters provide step-by-step information and ideas for an effective supervisory program. The staff orientation process receives special attention because it is viewed as a critical element of the supervisory process. Because directors often move into their positions from the teaching ranks, they may have limited opportunities to learn about supervision from that perspective and may have focused on the perspectives they held as teachers. These four chapters help directors move toward their new roles with specificity that they can adopt or adapt to their own circumstances. Finally, Section III, The Leader in Action, considers advanced aspects of the leader's role. Two chapters are devoted to the leader's roles as a change agent and as a professional. The latter focuses on the need for keeping current, for becoming an advocate, and for addressing ethical issues.

Because many of the concepts of the book are abstract, special features are designed to make it more readable and more meaningful. These features include:

- Scenarios, descriptions of directors and their roles, usually involving a particular challenge. Readers are asked to consider the approach taken by the characters in the scenarios and to analyze the scenario in terms of the text in that chapter.
- Reflections, opportunities for readers to consider their own perspectives on leadership ideas and principles. Readers are guided to think about their personal beliefs and to relate them to their current or future roles as leaders.
- Leader's Corners present a description of a leadership situation in the words of a director who had experienced that situation. These reports bring the real world of leading to the forefront.
- Class Exercises, activities which a faculty member may use (or modify) and have students complete in class
- Class Assignments, work that faculty may assign (or modify) to encourage students to move beyond the text and class material
- Working Papers, documents which can be used by working directors or can be completed by students in order to have a record of their understanding of textual material
- Leader's Resources, material specific to the profession that leaders can photocopy and use in their work
- Leader's Library, annotated print- and technology-based resources

Before beginning to read this text, students may find it helpful to familiarize themselves with the special features listed above. As you read, be sure to pause to use the Reflections. Considering your own ideas will provide depth to your understanding and will give you opportunities to decide whether you agree or disagree with materials presented and why. Because you will bring your beliefs to your leadership role, it is essential that you have a deep understanding of your own beliefs, rather than assuming that you have already thought seriously about all the facets of leadership.

Today, as more and more young children are receiving services from a wide range of agencies, we must prepare strong, knowledgeable, ethical leaders for those organizations. We hope that you will become successfully involved in such a role.

Acknowledgements

We gratefully acknowledge the cooperation, assistance and ideas we obtained from Chris Burroughs, Rene Daniels, Verline Dotson, Lisa Garofalo, Patricia Gleason, Cynthia Heinrich, Chris Kelly, Eila Roark, Denise Schnurr, Aimee Tillar, Sally Wehby, and Barbara Whitfield. We also appreciate the professional expertise of Erin O'Connor Traylor, Melissa Riveglia and Alexis Ferraro, of Delmar, Cengage Learning. The guidance of these women has helped make the book richer and more relevant to students and working leaders. We also acknowledge Vassar College for the use of their photos.

The authors and Delmar would also like to thank the reviewers for their many helpful comments.

Billie L. Armstrong
Mother's Helper Child Care & Learning Center
Columbia, North Carolina

Nancy Baptiste, EdD
New Mexico State University
Las Cruces, New Mexico

Toni Cacace-Beshears, MS
Tidewater Community College
Portsmouth, Virginia

Elaine Camerin, EdD
Daytona Beach Community College
Daytona Beach, Florida

Margaret King, EdD
Ohio University
Athens, Ohio

Nina Mazloff, MS
Becker College
Holden, Massachusetts

Mary Clare Munger
Amarillo College
Amarillo, Texas

Please note that internet resources are of a time sensitive nature and URL sites and addresses may often be modified or deleted.

Describing the Leader

CHAPTER 1

Understanding the Leader's Roles

8:00 A.M.: Kendra clicked on her office light and took a stack of folders from her brief-case. She'd work on them from 9:30 until 11:00. Mentally reviewing the day ahead, she knew that at one o'clock she'd be meeting with two of the staff, a teacher and an assistant. They had volunteered to begin the development of a marketing plan for the center based on the unique approach the staff uses. At 2:00, she'd be meeting with the cook, Sherlene, to discuss with her why USDA had required menu changes. She'd have to take a firm approach. Sherlene was used to her own style of cooking and didn't yet see the value in the balanced diet that the center supported. But Kendra also wanted to help the cook recognize her role as part of the staff. At three o'clock four leaders from other centers would be coming to her office. Together they planned to approach the local human services department with their concerns about the low reimbursement rate for child care services. Although the five of them were competing for the same dollars, they had

realized that a group approach would be more effective than trying to influence the department individually. Still it seemed risky.

As Kendra headed out to say good morning to each staff member, she smiled. Being director was indeed the right job for her and, barring unexpected challenges, it could prove to be a pretty good day.

Across town at the Mead Valley Child Development Center, Mindy clicked on her office light at 8:00 A.M. She removed a stack of folders from her briefcase and began working on the menus for next week. She wished the cook could do them, but she probably wouldn't get them right and then Mindy would just have to do them over. She paused and smiled to herself. She had an important surprise for the staff. She hadn't wanted to tell them she was applying for a Whitfield Foundation grant for playground equipment. Now that she knew that it was approved, she had placed the equipment orders, and delivery would be in two weeks—now she could tell them. Maybe later she would have time to see what was going on in the classrooms. She wondered how the two new teachers were getting along.

Mindy returned to menu planning, cheered by her realization that she was doing a good job of getting resources for the center even though the overall center budget was often overspent. Yes, she thought, I'm in the right job.

Kendra and Mindy are both directors. Both feel positive about their roles and about ways in which they are implementing them. Yet, there are major differences. Reread these vignettes and think about what the differences might be. What are the pros and cons of each approach?

Perhaps you noticed that both Kendra and Mindy seem happy in their jobs despite the heavy schedules each of them follows. However, also of major importance is the response of staff members to the director. Consider how Kendra's staff might feel under each of the circumstances listed in Figure 1–1 and how Mindy's staff might respond under the circumstances listed in Figure 1–2.

What do you think will happen when a director firmly tells a staff member what is expected? Would it be preferable to do parts of the staff member's job for them? Certainly, you have been given very little information about Kendra and Mindy, but you can begin to see some differences emerging. In Chapter 1, we will examine these differences and what they might mean to an organization.

Leadership in Early Childhood Education

Although over 1000 books on leadership are currently available, very few specifically address the early childhood director and other related fields. Nonetheless, child care is a

1. Kendra meets with a teacher and an assistant to work on center marketing plan.
2. Kendra firmly explains USDA requirements to the cook while working to emphasize the cook's role as part of the staff.
3. Kendra works with other directors to get increased funding.
4. Kendra makes a point of saying good morning to each staff member.

Figure 1–1 Kendra's Role

1. Mindy takes over part of the cook's job because the cook is not doing it correctly.
2. Mindy applied for a grant without telling the staff.
3. Mindy selected new equipment without staff input.
4. Mindy goes to classrooms if she has time.

Figure 1–2 Mindy's Role

business, and as such, needs a business leader. Furthermore, leaders in our field must work with a variety of business leaders, such as foundation officers, bankers, and contractors. They also work with school administrators, attorneys, legislators, and product suppliers. Early childhood education leaders must understand the business perspective on leadership and management in order to interface with their peers. As you continue reading this chapter, you will learn about the differences between leaders and managers. It will become apparent that you, as a director, may find it easy to see yourself as a leader, or you may find that you first have to practice as a manager and then mature into a leader in your position in our profession. You'll read about the differences in this chapter.

Early childhood education directors who have the leadership characteristics find that they are able to create more successful child care businesses. Keep in mind that success in child care means a balanced budget and a smooth operation in terms of business practices, but equally important is the well-being of the children, families, and staff. Early childhood education directors who have not yet recognized the importance of developing their own leadership to enhance staff motivation and involvement and to be proactive and creative in their work with parents and children will find that the business field has jumped ahead and is working hard to build a participative climate on the job.

Successful early childhood leaders are likely to obtain results that parallel those of business leaders in other fields. These results include:

- increased productivity
- more satisfied clients
- improved financial position

Increased productivity in early childhood education means that children have better quality interactions with teachers and that more of their time is spent in interesting, worthwhile learning. It means that teachers continue to develop professionally.

More satisfied clients refers to families of children enrolled at the center as well as to the children themselves. Centers with successful leaders are more likely to have clients who feel positive about the program and staff.

Improved financial position may occur as a result of better organization and management under a successful leader. More initiatives that produce grants or improved funding also may be a factor. However, in our culture today it is challenging to find leaders who are able to provide the kind of financial picture that allows them to do what should be done in terms of staff salaries in particular. This condition is affected by attitudes toward programs for young children. To date, these programs have not been seen as important as programs for older children in terms of funding.

In reviewing research evidence, Mitchell (1997) found that a limited number of early childhood studies pointed directly to leadership as a factor in high-quality children's programs. Mitchell also found that the factors that lead to high quality such as teacher's educational backgrounds, working conditions, and environmental factors (teacher-child ratios, group size, materials and equipment) do seem to be affected by the quality of leadership.

Defining Leadership

The business and social science literature contains almost as many definitions of leadership as there are books on the topic. Let us look at several definitions.

- "Leadership is a combination of traits and skills forming a personality with distinctive characteristics that cause others to trust and follow or collaborate with that leader. Leadership is the ability to cause others to perform at high levels for the good of the overall organization" (Dorsey, 1999).
- "Leadership is the ability to influence others, especially in getting others to reach challenging goals" (Chapman & O'Neil, 2000, p. 2).
- "Leadership is not so much a function of the individual leader as it is a condition of the culture . . . . Leadership is the task of creating harmony among the disparate, sometimes competing, organizational human, system, and program factions. It is a task of culture creation more than of development of charisma. It is an expression of community. It is a task of generalizing values and principles of action in ways that all stakeholders will find acceptable and energizing . . . . Leadership is the exercise of values that give preference to democratic participation in the joint enterprise" (Fairholm, 1994, pp. 7-8).
- Leadership is the facilitation of constructivist reciprocal processes among participants in an educational community (Lambert et al, 1995, p. 44).
- Leadership is "the ability to influence, inspire, motivate, or affect the thoughts, feelings, and actions of others . . . . [It] is sustained influence over others, shaping the course of events and bending the will of others by word or personal example" (Espinosa, 1997, p. 97).

Two of the themes that stand out in these definitions are:

1. involvement of staff as well as of the leader
2. the essential element of change

First, we can assume that leadership involves at least two people, one to lead and one to follow. If no one is willing to follow, then there can be no leader. Thus, part of the leader's role is to motivate others to follow. Leaders must, in some manner, influence the prospective followers so that they will become actual followers. Leaders must also guide followers to work toward the changes described in the organization's vision statement. This premise implies that the leaders are persons with vision and have inspired their followers to work together and with their leaders to create a vision for the organization. Considering these factors, leadership becomes a collective activity, rather than solely the charisma or talent of the leader (Fairholm, 1994). We'll look first at the relationships between leading and following. Later we will address the issue of change.

REFLECTION

As you consider the idea of the necessity of a follower, think about some-one whom you have followed in some way. Why were you willing to be led by that person? What motivated you? What influence did the leader have over you?

Leaders' Approaches Toward Influencing Others

Because one cannot lead without followers, the influence of the follower over the leader is a factor. However, more attention is generally paid to the leader's influence on fol-lowers. What are the sources of that influence? The power one can exert over another is the main factor in influencing others. That power or authority comes from a variety of sources (Yukl, 1989).

Legitimate Power

Legitimate power is the power obtained by virtue of position in an organization. In child care, directors have power because they have the title that carries with it the under-standing that they are in charge. Typically, staff follow the director because our culture ordains that we follow the designated leader. A person who refused to follow would usu-ally no longer be part of the group, thereby severing the leader/follower influence rela-tionship. When the leader has decision-making authority, staff are more likely to see that leader as one to be followed. When leaders must repeatedly go to a higher authority for approval, their authority is likely to be weakened.

In the opening scenario, you read an example of Kendra's use of legitimate power. She decided to talk to the cook about menus, using a firm approach. Kendra knew that she was ultimately responsible for the menus. She planned to work to help the cook un-derstand the rationale behind the requirements, but she maintained emphasis on the cook's responsibility, rather than taking on the job herself.

Legitimate power includes power to dispense rewards as a motivator, which en-courages some staff to follow a leader. Rewards may be financial, including raises, ben-efits, and bonuses. They may also be special privileges, extra equipment, or personal attention from the leader. Of course, the leader with legitimate power can also punish. Others may follow to avoid punishment in the form of undesirable job assignments or hours, little or no merit pay or rewards, or personal rejection. An example of the latter would be repeated failure to recognize the ideas of a follower.

Communication Power

Leaders influence followers by controlling communication. Effective leaders use com-munication to keep staff members and clients informed. They understand the differ-ences between the types of information staff need and are entitled to receive and what clients should have access to. For example, when the director informs the staff that an additional position is open, staff have the opportunity to apply. Imagine how awkward the situation would be if a position were advertised without staff knowledge and several of the current staff applied. Is the director now to assume that they plan to leave? Will the staff feel that they will be viewed negatively for considering leaving? Certainly, looking for a better job is not an indication of disloyalty, but much ill will can be prevented by keeping communication open.

Parents, on the other hand, need to know that a center is planning to add infant care. Surely, they would want the option of considering the center for their younger child, rather than hearing about it from neighbors. Parents appreciate hearing in advance that a new schedule is to be put into effect during the summer or that the center will be closed for certain holidays. Knowing that they have to provide alternate child care usually will not make parents happy, but advance knowledge is far better than sending home a hasty note about a change in schedule for the following day.

Good leaders also are alert to the significance of timing in communicating. Letting staff know that the board of directors has voted a smaller than expected raise before word gets out may not make it any easier to accept the feelings of dismay, but it will at least allow staff to hear the message together, preferably in a meeting at which the decision is announced by the director. This type of communication is particularly challenging for directors, because even though they disagree totally with the board's decision, directors must avoid negative comments. Directors may express their concerns and the rationale directly to the board or to the board president, but once a decision has been made, it is the director's responsibility to uphold that decision. However, a director in this position might work with the staff to begin immediately to plan ways to educate and encourage the board to create a better plan the following year.

Directors also have the great pleasure of communicating good news to staff. Timing is important here, too. If the long-sought decrease in class size has finally been approved, it is uncomfortable for staff to find out that one teacher was told in advance and that many people in the community know about the decision before they have been informed. Sharing the information with staff right away also gives the director and staff a very positive joint experience. The more opportunities for such shared celebrations, the more likely the staff are to work together as a team and to follow the leader.

In order to know what is going on in the organization, followers may recognize the importance of maintaining a positive relationship with the leader. Even when a leader is fair, the follower who is constantly trying to interfere with the leader in some way may find that the leader has a hard time being objective. Leaders wield communication power if they selectively communicate information to certain employees when all have the right or need to know. In fact, communication skills are one of a leader's most powerful tools. Good communicators motivate people to follow them by both their words and their manner. This power can be used for the good of the organization and its employees, including the director, or it can be used solely for the leaders' own benefit. They can motivate an employee through good communication to work unusually hard at a project that, if successful, will bring great rewards to them.

Employees too have access to some kinds of information that may not be available to the leader. Once again, the leader/follower relationship is reciprocal. For example, teachers will often be the first to know about parental concerns. When the leader communicates openly and fairly with all staff, communication is much more likely to flow in both directions.

In the opening scenario, Kendra used communication positively by involving staff members in designing a marketing plan and releasing part of her legitimate power to them, thereby demonstrating her confidence in them and in herself. Mindy, on the other hand, operated totally independently, treating the staff as though they were too inept or disinterested to participate in grant writing and choosing equipment. She sent the message, in effect, that they would not be able to handle the disappointment of possibly not receiving the funds. She may have been thinking that they might disagree about what to order. By her actions, she missed an opportunity to help the staff develop as a team.

Power over Work Environment

The leader has power over the work environment. In this case, the environment includes the physical plant as well as, in large part, the ambiance of the workplace. As you envision the difference between working in a dirty, cluttered environment and a clean, attractive space, you begin to understand the power leaders have here. They can ensure that clutter is eliminated, in part by motivating staff to work toward creating a better environment. They can also arrange, within budgetary limitations, changes that can improve the environment. Teachers whose classrooms are in dark basement environments find it difficult to create appealing spaces for children. Directors can arrange for improved lighting and can provide funds so that the teachers can choose wall hangings, light paint colors, and brighter halls and stairways. Or if the teachers' break room is furnished with dirty or broken furniture, the director may work to obtain one or two new pieces periodically. Occasionally, furniture stores will donate a sofa or chair that is being replaced with a newer line.

The organizational environment is also a factor in leaders' success. The organizational environment includes the organizational structure. A leader may ensure that this structure is lean or may insert several additional layers of "leaders" (in reality, managers), each of whom has to try to create a cadre of followers. The result may be that followers are being challenged to follow several layers of leaders, which may include assistant directors, educational coordinators, staff trainers, and consultants. The situation becomes even more complex when the leadership layers have varying approaches and goals. When multiple leadership layers are required because of the size of the organization, the leader with ultimate responsibility must ensure that the expectations are clear and that staff are not required to try to figure out who is responsible for what. If this is not done, staff may begin to play one layer against another and the various leaders may let tasks slide, pointing to one another as having failed to do something.

When people are given managerial or leadership responsibility, there is usually an explanation of whether the individual is in a staff or a line position. If the person is in a staff position, then he or she reports to the administrator, but other employees do not report directly to the person in a staff position. Thus, the administrator is still the person to whom workers report. For example, let us assume that a center director appoints an individual to manage the center's nutrition program. The job involves planning meals, ordering food, supervising the cook, and communicating with teachers about the food program. In this situation, it is clear that the cook reports to the nutrition coordinator. However, if the teachers do not return their food carts to the kitchen on schedule, the cook is unable to finish the daily work of cleaning the kitchen. In this case, because the teachers report to the administrator rather than to the nutrition coordinator, communication becomes essential. The nutrition coordinator has no power over the teachers, but in most cases, teachers will be willing to find a way to solve the problem by discussing their concerns with the coordinator. When that does not happen, the administrator must determine how the situation is to be handled.

If the cook fails to prepare lunch on time on a regular basis, then the nutrition co-ordinator, who is in a line position in terms of supervision of the cook, is responsible for finding out from the cook what the problem is and helping solve it, or coaching the cook so that the job will be completed on time.

LEADER'S CORNER

Christy, one of my teachers, and I arrived at the center at the same time early one morning. "I had the greatest idea over the weekend," she said. "Katy Rosen's family has a small apple orchard right at the edge of the city. Our children think apples come from stores. We could take them all to the orchard and they could see for themselves how apples grow." I agreed that this would be a good experience for the children. Right away Christy immediately contacted the Rosens, prepared permission slips, and began lining up volunteer drivers and chaperones for a week from Tuesday.

On Friday at the teachers' meeting, Tracy, our educational coordinator, announced that, based on the teachers' suggestion at the last meeting, she had arranged for Mr. Bronson, a local baker, to come to each classroom a week from Tuesday and help the children make bread. The next step was to work out a schedule for his time with us. At that moment, Christy knew she had forgotten to follow an important procedure, notifying the educational coordinator when she planned to take her class out of the building.

Even though in our center, the director is the leader, the educational coordinator has been given direct responsibility for working with teachers on program. I supported her and let her work out with Christy what would happen.

Director, large not-for-profit center

When the leader has created an organization that is workable and has provided a clear organizational chart to all employees, that leader is likely to get reasonable resolution of conflict with little wasted time and limited negative feelings. When the organizational structure is unclear or when the organizational environment is debilitating, conflicts are likely to arise frequently and to consume inordinate amounts of time.

Expert Power

The leader's expertise is another important factor in influencing others. This type of authority is often referred to as expert power. For example, when staff members recognize that the director has a strong knowledge base in early childhood education, they will be more willing to follow that person's lead. Furthermore, if the director can demonstrate the application of that knowledge in interactions with children, they will feel that this is someone who is even more believable and who can legitimately claim leadership.

On the other hand, the leader who doesn't seem to have any idea about what is going on in the field or even in the center quickly loses the claim to leadership based on expertise. She may not know early childhood terminology, standard practices, references and organizations in the field and may be completely removed from planning and visioning owing to lack of understanding of the situation.

Most early childhood directors come to their administrative roles from a teaching position. They do know about early childhood education and about teaching. However, their knowledge base about administration may be nonexistent or seriously lacking. Directors often learn their roles by trial and error, or from support groups. Today more and more courses for directors are being offered. As more states require that directors have a specific credential, more attention is being paid to helping directors obtain the expertise they need.

Loyalty as a Source of Followers

Some leaders may obtain followers as the result of loyalty. This loyalty may be based on the good will the director has built up with staff over time. Perhaps they have brought untrained people in to work at the center and nourished them as they grew into the job. Perhaps they have supported staff through various crises such as family illness. The loyalty factor may reach a crescendo when a crisis occurs. For example, if a competing program opens nearby, staff that have developed a strong affinity with the leader may, out of loyalty, reject feelers put out by the new center to attract them, even if the new center has offered higher pay. Following out of loyalty may lead staff members to stressful situations, causing them to be torn between additional support for their own families via higher pay and loyalty for the current director. Sometimes loyalty is a natural outgrowth of the personality of the director and her ability to attract followers. Such a person may be very friendly, enthusiastic, and confident. That person's welcoming approach gives staff the feeling that they are part of something very good and that by following such a person, they too will take on these attractive qualities.

In contrast, leaders who see themselves as the center of the universe are unlikely to have loyal followers. Such a director's staff members will readily leave for different jobs, even those with less pay. Or they may ridicule the director behind the scenes, resulting in a unified staff that opposes the director. Consequently, it becomes difficult or impossible for the director to lead.

Reciprocal Nature of the Development of Leadership

Leaders work to obtain followers in order to obtain commitment from them. When staff are committed, they respond very positively and quickly to both parents and children. They develop a genuine caring for the center's clients. When everyone is working together, children are more likely to feel comfortable at the center and families are more likely to work with teachers for the benefit of children.

When commitment is weak or nonexistent, productivity suffers. In many companies, productivity refers to the number of items produced. The more cars or DVD players workers produce, the more productive they are said to be. Productivity can also be measured in terms of sales. The more groceries or clothing a store sells, the more productive the business. In child care situations, productivity refers to the outcomes for children and families.

When employees are following the leader, both the leader and the followers participate in the Mutual Reward Theory (MRT). Mutual reward is a process by which each supports the other. It is sometimes referred to as referent power. In child care, perhaps the teachers establish an excellent curriculum in their classrooms, and the director benefits by directing a center that is highly regarded and provides very effective programming for children and families. The teachers (followers) benefit from the responsiveness of the leader (director). In addition, they usually will benefit in receiving spoken or unspoken satisfaction from clients (children and families) and from each other. Even more important is the internal satisfaction staff members receive when they know they have performed effectively and creatively. In these circumstances, the leader has exerted power appropriately. The appropriate use of power is essential in the leader/follower relationship.

LEADER'S CORNER

I have been director of Winton Corner Center in the inner city of a large urban area for fifteen years. When I came to the center, I enlisted a group of eight women from a local club to volunteer once a week. They worked with the children in the classrooms, usually reading stories to one child or a small group of children. Although I would have preferred to have one or two volunteers a day, the women decided they wanted to come as a group and then go out to lunch together. To accommodate that schedule, the staff and I decided to organize special cooking, woodworking, or field trip plans for the days the volunteers would join us.

It has worked so well that now several of the women also come one afternoon a week and do whatever families need. Maybe they'll drive a mother and her three children to a clinic, or they'll help them learn how to call the electric company when they are behind on payments. Sometimes, one of them will just sit and listen to a mom talk about how anxious she is about her role as parent or about her children's future. Some directors tell me they wouldn't like to have all those volunteers around meddling in their business. I find it to be the best day of the week. The children say "Here come the ladies!" The teachers appreciate the individual attention these women can give children. And as for me, well, I have learned that many people really do care about our children.

Director, Head Start center

Yukl (1989) describes the way in which leaders obtain power:

Leaders gain expert power and eventually legitimate power by demonstrating competence in solving problems that are important to the organization. . . . Demonstration of exceptional expertise may result in attributions of charisma by subordinates if the leader implements innovative strategies that involve high risk of personal loss. Referent power is developed during repeated interactions in which the leader provides appropriate benefits and treats subordinates in a fair and considerate manner.

Although leadership is an abstract concept, we have seen that leaders are people who get their staff involved. They accomplish this by influencing others based on the sources of power available to them. These sources include legitimate power available to holders of particular titles, communication power, power over the work environment, and finally, expert power. We turn now to the second theme related to leadership.

Leaders Recognize That Change Is Essential

Recall that the first theme emerging from the definition of leadership is involvement of the staff as well as the leader. The second theme emerging from the definitions of leadership focuses on leaders' recognition that change is essential. We will introduce the essence of this theme here and return to the topic in more detail in Chapter 7.

In the past, generations of workers were guided into or selected employment as they reached working age or even earlier. Career choices were considered to be for a lifetime. The young boy who was apprenticed to a blacksmith worked throughout his life as a blacksmith. During the industrial revolution, men entered the workforce at a factory or plant and assumed that they would spend a lifetime with that company, perhaps rising through the ranks to some degree. As women increasingly sought regular employment, they too chose a company and remained with it throughout their working careers. Stories abound of whole families and even whole towns being thrown out of work when a mine closed or a factory consolidated with a plant in another city.

Recently a newspaper report described the closing of a plant that had for years produced bicycles. The emphasis of the story was not on why the plant was closing, but rather on the stories of the generations within families, most or all of whom had worked for that company. These folks commented on their loyalty to the company and on their lack of thought or preparation for other work. Everyone knew everyone else at the plant and it was expected that their children would follow them in working there as soon as they were old enough. To an extent, the town's social and political life centered on the plant.

In child care also, women who entered the field often stayed at the same center. Even volunteers remained loyal, as shown in the Leader's Corner example in this chapter. Today, however, both staff members and directors seem to move from center to center, maintaining loyalty to the profession, rather than to a particular center or administration. Others leave for better paying, but often less satisfying, jobs. In part, effective leaders can forestall this short-term effect by creating satisfying work environments. At the same time, they recognize the importance of change for their organizations and their employees, as well as for themselves. Indeed, directors often welcome the opportunity to bring in new staff with fresh ideas and eagerness to advance those ideas.

Many child care center directors are accustomed to operating under the status quo. However, they must recognize the rapidity of change and they must work to envision what changes seem plausible and where their centers should be positioned relative to those changes. For example, as more and more women and men work from their homes, whether they own their own businesses or work for another company, what child care needs will these home-workers have? Will we see a return to part-day programs? Will parents look for programs that they can share with their children? Will additional in-home support be of interest? Effective child care leaders are needed to create solutions for work-at-home families and for a myriad of future situations. But rather than doing it by themselves, they and leaders in other related fields will develop the talent in their organizations, attract and retain new talent, and provide them with conditions that encourage the thought and creativity necessary to go beyond the status quo (Bennis, 1994).

REFLECTION

When you talk to grandparents, you may hear about dramatic changes that have occurred over their lifetimes, especially in the area of technology. What are some of the changes that *you* have experienced in technology and in other aspects of your life? Have they been positive or negative?

Change and influence coalesce in many leadership situations. For example, when a leader decides to leave a situation, either by choice or because of someone else's decision, followers may find themselves left behind. The leader may leave to pursue other interests, to retire, or to advance to a higher level of administration. In some cases, the leader may have been terminated or ousted through a political process that left no resources for the staff and no decision-making authority for the leader. The new leader may have been brought in to weed out staff. Thus, the mutual loyalty built by the leader and her followers may be overturned. In today's society, changes in leadership frequently occur. As a result, leaders have to work hard to develop a positive organizational climate and to undo any damage created by the departure of the previous leader.

We turn now to another perspective on the leader's role by contrasting leadership and management. Although both are essential, each requires different behaviors and skills. Many persons in early childhood education leadership positions began as managers and added the knowledge and skills needed while further developing the dispositions required to lead. In fact, Neugebauer (1997) suggests four managerial stages through which directors typically progress as they gain more knowledge and understanding of the realities of the role: pseudo managerial, premanagerial, concrete managerial, and formal managerial. These stages reflect the growth of the manager from basic lack of understanding of the role through competence in managing.

The Role of the Manager

The broad range of tasks expected of managers requires that they control or direct the operations of a department, organization, team, or agency. Although later chapters will include discussions of several of these tasks or responsibilities in greater detail, an overview of the expectations for managers will serve to clarify widely held beliefs. Yukl (1989, p. 129) proposes a taxonomy shown below. It contains four broad categories, eleven mid-level behavior categories, and many specific behavior components.

Figure 1–3 Integrating Taxonomy of Managerial Behavior

Reprinted with permission of Prentice Hall.

Figure 1–3 shows the four broad categories along the outer circle: 1) Giving and seeking information, 2) Making decisions, 3) Influencing people, and 4) Building relationships. Each of these categories is divided into several of the eleven mid-level behavioral categories, which are shown in Figure 1–4.

Networking: Socializing informally; developing contacts with people who are a source of information and support and maintain relationships through periodic interaction (e.g., visits, telephone calls, and correspondence, attendance at meetings and social events).

Supporting: Acting in a friendly and considerate manner, showing sympathy and support when someone is upset; listening to complaints and problems; looking out for someone's interests; providing helpful career advice; doing things to aid someone's career advancement.

Managing conflict and team building: Encouraging and facilitating constructive resolution of conflict; fostering teamwork and cooperation; building identification with the organizational unit or team.

Motivating: Using influence techniques that appeal to emotions, values, or logic to generate enthusiasm for the work and commitment to task objectives, or to induce someone to carry out a request for support, cooperation, assistance, resources, or authorization; setting an example of proper behavior by one's own actions.

Recognizing and rewarding: Providing praise, recognition, and tangible rewards for effective performance, significant achievements, and special contributions; expressing respect and appreciation for someone's accomplishments.

Planning and organizing: Determining long-range objectives and strategies for adapting to environmental change; identifying necessary action steps to carry out a project or activity; allocating resources among activities according to priorities; determining how to improve efficiency, productivity, and coordination with other parts of the organization.

Problem-solving: Identifying work-related problems; analyzing problems in a systematic but timely manner to determine causes and find solutions; acting decisively to implement solutions and deal with crises.

Consulting and delegating: Checking with others before making changes that affect them; encouraging suggestions for improvement; inviting participation in decision-making; incorporating the ideas and suggestions of others in decisions; allowing others to have substantial discretion in carrying out work activities and handling problems.

Monitoring operations and environment: Gathering information about the progress and quality of work activities, the success or failure of activities or projects, and the performance of individual contributors; determining the needs of clients or users; scanning the environment to detect threats and opportunities.

Informing: Disseminating relevant information about decisions, plans, and activities to those who need it to do their work; providing written materials and documents, answering requests for technical information, and telling people about the organizational unit to promote its reputation.

Clarifying roles and objectives: Assigning tasks; providing direction in how to do the work and communicating a clear understanding of job responsibilities, task objectives, deadlines, and performance expectations. (Yukl, 1989, pp. 129–130)

Figure 1–4 Yukl's Managerial Behavior Categories

Reprinted with permission of Prentice Hall.

Yukl's (1989) Managerial Behavioral Categories refer to businesses. Managing a child care center involves the same strategies. Because each business has its own unique characteristics, let's look at ways in which Yukl's behavioral categories might apply to child care management. Figure 1–5 provides examples.

Leadership Contrasted with Management

In early childhood education, the leader is often referred to as the director, particularly in child care centers. Other early childhood organizations, such as resource and referral agencies and advocacy groups may have administrators, but whatever title the lead role carries, the basic responsibilities are the same. Today many child care directors are managers; a few are leaders. The literature in the field is pointing directors toward the

Networking: Early childhood directors develop contacts with other directors, with leaders in other businesses, and with professional organizations.

Supporting: Directors form support groups, meeting to discuss mutual problems. Directors listen to teachers and parents who are experiencing challenging situations.

Managing conflict and team building: Child care directors facilitate problem-solving among staff and between staff members and families. They coach staff in ways to help children develop conflict management skills.

Motivating: Early childhood leaders set an example for other staff. They encourage staff on rough days and congratulate them on successes. They are quick to recognize good work.

Recognizing and rewarding: Although tangible rewards in the early childhood field are generally limited, directors work to acknowledge staff members' accomplishments and encourage the whole team to support one another.

Planning and organizing: Preplanning and organization are essential in the child care field. Because the unexpected frequently happens when young children are involved, directors must be organized to keep things running smoothly. The director's job is so broad that efficiency is essential.

Problem-solving: The hallmark of the director's role is the flexibility to solve problems ranging from repairing plumbing to balancing budgets.

Consulting and delegating: Early childhood directors conduct regular staff meetings, communicate by being in each classroom daily, and turn over to teachers most of the decision-making about what happens in the classrooms.

Monitoring operations and environment: Early childhood managers collect information from staff and families on a regular basis to determine how well the program is doing. They also participate in an accreditation process.

Informing: Early childhood directors are usually responsible for a newsletter, for marketing the program, and for communicating with staff and parents.

Clarifying roles and objectives: Directors assume responsibility for orienting new staff and for assessing staff members' work. They communicate with families and the public to ensure that the center's goals are clear. They may also present information about early childhood education in a broader arena.

Figure 1–5 Examples of Early Childhood Directors' Application of Managerial Behaviors

leadership role (Culkin, 2000; Kagan & Bowman, 1997). Are there differences between leaders and managers? Often we use the terminology related to management. Are we being precise? Are we aware of the differences in behavior, goals, and relationships?

All leaders must also be managers in a sense, but not all managers are leaders. A manager is responsible for all the details of running a program. For example, the manager of a child care center is responsible for reports to funders, for hiring and firing, for evaluating staff, for working with licensing agents, and so forth. The manager keeps things going within the organization on a day-to-day, month-to-month, year-to-year basis. According to Chapman and O'Neil (2000, p. 16), "[m]anagement means planning, organizing, communicating, controlling, and evaluating." Managers resolve conflicts, set goals, and help employees move toward them. It is the manager's responsibility to use resources effectively and to maintain working conditions that enable employees to accomplish what is expected. See Table 1–1.

Only recently has the distinction between leadership and management been drawn as more and more researchers examine the qualities and traits that comprise a leader. Indeed, in today's work environment, which is heavily influenced by a global economy, management alone will not suffice. Although managers are still needed, an increasing number of companies are reducing the number of management levels and focusing on empowering employees supported by effective leaders. Companies are selecting leaders who delegate enthusiastically and take calculated risks in order to advance their operations.

Bennis (1994, adapted from p. 45) takes a slightly more poetic approach stating that:

- The manager administers; the leader innovates.
- The manager is a copy; the leader is an original.
- The manager maintains; the leader develops.

Table 1–1 Comparing Managers with Leaders

"The differences between an excellent leader and a successful manager are subtle and difficult to define. Sometimes a manager is a leader in one or two areas, but not enough to make an impact. Others start by extending themselves (stepping out in front) in a few instances and then, as their confidence grows, venturing further into leadership roles. While most people move from management into leadership. . . . in a haphazard, uncharted manner, more and more emphasis is being placed on leadership training."

Managers	**Leaders**
Protect their operations	Advance their operations
Accept responsibility	Seek responsibility
Minimize risks	Take calculated risks
Accept speaking opportunities	Generate speaking opportunities
Set reasonable goals	Set "unreasonable" goals
Pacify problem employees	Challenge problem employees
Strive for a comfortable working environment	Strive for an exciting working environment
Use power cautiously	Use power forcefully
Delegate cautiously	Delegate enthusiastically
View workers as employees	View workers as potential followers

Adapted from Chapman & O'Neil, p. 4. Reprinted with permission of Prentice Hall.

- The manager relies on control; the leader inspires trust.
- The manager asks how and when; the leader asks what and why.
- The manager imitates; the leader originates.
- The manager does things right; the leader does the right thing.

What Followers Want from Their Leaders

We have described the importance of the follower to the leader. Now we turn to the importance of the leader to the follower. According to Bennis (1994), followers (staff members) want three things from leaders:

- direction
- trust
- hope

REFLECTION

Think about whether direction, trust, and hope are what you want from a leader. Are there other things that are more important to you?

Direction

If they are to feel successful, employees must know and understand what is expected of them. The leader's responsibility is to provide the guidance they need and in addition to provide the training, support, and encouragement that will allow them to do the job and to be as autonomous as possible. Some workers have to ask permission at every turn. Others are left to their own devices and then fail to do well or are criticized for not meeting the leader's expectations. Although these workers may continue to follow their leader, they will not be committed.

LEADER'S CORNER

When I was a teacher, my director had lots of rules for us to follow. One rule was that we had to be out on the playground at a very specific time, no earlier, no later. One day, one of the children's fathers was visiting my class. He had participated in our group time by telling the children about how he had learned to play the clarinet. He played for them and then said they could each have a turn to come up and press one of the keys. The children were fascinated and quite attentive. As a result, we were ten minutes late getting to the playground.

The director came to my classroom during lunch and said, in front of the children, that she had noticed that we weren't following the schedule. She didn't even ask me why, just said that she didn't want to see it happen again. I know other classes have to use the playground and we were getting ready to come in when the next class came out.

When I became a director, I knew right away that I would try to be flexible and also to listen to what teachers have to say before judging their actions.

Director, private center

Trust

Followers expect to trust leaders and to be trusted by leaders. But in order to establish trust, each individual must first have accurate knowledge of the other person and often of the particular situation in which trust is being established. Trust develops slowly and evolves from informal analyses of a range of situations. Does the leader provide what the follower needs? Does she avoid behaviors that cause resentment, embarrassment, or confusion? Followers watch closely. Does the leader follow through with what she has stated or does she agree in a staff meeting to something that the staff requests and then fail to take the necessary action to implement the plan. Followers would rather have a leader who openly disagrees with a request or points out why it will not be implemented than one who gives lip service but does not act. Followers are looking for leaders on whom they can depend, who will not change a story depending on with which staff member they are meeting. In a child care center, where flexibility is key, staff depend on being able to trust their directors. In fact, based on the rate of change extant in today's world, most workers need the stability of a trustworthy leader. Bennis (1994) opines that "[w]ith respect to the spastic changes taking place in the world today, the trust factor will reign as the most pivotal factor of a leader's success, whether at the U. S. presidential level or the chair of the PTA" (p. xiii.).

Hope

Workers expect to be able to look to the future. They want a leader who has a vision for that future for their organization and, particularly when they have a part in creating that future, they are willing to join with the leader in creating it.

When leaders recognize what employees want and need and tailor interactions with them to meet these needs, they are demonstrating understanding that indeed the employees are the organization's internal clients (Fairholm, 1994). When workers' needs are not being met, they lack commitment and may even be unwilling to comply with leaders' expectations, thus almost forcing leaders to move to a management approach (Fairholm, 1994). The loss to the entire organization and its clients could be staggering.

REFLECTION

Think about the traits you expect in a leader. It may help to consider a group to which you currently belong and to reflect on the traits that the leader of that group does or does not exhibit.

The Special Role of the Early Childhood Leader

Since its inception, many individuals have looked on the field of early childhood education as similar to babysitting, viewing it as a totally nonprofessional field. Legislators balk at allocating funds necessary to employ professional teachers. Parents resist paying tuition which would provide enough income to support even living wages for their young children's teachers. Directors recognize that not all families can afford the cost of child care and a number of government funded programs have been created to meet this need. However, the cost is still high based on the required and recommended teacher-child ratios.

Some owners see child care primarily as a way to make money easily. We hasten to add that many dedicated professionals have worked in early childhood education over the years and a number of owners have made major personal financial sacrifices in order to maintain high-quality child care programs. However, overall there has been a general failure to see early childhood educators as professionals.

As directors—who may have heretofore focused on themselves as managers—now recognize the importance of their roles as leaders, a new opportunity presents itself. In taking on the role of leader, early childhood educators can advance the field as a profession. Neugebauer (1997) states that "A leadership development effort that makes a difference must have the goal of developing visionaries and keepers of the faith."

To reach this goal, we will need to recognize the attributes of a profession and its professionals. Bergen (1992) lists three characteristics:

1. an extensive understanding of the body of knowledge that composes the area of professional expertise;
2. a high level of competence in the practice of the skills identified as essential for effective professional performance; and
3. a conscious commitment to the ethical standards embraced by the group of professionals who comprise the field.

These characteristics can be used as important guides as you work toward enhancing your own level of professionalism.

Summary

The expectations of a leader can be overwhelming to one considering taking on a leadership role. Because most researchers have found that leaders are made, not born, aspiring leaders must begin to form themselves as leaders. Prerequisites are the technical, conceptual, and interpersonal skills that are used by leaders, as well as the reinvention of and deep understanding of self (Bennis, 1994; Fairholm, 1994). Leaders must constantly attend to the need for balance.

Class Assignments

1. Return to the opening scenarios regarding Kendra and Mindy. As you reread them, consider what aspects of the information presented in this chapter these scenarios bring to mind.
    Would you recommend any changes to Kendra's or Mindy's approach to the director's role? If so, what changes would you suggest and why?
    Write your answers on Working Paper 1–1.
2. Interview a director and find out whether he or she considers himself/herself to be a leader or a manager. Do you agree with this director's assessment of the role he or she has assumed? What factors led you to your response?
    Write your answers on Working Paper 1–2.
    Be sure to write a thank you note to the director.
3. If you are currently directing a child care center or other agency or organization, what qualifications and behaviors do you believe you have that allow you to be successful in your role? Write an essay explaining your perspective.

If you are not a director, write about what you believe you could do that would make you a good director. What qualifications do you currently have?

Write your responses on Working Paper 1–3.

4. Check the Internet for books on leadership. Find out how many are listed.
   a. Find out how many leadership books are about educational leaders.
   b. Find out how many leadership books are about leaders in early childhood education or child care.

   Write your answers on Working Paper 1–4

Class Exercises

1. With a small group of peers, discuss whether each of you considers yourself to be a manager or a leader.
2. Review the criteria for leadership described in this chapter. In your small group, discuss whether or not you agree with the categories presented. Would you add or delete any? Why?
3. Volunteer to participate in a debate with a classmate on the topic, "Leaders learn from others, but they are not made by others" (Bennis, 1994).

Working Paper 1–1

Recommended changes to Kendra's and Mindy's approach to the director's role:

Working Paper 1–2

Director Interview

Director Interviewed: ————————————————————

Date of Interview: ————————————————————

Type of Program: ————————————————————

Director's statement about her/his role:

Your assessment of director's role:

Working Paper 1–3

Director Qualifications

Qualifications you possess that would enable you to be a director:

Behaviors you engage in that do (or would) help you be a good director:

Working Paper 1–4

Books on Leadership

How many books on leadership did you find?

How many of these are about leaders in education?

How many are about leaders in early childhood education or child care?

What is your reaction to this information?

References

Bennis, W. (1994). *On becoming a leader.* Reading, Mass.: Addison-Wesley.

Bergen, D. (1992, Autumn). Defining a professional and developing professionals. *Journal of Early Childhood Teacher Education.* National Association of Early Childhood Teacher Educators.

Chapman, E., & O'Neil, S. L. (2000). *Leadership: Essential steps every manager needs to know.* Upper Saddle River, NJ: Prentice-Hall.

Culkin, M. L., ed. (2000). *Managing quality in young children's programs: The leader's role.* New York: Teachers College.

Dorsey, R. W. (1999). Case studies in building design and construction. Upper Saddle River, NJ: Prentice-Hall.

Espinosa, L. M. (1997). Personal dimensions of leadership. In *Leadership in early care and education.* Kagan, S. L., & Bowman, B. T., eds. Washington, D.C.: National Association for the Education of Young Children.

Fairholm, G. W. (1994). *Leadership and the culture of trust.* Westport, Conn.: Praeger.

Kagan, S. L., & Bowman, B. T. (1997). *Leadership in early care and education.* Washington, D.C.: National Association for the Education of Young Children.

Lambert, L., Walker, D., Zimmerman, D. P., et al. (1995). *The constructivist leader.* New York: Teachers College.

Mitchell, A. (1997). Reflections on early childhood leadership development: Finding your own path. In *Leadership in early care and education.* Kagan, S. L., & Bowman, B. T., eds. Washington, D.C.: National Association for the Education of Young Children.

Neugebauer, R. (1997). Commentary. In *Leadership in early care and education.* Kagan, S. L., & Bowman, B. T., eds. Washington, DC: National Association for the Education of Young Children.

Yukl, G. A. (1989). *Leadership in organizations.* 2nd ed. Englewood Cliffs, NJ: Prentice-Hall.

CHAPTER 2

The Leader as Role Model

Morris arrived at the parking lot and checked his watch. Oops, 10:15! He was due in at 8:30. Morris directs an agency that serves parents and their children, particularly in times of family crisis. The agency provides parenting training prior to the birth of a baby and continuing until the child reaches age three. Morris had been a teacher in a child care center sponsored by this agency. The children who attended had been abused by family members or had experienced some other major trauma. He had been a good teacher but he was soon tapped for the agency director's position when the former director, Felicity, left to transfer to another state with her husband.

Although he had no real preparation for this job, he had observed Felicity when he was her subordinate. She had been a stickler for following policy and procedures. Most of the agency's employees had liked her. They had considered her to be fair and they had recognized that she, too, had followed the same procedures expected of them.

Morris chuckled to himself. 10:15! He would have been reprimanded had Felicity still been director. But he had stopped at the barber on the way in and as usual he had had to wait about fifteen minutes. Still it was important that he look good for the afternoon agency personnel committee meeting. Certainly, those people would expect the agency director to look professional. As he entered his office, he greeted the receptionist who nodded. "Uh-oh" he thought, she's in the middle of another one of those long personal phone calls again. I guess I'll have to take action." Just last week, several callers had commented on how hard it is to get a real person on the phone. The board members had noticed that, too. They had said that a personal answer is essential, especially when a parent calls.

Morris put his briefcase down on his desk and checked his calendar for the day. First order of business was to call Sam about a tennis game they had scheduled for the next morning. Morris was beginning to feel a little guilty. He couldn't be that late two days in a row. He reached Sam immediately. Twenty minutes later, when the receptionist came to the door, she heard him say, "Well, I gotta get going, Sam. I'll arrange that appointment with you in a day or two," and then he turned his attention to the doorway to find out what the receptionist needed.

REFLECTION

Have you ever worked for a boss whose behavior was similar to that which Morris displayed? How did his or her behavior affect you?

One of the most important roles of leaders is serving as role model. According to Yukl (1989), subordinates tend to imitate leaders with whom they identify. Therefore, "the leader should set an example of appropriate role behavior by performing duties in a responsible and dedicated manner and avoiding improper behavior" (p. 48). This seems to be true in a wide range of organizations, but is perhaps even more significant in early childhood programs. In this chapter, we will discuss appropriate role behavior and then address why this principle is particularly applicable in child care organizations.

Modeling Expected Practices

Whenever certain practices are expected of staff members, the leader must follow those same practices. For example, because all staff are expected to arrive for work on time every day, leaders must also follow that practice. Their hours may vary considerably, but they should be scheduled and adhered to. For example, many child care center directors alternate weekly arriving early or staying late on a weekly basis. With such a schedule, they can be available to parents who drop children off early as well as to those who pick their children up at the end of the day. A director who works only the early morning start time would see little of part-time workers who are on site until the last child leaves. Early shift directors would have little idea of situations that may arise at the end of the day and may find it difficult to solve problems that occur specifically at that time. Note that in the opening scenario, Morris seemed to have his own "rule" for time to be spent on the job. In addition, although he disapproved of staff members' personal phone calls, he seemed to feel that he could do whatever he chose.

However, leaders often have job responsibilities away from the center. They may be attending meetings called by the Department of Human Services to discuss a new funding stream. Perhaps the board's executive committee has called a meeting at the chairperson's office and has asked the director to be present. Some leaders direct community programs that do not provide direct daily services to children. These leaders spend many hours in meetings in order to plan, collaborate, fund and implement programs for children and families. All early childhood leaders should spend some time on advocacy, sometimes meeting with legislators. In one city, several advocates took council members on tours of high-quality centers to enable them to see what kind of care all children need. In another city, United Way committee members were invited to tour centers with early childhood leaders to encourage them to support programs for children. These duties keep leaders away from their desks and may give employees the feeling that administrators can set their own schedules and can decide which policies, if any, they will follow. Leaders must explain to staff that their responsibilities are varied and require both on-site and off-site presence. Note that Morris, in the opening scenario, failed to keep his staff informed of his whereabouts, making it difficult for them to do their jobs well and possibly causing ill will in the community.

When leaders must be away from their office, it is essential that the staff understands who is in charge, particularly in case of emergency. If absence from the site is not at a regularly scheduled time, the leader should post a notice on the staff bulletin board or via e-mail, informing the staff of the situation and letting them know who will be in charge in her absence. By no means does this imply that it is acceptable for a child care center director to be off site a majority of the time, nor does it imply that staff have to be told details of the leader's whereabouts. In many cases, staff will be quite disinterested. In other instances, the destination may be somewhat confidential. For example, the organization may be interested in purchasing a particular piece of property, but to make that widely known may raise the price of the property considerably.

Leaders must assume responsibility for designating alternate leaders during their absence from the site, whether it will be for an hour or a week. They must prepare their alternates by providing the information and skills they will need. Plans must be in place to cover the responsibilities of alternates when they are assuming the leaders' roles. Although alternates have been designated as having authority, they may seldom need to use it. Nonetheless, it is essential to be prepared.

LEADER'S CORNER

I learned how essential a back-up director is one day when I returned to the center after a meeting with our funders. As I approached the center, I could see two police cars with lights flashing. Parking quickly, I rushed inside and found an irate father and six other adults shouting at the police men and women. Our assistant director had been asked by the police to leave the room. She had not given the parent the information he wanted but had explained that the child they were seeking had not come to the center that day. Although other staff were not aware, I had alerted the assistant director that the child's mother had been working with a social worker and was afraid her husband would harm their child. The mother had confided to me that she wanted to leave her abusing husband, but ethically I felt that I was unable to discuss it further with the social worker. The assistant director had also communicated the code to the receptionist that alerted her to call the police and to signal teachers to keep children in their classrooms. When calm was restored, I breathed a sigh of relief for having had such a quick-thinking assistant. She had been prepared and she averted what could have been a real tragedy.

Director, full-day center

Modeling Respect for Others

Although procedures such as being on time for work and signing in and out are necessary, even more important is the interpersonal behavior among staff members and toward clients. Leaders set the stage by showing respect for others, even when they are very busy. Treating others fairly and courteously is expected of all employees, but the behavior can quickly disintegrate if leaders demonstrate that they have time to listen to only a few chosen staff. Others may be ignored, particularly those whose roles are less prestigious, such as cleaning staff or cooks.

Leaders show respect when they consider the ideas of others, when they commend them for jobs well done, and when they pay attention to the needs and interests of each employee and client. You should expect to see leaders in early childhood programs:

- greeting parents warmly and calling them by name.
- welcoming hugs even from poorly clothed children with hair that needs washing.
- positioning themselves at child level when they stop to listen to a child's story about the classroom pet that died or the trip to the library.
- asking staff and parents how an ill grandma is doing or whether they are enjoying their new job.

When one hears and sees these demonstrations of respect modeled by the leader on a regular basis, the behavior is bound to become contagious.

Notice how pleased you are when someone shows you respect. The feeling is so positive, that it is then easier for you to respond in similar ways to others around you. If this feeling is not widespread throughout an organization, leaders must assume responsibility for discussing it with employees. They must let them know that this kind of behavior is expected and they must set limits when counter examples occur. In many cases, they must provide specific training about how to handle situations respectfully.

If staff are not respectful of persons from cultures other than their own, the leader will need to provide specific training on this topic. It may be that some staff are not aware of cultural behavior patterns. They may expect that everyone should think and behave in ways that they themselves know and understand. They may also be unaware of personality differences that lead to different ways of communicating. Although leaders cannot always change employees' attitudes, they can require respectful behaviors.

Modeling Good Communication

One of the most important ways in which leaders serve as role models is through their use of communication. Communication includes both verbal and written avenues of sharing information with families, staff, and community. Leaders must be able to present ideas that are clear and concise. They must consider the recipient and frame messages in ways that would be meaningful to them. When receiving a reply, whether written or oral, leaders must pay close attention to the feelings being conveyed as well as to the content of the message. It is a good idea to check with the speaker or writer to make sure that the message has been correctly understood. Taking time to do this can prevent misunderstandings.

When communication is spoken, leaders must consider the importance of body language. Leaders who make eye contact, whose facial expressions reflect the message being sent and received, and whose tone of voice is calm rather than shrill or harsh are more likely to be heard and appreciated. They must consider their posture and gestures as well as their words. In using written communication, wise leaders re-read their messages before sending them. This practice provides an opportunity to correct errors in spelling, punctuation, and grammar. It also gives the writer a chance to review the feelings and content of the message to ensure that what was intended is what is being conveyed.

Leaders must ensure that staff and families are informed in a timely manner whenever information is available that could benefit them. Some leaders take the approach that all meetings and events will be scheduled a year ahead and that staff and families will be notified prior to the beginning of the year only. This approach works well for some recipients, but can be frustrating to others. People who use electronic organizers that beep at them when something is scheduled for that day may find one notice sufficient, whereas others prefer a weekly notice to be posted on the bulletin board or placed in mailboxes.

Communication of a Business Nature

Much of the communication usually considered important to parents and staff relates to policies and procedures. Everyone involved needs to know who decides who will be admitted to the program and what the criteria are, including availability of program openings within teacher-child ratio, age of the child, and physical space in the center. The family, the center, the funders, or a combination of these must be able to cover tuition. When there are specific funding criteria, information about these must be available to applicants. Some staff may not need detailed information on this topic, while others must be well-versed in the procedure because they have full or partial responsibility for implementing the policy. All staff should know to whom to refer potential clients.

All center employees should know the days and hours of operation of the program, even when their own working hours vary from the hours for clients. They should be able to tell families where to obtain a calendar for the program's activities. Similarly, other routine information should be at their fingertips, such as where to find lunch menus and how the center decides who is too sick to stay there. The ability to communicate basic program facts demonstrates that the employee is engaged in the work of the center, rather than in merely doing a job. You may have worked in a grocery store. If you felt that your job was stocking shelves, you may have focused primarily on your next break or on "when you get off." But if you believed that your job was serving customers, your attitude was probably different and may have included smiling at customers and speaking to them, perhaps even thanking them for coming. You may have offered help to a customer with a perplexed look on her face and been willing to accompany her to the area for which she was searching. Notice how much more client-oriented these latter behaviors are. Whether the employee is working with children or is selling products, the clients (families and children) come first.

Everyone who works at the center should be very familiar with the organization's purpose and goals. When you read the chapter on orientation, you will learn how this information is communicated to new staff and how the leader ensures that employees understand the center's philosophy. Later in this text you will read about supervising staff. This process verifies that staff members have understood and are implementing the philosophy presented during orientation.

Leaders must decide how important communication is to be disseminated. Often the communication flows from the leader to the rest of the staff and to families. Leaders must set the standard for timely and clear messages. Would-be leaders, such as Morris in our opening scenario, who spend inordinate amounts of time in personal conversation or doing personal errands usually are too busy to communicate effectively. Leaders listen to staff and families, are available to hear from them, and care enough to ensure that several points of view are considered.

Some communication comes from parents. Perhaps the parent group decides to have a picnic. How will that information be shared, by whom, to whom, when, and by what means? Typically, all communication that concerns the center officially goes through the director or a designee. When this does not occur, conflicting messages may inadvertently be sent.

LEADER'S CORNER

Recently the five centers in our group decided to have a joint parent meeting to share information that would apply to all our center parents and their children. The program was prepared and distributed and included the location as Eastside Center. The day before the event, Eastside Center developed a major heating problem and had to close for several days. The director contacted Westside's director and arranged to have the meeting there. No one notified the parents. This fiasco definitely had a negative effect on our efforts to establish positive relations with our families. Of course, we sent a letter of apology to each family, but we'll have to work hard to rebuild that trust. It was a major lesson for all of us to check and re-check communication.

Director, preschool program

Communication at a Personal Level

In addition to official or business communication, the leader models personal communication with all staff and families. As discussed earlier, communication must always be respectful. Leaders should generally avoid close personal friendships with one or a few favored employees. Such friendships might lead to discussion of business and personnel issues to which the employee should not have access. More important, close personal friendships may be divisive in that other employees may feel that a few are receiving special treatment and benefits. As a result, cooperation among staff members may be impaired and some staff members may try to undermine the leader's authority.

For example, staff members who feel excluded may begin to be lax about preparing reports, writing lesson plans, or keeping classrooms orderly and attractive. If the director does not notice or lets both her behavior and staff behavior continue, it will be very difficult to rectify the situation in the future.

Modeling Professional Behavior

Often when the term "profession" is used, it refers to specific roles such as doctor or lawyer. However, leaders can help all employees view themselves as behaving professionally by following the expectations that their jobs demand. For example, child care center cooks do their jobs professionally when they prepare nutritious food on time and serve it attractively. Their products may not look or taste like those of gourmet cooks, but that is not what is expected nor would it be appropriate.

Teachers in child care programs are expected to deport themselves professionally in part through their personal behavior during working hours. For example, a teacher who is making loud noises with chewing gum would not be behaving professionally. Teachers who use poor grammar or repeatedly make spelling errors in notes to parents or on classroom materials are not behaving professionally. Teachers who leave the same dusty objects on the shelves for months or whose classrooms are in such disarray that children cannot find materials are not behaving professionally. Teachers who plan in advance, who arrive in the classroom ready for the day, and who work to develop positive relationships with staff, families, and children are behaving professionally.

Once again, leaders serve as role models. When they prepare reports accurately and in a timely manner, they are behaving professionally. When they come to staff meetings prepared to discuss items that staff have asked about, they are behaving professionally. If, however, leaders neglect the staff, paying little or no attention to them and to center clients, they are behaving unprofessionally.

Personal Appearance

Leaders model the importance of personal appearance. This aspect of professional behavior takes a variety of forms based on the role the individual plays in operating the program. Leaders must dress appropriately for their roles. Although early childhood leaders who work in office buildings rather than in centers will usually dress in business or business casual attire, leaders who are working directors of child care centers face challenges regarding clothing. They must model dressing so that they can interact with children because they will be going into classrooms, if only briefly, on a daily basis. They should also expect, and hope for, visits from children during the day. At times, they may be pressed into service in the kitchen or in a classroom. There will also be days on which the director is expected to meet with business people and to be dressed appropriately for those occasions. Perhaps the best guide is flexibility. The addition of a jacket, a tie, or a scarf and attractive pin may be just what is needed to move from one setting to another. An extra pair of comfortable shoes and a smock or apron kept at the center can make an emergency day in the classroom much more comfortable.

Just as teachers encourage parents to bring their children to school in clothing which allows them to participate fully in the range of classroom activities, so too must leaders help staff members understand the type of clothing and personal appearance that is expected of them in various roles. Creating detailed dress codes seldom encourages employees to do a better job. However, clarifying what is acceptable makes it easier for employees to present themselves appropriately. For example, maintenance staff generally need rugged clothes and work shoes that can stand up to grease, various kinds of dirt and waste materials, and some heavy work. Kitchen staff must make cleanliness a major priority. If they do not wear uniforms, they generally wear clean aprons. Frequent hand washing is a must and is usually required by boards of health.

Teaching staff must be prepared to sit on the floor and to be involved in activities that can stain clothing, such as paints and cooking activities. They must be able to move quickly and easily from one part of the room to another as children need them. Therefore, cumbersome shoes, tight clothing, and dangling jewelry are not appropriate. Teachers must also consider that they will frequently hold children on their laps and must think about how their clothing might feel to children. Is it scratchy? Might a child be hurt by a sharp belt buckle? Teachers must also consider whether their overall appearance is professional. Anything that is overdone or extreme such as heavy makeup, extra long and elaborate fingernails, and clothing better suited to the beach or the dance floor, usually is not professional. Teachers must also be prepared to go outdoors with children in a range of weather conditions. Boots and gloves encourage teachers to take their children out to enjoy falling snow, whereas shivering in a lightweight, albeit attractive, jacket does not meet the criteria for appropriate attire.

Whatever the role, clothing with messages generally should not be worn. Whether the message contains personal beliefs, obscenities, or famous quotations, clothing at work is not the place to declare one's ideas. In addition, secure storage must be provided for staff so that they can store purses, hats, and items that they may want to change to for after-work activities.

When leaders model appropriate personal appearance and grooming, they encourage staff to follow suit. Nonetheless, statements in the policy manual should make it clear that professional appearance appropriate to the role is expected of all workers. It is the leader's responsibility to see that this policy is carried out.

Significance of the Role Model in Early Childhood Programs

Based on conditions often found in early childhood settings, the primary person available to be a consistent role model for the entire staff is the director, program administrator, or educational coordinator. Some programs may use different titles, but the person who is responsible for the entire organization, its staff, and its program is the person who will be in the most prominent position as a role model. Although directors may change jobs, their rate of change does not appear to be as rapid as is that of teaching and support staff. Thus, the leader becomes the key to transmission of the organization's culture.

Staff are likely to imitate good leaders; however, some employees may chose to leave rather than respond. Some staff may have come from centers at which minimal expectations were the norm. At first, they may feel irritated or even express animosity toward the director. In time, most people appreciate being treated as professionals—treatment they earn by behaving as professionals. Very young staff who have just completing schooling at which limited attention had been given to their behavior may also rebel. Staff who have worked at the center for many years may find it hard to accept a new director who expects them to behave in certain ways. Nonetheless, knowledgeable leaders are cognizant of their responsibility to serve as role models.

Earlier in this chapter, we pointed out that early childhood staff may depend more heavily on the leader as a role model than do employees in other types of organizations. This need may occur for several reasons:

1. Many staff members have limited education and training for their jobs.
2. Early childhood jobs often require working alone in a classroom or with another minimally prepared staff member.
3. Early childhood professionals are required to be role models for their clients (children and parents).
4. Early childhood programs differ from other kinds of education programs as well as from other kinds of businesses.

We will examine these four reasons in the following sections.

Working with Minimally Prepared Staff

Major efforts are being made to ensure the presence in each classroom of a teacher who is well-prepared and experienced in the field of early childhood care and development. However, based on available staff, salaries, and benefits a severely limited pool of knowledgeable teachers and assistants is available. Therefore, large numbers of leaders in our field must bring new staff into the field with little or no preparation. These leaders introduce new hires to the profession and socialize them to the particular program in which they have found employment. At the same time, the new employees often begin working with little or no lead time in which to process what is expected of them. A challenge occurs when the new employee begins working and bases her practice on her current understanding of child development. As she begins to learn more about children in groups, she has to break established habits. Breaking habits and substituting new behaviors is a slow process that generally requires support. Sometimes, even when new habits have been established, it is easy to return to old behaviors unless support and encouragement are readily available. Certainly, workers in these categories need a strong role model.

In some cases, the culture of the community relative to work may be similar to the new staff member's culture. As the new staff member regularly encounters parents or community members who speak about the "boss" as someone to circumvent, it may be difficult to accept the culture the director is attempting to inculcate. In such cases, the director would be wise to establish a support person or group from the existing staff for the new person. It will be much easier to learn a culture by associating with a peer or peers in whom that culture has already been established. Later chapters on orientation and supervision will provide a detailed approach to the leader's role in working with staff in these situations.

REFLECTION

Think about a habit that you had established and had to work to break. Were you successful? What process did you use? For example, were you or someone you know eating a poor diet and becoming overweight? Perhaps you were spending beyond your means, incurring huge credit card debt and interest charges. Was there a person or organization available to help create new dietary or spending habits?

Considering Isolation in the Classroom

Many early childhood teachers work in classrooms by themselves or with other minimally prepared staff members. They may even be responsible for supervising others who work in the classroom with them. They have little or no contact with strong role models. Often teachers go immediately to their classrooms upon arriving at the center and leave for home when their work day is over. Breaks during the day are usually scheduled so that only one or a few staff are out of the classroom at a time in order to maintain appropriate teacher-student ratios. When staff do assemble for a staff meeting, typically a full agenda is planned. Certainly, these staffing patterns are not designed to isolate staff; rather they relate to the economic realities of staffing programs. In these situations, a strong early childhood role model is needed.

Perhaps the leader can arrange for an experienced staff member who is knowledgeable about the field to work with the under-prepared staff member. Another option would be to try to arrange their breaks simultaneously or to assign them a joint project to complete. As trust builds, the new member is likely to turn to the experienced staff member for guidance. This may be more comfortable than relying on the director. It also gives experienced staff an opportunity to enrich their work and assist the director.

Serving as Role Models for Children and Families

Despite the fact that many teachers have limited opportunities to develop their early childhood knowledge base, they are still seen by children and families as role models. Many behaviors that children exhibit are traceable to the behaviors demonstrated by the adults in their lives. Because children, particularly those in full-day programs, spend many hours and even years with teachers, they often adopt the behaviors they observe in their teachers. The teacher who tells a child, "I'll write a note to remind me that you want to sit next to Ramon tomorrow," may find that over time, children are talking about and writing notes to remind someone of something. By the same token, the teacher who screams at children, labeling them as babies, brats, or stupid, should not be surprised to hear children screaming at others and calling them inappropriate names.

Family members, too, look to the teacher as the expert in how to help children. Although not all of them will accept or adapt what the teacher does, it is quite encouraging to hear a parent talk to her child about going home now and coming back tomorrow, especially if that parent was someone who formerly yanked a child's arm and shouted belittling remarks. Parents often adopt the words and actions they have observed teachers using. What a great compliment to teachers! At the same time, what a great responsibility to model appropriate practice.

The responsibility for serving as a role model is challenging for the experienced teacher; it is far more challenging for new teachers trying to find their way in the classroom. Working to be a good model may put stress on teachers. This kind of stress usually is not as pronounced in other fields. These factors make it essential that directors assume responsibility for serving as a role model for teachers. One way to do that, while encouraging continued growth, is to commend teachers for specific progress they demonstrate. We all want our work to be recognized. Directors who do so are modeling an appropriate behavior for staff. At the same time, they are providing specific support.

Recognizing Early Childhood Issues

When individuals become teachers in schools for older children, they are required to have a certificate or license from the state. This license usually requires specified preparation and testing designed to demonstrate that the new teacher is qualified for the job. It would be unusual for a school system to accept someone with a preschool teaching license to teach third grade or seventh grade. Yet many directors believe that a license in elementary education prepares teachers to teach in preschool. This type of outlook does not apply in other fields. For example, being licensed as a surgeon does not qualify one to be a psychiatrist or vice versa.

In other lines of work, specific preparation is required for all except very basic entry level positions. The owners of a much-loved bakery recently closed their shop for lack of qualified bakers. They explained that it takes three years to become a good baker and that most people were unwilling to work at low wages while they acquired these skills. Incidentally, the hourly rate being offered exceeded what many child care workers were receiving. Even when a baker, cashier, or salesperson is operating relatively independently, a supervisor is often working nearby and can catch and correct inappropriate behaviors immediately. This is not often the case in early childhood education.

LEADER'S CORNER

Yesterday I stopped at a coffee bar for an espresso. While the clerk was taking the order of the customer ahead of me, he answered the phone and answered questions about the store's hours of operation. As soon as he finished with the phone call and the customer, the manager, who was nearby, said, "Jim, focus on the customer you are working with. Then answer the phone." The manager's direction was given in a positive manner, but it was immediate and let the employee know exactly what to expect. As director of a child care center, I wish I could always be nearby my employees to coach them in this way. Although I really enjoy coffee, I could not help thinking how much more critical it is to be able to coach staff who care for children than to coach those who prepare my coffee.

Director, franchised child care center

REFLECTION

Have you ever been in a restaurant and found that another person was following your waitress, listening to everything she said and writing down your order too? Perhaps you have been the wait person or trainee in a similar situation. Although wait staff typically do not take courses to learn their trade, nonetheless, they are still trained by a mentor who coaches them until they demonstrate that they are able to work independently. Are you prepared to coach a new employee?

Conflict Resolution

Although early childhood programs differ in many ways from other organizations, they are like every other organization in that conflict is inevitable. Good leaders understand this inevitability and are not threatened by it. Instead, they prepare to manage conflict and to ensure that their staff members know how to do that, too. Leaders also recognize that relationships are the backbone of the service provided in early childhood programs and that when conflict occurs in those groups, it often indicates a breakdown in interpersonal relations. Poor communication skills also may induce conflict. When a person or group is unable to explain their perspective with clarity, it will usually be difficult for others to accept it. In recognizing this, the leader may need to put additional emphasis on developing communication skills among staff.

However, leaders must also recognize that conflict within the organization is inevitable and is often a healthy sign. When staff feel free to challenge one another and when they have invested time and energy in thinking about differences, they are signaling to leaders and peers that the organization is important to them. They want to be involved in decision-making. However, when conflict is all-consuming, it can become the standard, thereby consuming energy and time that could be better used to work toward program goals. Because early childhood programs are based heavily on values, disagreements among people with differing, deeply held values are likely to occur. Early childhood programs also focus on practices that have been handed down, often from parent to child. Beliefs and practices coming from these sources are very personal and challenging them may cause individuals to feel that their very being is being attacked. When the conflict appears to be personal, many individuals have difficulty distancing themselves from the issues. Leaders must work toward a balance of healthy conflict and attention to the work of the group. They must coach staff until they are able to resolve conflict on their own, rather than depending on a higher authority, and they must set limits on quarrelling, name-calling, gossiping, and rumor-mongering.

When conflict does occur, all parties involved can benefit if they are willing to participate appropriately. In some cases, a person will agree primarily to end the conflict, although still disagreeing strongly with the outcome. When this occurs, the conflict will appear to have ended, but feelings will fester and erupt at some future time, often with great intensity. Therefore, leaders watch to assure that each person has reasonable opportunities to share his or her thinking and to consider others' points of view. Sometimes an individual pouts, remaining silent and brushing off concerns with "Whatever you decide is fine with me," while inwardly seething. Such a person is likely to drop out of the workplace emotionally, coming to work but limiting effort. Others may begin a subtle campaign to convince co-workers that the leader is unfair or incompetent. Even more serious is the problem of the worker who takes a grievance to clients, in this case parents.

LEADER'S CORNER

Last year I had to terminate a well-liked employee, Ms. A., because she was stealing from the center. Efforts to work with her on this issue were to no avail. Of course, I did not tell the staff why she no longer worked here. Instead, I said she was pursuing other interests.

Things were calm for about a month. Then one day, three parents set up an appointment with me and demanded to know why I had fired Ms. A. Their children had been in her class last year and they were quite fond of her. This year their children were in the class of Ms. A.'s very good friend. She had told them I had it in for Ms. A. and that I had fired her on trumped up charges.

Of course, I couldn't tell parents what had really happened. I assured them that the confidentiality they expected for their children and families at the center had always been respected and that we extended the same ethical principle to our relations with teaching staff. I listened carefully to how much they had valued Ms. A. as their children's teacher, how much she had supported them as young parents, and how glad they were to have their children in a class with Ms. A.'s good friend. I acknowledged their feelings, including their frustration at not being able to change what had happened to Ms. A. They left seeming to feel that I had heard them even though I hadn't changed my decision. After cooling off that afternoon, I contacted Ms. A.'s teacher friend and scheduled an appointment to address her discussion of personnel matters with parents. I put a letter in her file after showing it to her and explaining that, based on center policy, it would remain in her file for three years. If no further disciplinary action were necessary, the letter would be removed.

Director, employer sponsored child care center

In the case of Ms. A., the director may not have been clear enough in her discussion with the staff. The director must tell staff members that decisions to terminate a person are based on policies, not on personal preferences. Staff must also hear a clear message that personnel decisions are not to be discussed outside the center. They are free to register their concerns and complaints with the director, but not with parents or community members.

Providing Training in Conflict Resolution

In any organization, modeling conflict resolution is a key role of leaders. When leaders demonstrate that they can work to resolve conflict, even though the process may take a long time, staff members see that it can be done and that this is an expected process. To begin, leaders must analyze their personal conflict resolution style. Although many conflicts will not directly involve leaders, disagreements with leaders will occur often enough for them to invest time in learning in order to change their own ineffective ways of addressing conflict. Only when that has been dealt with will they be able to help others manage conflict.

Good leaders will have provided specific training in conflict resolution for all staff. They often use the following widely accepted model.

1. Listen to the problem actively.
2. Restate the problem so that both parties agree on the content.
3. Generate all possible solutions.
4. Agree on the solution that is comfortable for both parties.
5. Begin using the solution.
6. Evaluate progress at an agreed upon time.

Using this approach will require practice, coaching, and encouragement. Many employees will have to unlearn habits of insisting on their own way, drowning out other speakers, using gestures and facial expressions to display their negative opinions of others' ideas, or crying or leaving the room (Yukl, 1989). In such cases, the leader should listen to and reflect on that person's feelings. If similar situations occur repeatedly, the leader may need to listen to that person privately. Perhaps the leader has unwittingly or purposefully manipulated staff to express a particular point of view. Staff members may feel intimidated and thus unwilling to speak up or they may be disinterested and decide that the easiest and quickest way to resolve an issue is to agree with the leader. Therefore, the leader must be quite certain to listen carefully to the person who disagrees. If that has happened and the leader and staff member are still in conflict, a negotiator or neutral party may be asked to listen to both sides if magnitude of the situation warrants it. If the issue is not critical but continues to be disruptive, an assertive limit-setting response is essential. Each of us brings our own points of view to a situation, but when one person's perspective is always out of synchrony, that person may be in the wrong organization.

Sometimes the conflict may occur in the presence of persons who are not directly involved. For example, an irate bus driver may rush into the classroom with a group of children while the director is visiting that class. He may verbally accost the director with charges of poor management, unfair treatment, or any number of accusations because once again some "inconsiderate" parent has parked in the space that has been reserved for the bus so that children can be easily and safely unloaded. When the director quickly and calmly moves the driver to her office, staff are introduced to the importance of protecting the children from what might seem frightening to them, and possibly preventing serious harm to someone. The leader models her willingness to listen to the staff member: "Let's go to my office, Mr. Jones. I'll be able to listen to your concerns more carefully there."

Once in the office, the director offers Mr. Jones a seat and listens to the details of his legitimate concern. She reminds him of the procedure which they had established. He is to keep the children on the bus until the safe unloading spot is available. Meanwhile he is to use the cell phone that is kept in the bus, to alert the director or receptionist of the problem so that if the person parked in the space is in the center, that vehicle can be moved. The director then discusses with Mr. Jones some possible solutions. He suggests expelling the child whose parent parked there. His next idea is to send a letter home to all the parents. The director suggests that they repaint the spot for the bus as well as the sign because both have faded. Together they agree on Mr. Jones suggestion about sending a letter home and on repainting. Mr. Jones agrees that meanwhile he will follow the procedure set forth earlier and will not erupt in the classroom if other problems occur. He agrees to go directly to his supervisor, the director. Together they decide to talk briefly in two weeks to check on how effective the letter and painting have been. The two shake hands and the director thanks him for his concern about the children's safety as he leaves.

Imagine what might have happened if, instead of remaining calm, the director had shouted back at the driver, "How dare you burst into this classroom like that," followed by a heated face-to-face exchange that grew louder and more animated while all the children watched. Surely, some of the children would have been frightened. The following are some possible consequences.

1. The driver and director will now respond to each other with animosity.
2. The driver may try to circumvent future directives and requests from the director.
3. The director may berate the driver for every minor infraction, real or imagined.
4. Staff will see and perhaps imitate a negative role model.
5. Parents will hear accurate or distorted accounts from their children about the incident.
6. Children may be frightened by the driver and the director.
7. The director and driver may be embarrassed or may need help to undo the damage.

Supporting Conflict Resolution

When leaders are not directly involved in a conflict situation, they should allow employees to work it out. If the center culture has been well-established and appropriate training has been provided, reasonable adults should be able to handle a variety of situations openly. For example, when equipment, such as a video camera or musical instruments, must be shared, staff members should resolve the problem without going to the director. When the cook is upset because the assistant teachers are not picking up the food trays on time, they should be able to set a time to discuss and resolve the issue. Adults who have major responsibility for young children's education and safety must be able to act maturely in their relations with other adults. When this is not happening, leaders must step in, bring the staff together and help them solve the problem of becoming problem solvers.

Some adults, especially those who have limited work experience, may prefer to have the leader serve as arbitrar in all situations. However, once they gain confidence, they are likely to join other staff in wanting to have a voice in decision-making, and they find that they are not comfortable with authoritarian leaders whose focus is on controlling staff. Experienced workers also do not favor laissez-faire leaders who let staff do pretty much what they like whenever they want. Persons who consider themselves to be leaders yet have such attitudes are either lazy or incompetent. All workers need some direction. They need authoritative leaders who guide the staff, take a personal interest in each person, yet set limits when needed. Workers can trust this type of leader and are likely to become involved in resolving conflicts, rather than depending on the leader or avoiding legitimate conflict.

In early childhood organizations, leaders play major roles in accepting conflict and managing it when appropriate. They must be well-versed in understanding the role of conflict and approaches to conflict resolution. To accomplish this, they must have established a foundation of trust and sound communication.

Summary

The business literature, as well as our own lay observations as we go about our daily lives, demonstrates the importance of leaders who are role models. Whether we have read about this phenomenon or experienced it ourselves as employees, clients, or customers, it is relatively easy to find the impact that a good model has. We have also considered the negative effect of poor models on the behavior and morale of staff. We recognize that early childhood staff, even at entry level positions, are given far more responsibility than entry level staff in other types of organizations. Therefore, leaders in early childhood programs play a major role in assuring that staff understand and follow the expectations set for them and demonstrated by the leaders themselves. At the same time, leaders work to empower staff members to assume responsibility for their own behavior and for supporting the work of the group. Of special significance in every aspect of the early childhood profession is the ability to model and implement sound conflict resolution strategies.

Class Assignments

1. Read the following scenario and decide what you would do if you were in a leadership role. What would you say to the teacher or the assistant teacher? What do you think might happen? Think of as many outcomes as possible. Write your responses on Working Paper 2–1.

    Scenario: As Marie, the center director, walks down the hall to talk with the cook, she hears Debby shouting at her assistant teacher. "José, for Pete's sake, why did you let those two children sit next to each other? You know they are going to cause trouble. I'm sick and tired of having to tell you exactly what to do all the time."

2. In the opening scenario in this chapter, Morris is concerned because the receptionist repeatedly has long personal phone conversations. He himself has just had a long personal conversation that she may have overheard. In this situation, how would Morris describe the problem? How would the receptionist describe the problem? What could be done to solve their problems? Write your response on Working Paper 2–2.

3. Using the Internet, locate an article on the leader's role as a model. Read the article and write a summary. Include your comments about whether or not you agree with the points the author makes and why. Write your response on Working Paper 2–3.

Class Exercises

1. Discuss with your classmates what their current (or previous) jobs are. How satisfying are those jobs? Find out what factors each person feels contribute to job satisfaction.

2. Visit a store and note the behavior of clerks as they interact with customers. Did you observe any efforts to pay attention to the customer? Did you observe any behaviors that indicated that procedures were being followed but that the customer was basically ignored? Report your findings to your class. Do not reveal the names of the businesses or the clerks.

3. Suppose a director asked a parent group for field trip suggestions. The goal was to involve parents. One parent group decided that their children would enjoy a boat ride. They contacted a boat company, arranged a date, and began telling children and teachers. The director found out about it when a teacher asked if there were any funds for children whose parents couldn't afford the cost of the trip. Upset at not having been informed of these plans, the director called a halt. She asked parents who had been involved to meet with her and she expressed her concerns about the staff members' ability to supervise children even if a few parents were able to leave work to participate. At first the discussion was heated, with parents charging that they had been asked to plan and when they took initiative their plan was squelched. The director countered that she had just wanted ideas for the staff to consider.

   Discuss with your classmates why this situation happened and what might have been done to prevent it. Then decide how you would resolve it if you were the director.

4. In scenario number 3 the solution which the director and the parents reached was a compromise. The boat ride would be held early in the evening and each family would accompany their children or designate another adult to accompany the child. Younger and older siblings could attend if families could provide the supervision. Staff would also attend and could bring their families. The director had a contact in the community who arranged to provide partial funding for this special event so that all could participate at a reasonable cost.

   Discuss with your classmates whether this solution was appropriate. Why or why not?

Reference

Yukl, G. W. (1989). *Leadership in organizations.* 2nd ed. Englewood Cliffs, NJ: Prentice-Hall.

Working Paper 2–1

Write your response to the situation involving the teacher yelling at the assistant teacher. Assume you are the director. Describe what you would do.

Working Paper 2–2

Write your response to the situation involving Morris and the receptionist. State the problem from each person's perspective, then describe in detail how the problem might be solved.

Working Paper 2–3

- The Web site I used was:

- The title of the article is:

- The article was written by:

- Summary of the article:

- My reaction to the content:

Supervision 101

CHAPTER 3

Setting the Stage for Effective Supervision

The center leader is the key player in setting the stage for effective supervision. A credible authority figure who is the established, trusted leader can inspire the organization's staff to perform with dedication and enthusiasm as they strive to refine their professional practices and contribute to maintaining program quality (Greenman, 1998). The credible authority figure—the director in most centers—has a significant role in developing the common culture, describing the program, and defining the expectations for the staff.

The framework within which the supervisory and evaluation process can be effective is when the established leader, who is often the director, and all staff share in the common culture, know what the program is about, and understand what is expected in their respective roles in the organization.

Developing the Organizational Culture

Every organization has its own unique culture. Whether large or small, for-profit or not-for-profit, public or private, the culture of the organization is the unifying force that shapes the day-to-day practices of everyone involved. The culture is essentially the sum of "the way we do things here," and it applies to both large and small businesses—from Procter and Gamble or General Electric to Bright Horizons, Kindercare, or the half-day church nursery in Cedar Grove, Montana. Jack Welch, who recently stepped down as CEO of General Electric, noted that, when he took over that position, while he dealt with each day's irritations and distraction, he concentrated on reforming the culture of the organization which would then infuse the way business was done in this behemoth of the business world (Colvin, 1999). "A critical role of the supervisors *(leaders),* is to understand the culture and to work with staff to build and maintain a positive school culture" *(italics mine)* (Caruso & Fawcett, 1999, p.70). The culture of the program is what shapes how its members think, feel, and behave. It is key to improving and maintaining quality because it underlies and permeates all staff development and supervision activities.

Andrea is the administrator of a new, very large corporate-sponsored child care facility. She brings a wealth of knowledge and experience, but has never before enjoyed the challenge of a new beginning with a new building, all new staff, and an entire population of new families and their children. "It is an opportunity to build a culture! One which reflects my values as well as those of my newly assembled staff and the families we serve!" During meetings with the new staff before the center opened, discussions centered on past experiences where things were not exactly what this assembled group respected or appreciated. Now, with Andrea leading them, together they articulated what they valued. She recognized that the core values of the evolving culture in this new center were quality and teamwork. With Andrea's help, the new staff generated a "team-work" statement which they signed and posted. As center enrollment increases, new staff and families are joining this community each week, and the core values of quality and teamwork are conspicuously evident to them. Here children and families are valued, quality is apparent, and teamwork is obvious. Andrea also realizes that because she values quality and teamwork, she has modeled such values, and, in her quiet style, has led the way in shaping this culture.

Culture Is What We Are and Who We Want to Be

What are our shared beliefs? What are the norms that determine the basis of our day-to-day practices with children, with families, and with each other? How is our practice affected by our history, culture, and traditions? What values do we share as a staff, with our families, and with our community? Some of the answers to these questions can be gleaned through discussion and reflection. As ideas, concerns, and beliefs about ourselves are articulated and shared, our common culture emerges and "who we are" is defined for us.

Although the culture is but one piece of what the total organization is and does, it is the piece which has a huge impact on what the feeling tone of the center is for families and children as well as the entire staff. Their first impressions as they enter the space and encounter members of the center community give them a cameo view into the culture. As families and staff are assimilated into the culture, they become part of its shared values, beliefs, attitudes, behavioral norms, and expectations. It is not unlike being born into or marrying into a family where one is influenced by and embraces the history, lifestyle, ritual, and taboos of the family culture. These newcomers also contribute to the culture as well. "Shared meanings contribute to the development of cultures and lead to understandings that are taken for granted among members of the culture" (Lee, 1991, p. 85). Culture evolves, enriched by newcomers, while established members maintain the core values and traditions and give it stability.

REFLECTIONS

Think about the first time you observed in a child care center program. Perhaps it was a visit connected with a course in child development. It may have been the time you were visiting centers to select a program for your own child. On that first visit, what did you notice first? The noise level? The spaciousness and light? The odors? What were you feeling during the first five or ten minutes of that visit? Welcomed? Annoyed? Fearful? As you left, what did you remember about the experience? How would you describe the climate of that center?

Every person entering the center, whether a child or parent, a prospective employee, or a delivery person, quickly senses what this place is about because elements of the culture are obvious immediately. The feeling/tone of the space is apparent and reflects the center values and beliefs. The leader may not be the person who greets each newcomer, but he is the one who has modeled for and coached everyone on the staff. Staff interpersonal interaction with newcomers will reflect the tone set by the leader of the program, and those who enter the space will quickly sense what this place is like.

- This is a friendly welcoming place.
- This is a scary, noisy place.
- People here seem to be nice.
- People here are ignoring me.

Other dimensions of the culture are less obvious to a newcomer, but become more apparent after encounters with the director or other staff who share in the program norms and expectations.

- These folks cooperate with one another to get things done.
- It seems that no one here understands or knows what others are doing.
- This is a place where people learn from one another.
- Someone is always available to help me here.
- I am beginning to feel I can trust this director.

New staff who have participated in the orientation process and assume their responsibilities, whether in the classroom or in other positions at the center, become acculturated to the center community. Their day-to-day interactions impart much of what is shared and valued among the members of the community. The leader and the staff model behavioral and attitudinal expectation inherent in the culture. The newcomer is shaped by and accommodates to the common culture, assimilates it, and becomes an advocate for it.

- We are proud of the reputation we are establishing in this community.
- I have come to appreciate the importance of the family and I love learning about what it means to work in a family-centered program.
- Sometimes my supervisor and I agree that neither of us has the answer to my problem, but we agree that we will work on it together.

The elements and dimensions of the center culture shape the thinking and behavior of the members of the community and they, in turn, contribute to the common culture as they participate and collaborate in program changes and personal growth. The leader plays a seminal role in the entire process of developing the culture and helping members of the community accommodate to it. The director's words and actions set the tone. Descriptive documents about mission, philosophy, ethics, history, and organizational structure also reflect the common core of beliefs and practices and further define expectations for staff and families who are part of the center community.

The Center Program

There are many different kinds of programs for young children ("programs" is used here as an inclusive term covering all physical and human resources and activities). There are both part-time and full-time programs for different age groups. Programs may be located in a church basement, a school building, on-site at a factory or office building, or in a facility designed and built specifically for young children. Programs have different administrative structures, different regulatory restriction, and various funding sources and differ greatly in size and scope. The theoretical and philosophical bases for programs vary and are then reflected in different curricula, each with unique classroom practices and expectations. Whatever the program, the leader must have a clear understanding of its focus and content, which then must be communicated to all staff.

Information individual staff members should have about dimensions of the program will vary depending on their level of responsibility, but there are some things that all staff must understand. It is clear that everyone must feel a part of the center community and must know something about the type of program offered and the families served. But although a classroom teacher needs to know what is expected based on the program philosophy and curriculum model, the cook will find it more helpful to know the sanitation regulations regarding food preparation and kitchen maintenance. Organizational structure, on the other hand, is important to both individuals because each needs to know who reports to whom and where to find out about purchase orders and paychecks. All must understand the bottom line: Everyone strives for quality in every aspect of the program for children and families.

Documents Describing the Program

Center directors and experienced staff, in their cooperative efforts to communicate program content and expectations to other staff, can discuss and model practices and procedures with new staff, student teachers, volunteers, and families. However, it is essential that detailed written documents describing various components of the total program be available for distribution to all center staff and others where appropriate. Such descriptive documents further spell out "who we are and what we do here," thereby giving everyone a greater appreciation of their respective roles in the center community and what is expected of them.

In the case of a new center, the daunting task of developing and writing program documents is usually assigned to the center director. However, it is unnecessary to try to reinvent the wheel; rather it is a good time to draw on resources and help available from other centers in the area. There are ample samples of program documents that can be adapted and reworked to match the needs of the new center. When new sites are opened in an existing corporate structure, program documents will be readily available from corporate headquarters and thus should require only minor adjustments. All program documents should be regularly reviewed and revised as the leader facilitates program growth and changes its size and scope.

LEADER'S CORNER

When I first opened our center, 18 years ago, in a rural area of New Mexico, I was aware of the need for having documents such as personnel policies, program descriptions and parent handbooks, but had no one to help me figure out what should go into those documents. A former professor of mine referred me to the closest local NAEYC organization where I met other early childhood education (ECE) administrators who were willing to share what they had. They also reminded me that I had several text books from my course work which included sample documents. Today, if I faced that same problem, I would first turn to the Internet and check what I could find there.

Director—corporate center

The content of program documents will differ based on the overall structure of the sponsoring organization or corporation, the size and scope of the program, and the program's mission and goals. The basic documents covering regulations related to health and safety and those describing policies, procedures, and practices related to personnel and to classroom activities govern the day-to-day activity in most programs. Head Start education programs have additional written guidelines, including some which address lesson planning, family involvement, home visits, and screening and testing children. An employer-sponsored center may follow personnel policies used by the larger corporation, whereas a small church-sponsored half-day program will have simpler personnel policies for the preschool staff.

Documents related to curriculum and classroom practice are based on the program's philosophy and curriculum model, whether it be developmental/constructivist, Montessori, Reggio Emilia, or some other program base. (For further discussion of program philosophy and curriculum, see Sciarra & Dorsey, 1998.) But the common core for all quality programs is that practice be developmentally appropriate. Therefore, the National Association for Education of Young Children's (NAEYC's) *Developmentally Appropriate Practice* (DAP) *in Early Childhood Education* will apply to all programs (Bredekamp & Copple, 1997).

The orientation program for new staff is the first opportunity to share a selected sample of documents with each new hire. Individualized orientation packets can be assembled, including those documents relevant for the position being filled (see Chapter 5 for discussion of orientation programs).

The following list of program documents and forms, although not exhaustive, includes a sampling of descriptive materials which can be used with new staff to help them better understand your program.

- Mission Statement—Goals and Vision (sample in Leader's Resource 5–5)
- Program Philosophy—(sample in Leader's Resource 5–5)
- Summary of Organizational Common Culture—Values, Norms, and Shared Beliefs
- Handbooks—Parent and Staff (Sciarra & Dorsey, 1998)
- *Developmentally Appropriate Practice* (DAP) *in Early Childhood Programs* (Bredekamp & Copple, 1997)
- Organizational Structure (sample in Leader's Resource 5–5)
- Personnel Policies (sample in Leader's Resource 5–5)
- NAEYC Code of Ethical Conduct (Leader's Resource 3-1) (NAEYC, 1992)
- Read's "Guides to Speech and Action" (Read, Gardner, & Mahler, 1993)
- Head Start regulations (if it is a Head Start program)
- Holiday Policies (sample in Leader's Resource 3–2)
- Helpful Hints and Don'ts (sample in Leader's Resource 3–3)
- List of Resources in Staff Library

As a leader in a complex hospital/private-for-profit company partnership, James faced the huge challenge of staff turnover and burn-out among teachers and his site administrators. He realized that he and his site managers had to do a better job of hiring. They had to seek out creative teachers who were passionate and "wowed" by preschoolers' energy and curiosity. But, once hired, how could he and his managers make certain that his new teachers were clear about what was expected in his exemplary programs? His analysis of the turnover data was that, in many cases, there was a poor "fit" between the new teacher and the center culture, or there were basic disagreements or misunderstandings about expectations. He initiated several preliminary group meetings with site managers and selected staff in order to explore what needed to be done. One thing became clear as this group met: they not only had to do a better job of screening potential employees but, even more important, they had to develop a carefully thought out staff orientation plan.

Establishing Expectations

Blending into the common culture of the center community, becoming familiar with the program through experiences with other staff, and engaging in a guided reading of program documents with the director introduces new staff to what will be expected of them. They will also gain insights into what they can expect from the organization, from other staff and families and, most important for our purposes, from their supervisors.

The center leaders and others who may be in supervisory roles are responsible for defining expectations for staff. Expectations will be different depending on the staff position and level of responsibility, but all must be clear about what supervisors expect. For example, it may be that all classroom staff are expected to contribute to planning for children and keeping daily anecdotal notes on the children, but it is usually the lead teacher who completes the lesson plan, which is reviewed by the supervisor. The lead teacher also compiles anecdotal notes and prepares them for use in conferences with other staff, consultants, or parents.

All classroom staff—whether experienced or new, volunteers or student teachers—have ideas about what they should do in the classroom. These ideas are based on their life experiences as a child, as a parent, as a student in early childhood education or a related field, or as a teacher at another center. Ideas from past experiences must be respected and then shaped into what is expected in the current position. The shared experiences with center leaders and peers combined with classroom observation and review of program documents during the orientation program will help to clarify "what we do here and how we do it." As behavioral norms and expectations become more apparent, new staff will soon understand what kind of a place the center is.

The center is a "place for children," where children are valued and respected. Adults stoop down and speak to children at their eye level when they meet in the classroom or the playground. Children's voices are heard above those of adults. Adults guide and protect children, who are encouraged to problem-solve and become autonomous.

This is also a "place for families," where classroom staff offer support for parents when they bring children in each day and pick them up after work. A caregiver helps the baby transition from Dad so he can leave for work feeling that his baby is with a caring, nurturing person. When Mom picks up her preschooler, she is greeted by a relaxed teacher and a child who is tired from play and is pleased to see Mom.

Finally, this is a "place for staff," where caregivers take scheduled breaks in a pleasant staff lounge because folks here understand that caregivers need time to relax and refuel. Encouragement from supervisors who stop by the classroom each day helps the teachers feel appreciated and valued. Calls for help in the classroom are answered promptly and capably, and a teacher never feels that other staff are thinking, "Why can't you manage these crises by yourself?"

Understanding how people treat each other in the center is a significant piece of understanding expectations. This, along with information from program documents relating to philosophy, curriculum, personnel policies, and others help set the stage for effective supervision.

It goes without saying that classroom staff must understand how the philosophy and curriculum translate into developmentally appropriate practices. Supervisors and staff offer support and encouragement to each other as they all carry out the center's mission to provide quality programming for children. Supervisors coach, mentor, provide on-the-job training, call in consultants, and arrange for staff to take classes and attend conferences, all in an effort to help staff grow personally and professionally. Supervisors lay the groundwork for effective supervision so there will be "no surprises" for those they supervise.

At Randy's center, lead teachers are responsible for supervising other classroom staff and Randy recognizes that it is his responsibility to help his lead teachers understand what their assistants and aides expect of them. He models for his lead teachers what he expects them to model for their classroom staff. Just as he sincerely believes his lead teachers want to succeed, so he expects them to feel positive about their classroom helpers. He never lets issues "fester"—he is upfront and honest when he must confront or correct. For Randy, evaluation is not punishment or criticism, but an opportunity for growth, and that is the tone he sets when he communicates with his lead teachers. When a member of his staff confronts him with helpful criticism, he listens carefully and recognizes this as a new personal challenge and an opportunity to model problem-solving with that staff member. His lead teachers are responsible for what happens in their rooms. He offers support as they supervise other staff, but he recognizes that he must be careful not to undermine their position relative to their staff. He tries to work collaboratively with lead teachers who, in turn, help their classroom assistants, thereby helping everyone at each level to better understand expectations.

Staff expectations of supervisors change as staff members grow and mature professionally. Supervisors are expected to individualize their supervisory practices with staff just as they expect staff to individualize their planning and practices for each child in the center. Whether a beginning teacher, an experienced teacher, or an accomplished teacher, there are basic qualities such individuals expect of their supervisors (Sciarra & Dorsey, 1998).

What do teachers expect of their supervisors? According to Caruso and Fawcett (1999), they expect supervisors to:

- be honest with them
- offer helpful critiquing
- spend time with them and listen to their thoughts and feelings
- be knowledgeable
- accept criticism from teachers when it seems appropriate
- offer resources
- support reflection and self-assessment
- enjoy problem-solving and handling conflict.

The success of the supervisory program, as well as the health and well-being of the entire center program, is built upon the leader's ability to "enjoy problem-solving and handle conflict." Conflict is a fact of life in every organization as well as in every relationship, and ". . . there is no way a director can, or even should, drive all conflict out of the life of the center" (Neugebauer, 1998, p. 236).

Dealing With Staff Conflict

Neugebauer points out that some conflict is healthy for the organization and for relationships between and among staff. When conflict generates new ideas or forces examination of what the center is doing for children and families, it can energize staff and lead to change. A wise supervisor will refrain from dampening the enthusiasm generated when, for example, staff excitedly express their opinions and objections in a discussion about putting computers in all classrooms or the idea of having mixed age groupings in all classrooms. It is important to listen, ask questions, and take time to reassure teachers that you welcome healthy conflict. Accomplished, mature supervisors are usually able to create an atmosphere where staff can express opinions on controversial issues and feel confident that there will be no repercussions (Neugebauer, 1998).

A personal feud where staff members take sides and the resulting acrimony erodes morale is an example of destructive, unhealthy conflict. In these situations the supervisor can prevent escalation of the flare-up by stepping in to mediate, without taking sides or making judgments (Neugebauer, 1998).

In the role of mediator, it is helpful to try to flush out the facts by listening carefully to all the stakeholders in order to define the problem. The next step is to bring the key players together to talk about possible solutions. The goal here is to explore possible solutions which everyone can accept and then develop a plan for implementation. The following are the four steps for dealing with conflict.

1. Gather information to define the problem.
2. Bring the stakeholders together to brainstorm possible solutions.
3. Help the group reach a decision about a solution.
4. Facilitate the planning to implement the solution.

Successful facilitation of the conflict resolution process not only helps solve the problem, it also strengthens the relationship between the supervisor and staff.

Summary

The center leader, who is often the director and also the supervisor, is a key player in setting the stage for effective supervision. Directors play a critical role in developing and then sharing the unique culture of the center with all members of the center community. Community members share in the values, behavioral norms, and rituals as they assimilate and accommodate to the common culture of the center.

Center leaders are responsible for preparing and sharing program documents with staff, who must not only feel a part of the center culture but must also understand the program. Understanding the program and being a participant in the common culture of the community give the staff the information and experiences they need in order to define their role in the setting and know what is expected of them. Knowledge of the program and of expectations by staff who have a trusting relationship with a supervisor who advises, coaches, and helps solve problems sets the stage for an effective supervision program.

Class Assignments

1. Arrange an interview with a center director in the community. When you call to make the appointment, explain that you would like to ask some questions about the program and perhaps have a copy of some program documents given to new staff.
    a. Use the questions developed by the groups in class (see Class Exercise 1.)
    b. Read the documents you received and review other information from the interview. Write a brief paper (four or five paragraphs) describing what you learned about the common culture of this center. Include:
        • shared beliefs and values
        • behavioral norms
        • shared attitudes
    c. Turn in your copy of the list of questions developed in class (Class Exercise 1) with the documents you received and your description of the culture.
2. Read NAEYC's Code of Ethical Conduct (Leader's Resource 3–1). Answer the following questions:
    • Why do you think each staff member should have a copy of this document?
    • How do you see this document relating to the understanding of the program and affecting expectations of staff?
    • In the Code of Ethics, Section II, under *Ideals,* select 1-2.3, 1-2.4 *or* 1-2.5. Reflect on the item you have chosen and describe how well-prepared you feel you are to handle issues that might revolve around that particular item in the Code.

Class Exercises

1. Divide into groups of four or five students and develop a list of questions to use in an interview with a center director (see Class Assignment 1). Keep in mind that you are attempting to get a feel for the common culture of this center. When the class assembles as a whole, review all the questions generated by the groups and

decide which four or five questions to use in the interviews with the center directors for Class Assignment 1.

2. Choose a partner in class and compare feelings and responses to the sections each of you selected from the Code of Ethics for completing Class Assignment 2.

3. In groups of three, assign the roles of the two teachers and the supervisor in the following scenario, and follow the steps described on Page 53 for solving this problem.

Lowlette and Maggie are infant teachers in the same classroom and Gerry is their supervisor. Lowlette has come to Gerry three times in the last two weeks complaining that Maggie always finds ways to get out of sanitizing the toys in the room and doing the laundry. She insists that Maggie is lazy and that she does not do her share of the housekeeping chores.

Maggie has been in to see Gerry because she says Lowlette is always bossing her around and acts like she knows more about taking care of babies than Maggie. In addition, she says Lowlette criticizes the way she does the laundry and sometimes does it over.

Gerry has arranged time for both of them to meet with her in the staff lounge.

a. In groups of three, decide on roles for each member of the group. It is Gerry's responsibility to start the discussion.

b. Follow the four steps in the conflict resolution process listed on page 53. Try to reach a solution that is comfortable for Lowlette, Maggie, and Gerry.

c. At the end of the role play, talk about your feelings during the process and discuss how comfortable you were with the solution.

Leader's Resource 3–1

CODE OF ETHICAL CONDUCT AND STATEMENT OF COMMITMENT

Guidelines for Responsible Behavior in Early Childhood Education
NAEYC National Association for the Education of Young Children

This Code of Ethical Conduct and Statement of Commitment was prepared under the auspices of the Ethics Commission of the National Association for the Education of Young Children. Stephanie Feeney and Kenneth Kipnis did extensive research and prepared a "Draft Code of Ethics and Statement of Commitment." Following a five-year process involving the NAEYC membership, the Code of Ethical Conduct and Statement of Commitment was approved by NAEYC's Governing Board in July 1989.

Responsibility for reviewing the Code and preparing recommendations for revisions is assigned to NAEYC's Panel on Professional Ethics in Early Childhood Education. The first set of revisions was adopted in 1992 and the second set was approved by NAEYC's Governing Board in November 1997. The Code is reviewed for possible revision every five years.

The Statement of Commitment accompanying the Code is a recognition that the ultimate strength of the Code rests in the adherence of individual educators.

Stephanie Feeney, Ph.D., is Professor and Early Childhood Education Specialist at the University of Hawaii at Manoa. She is a former member of NAEYC's Governing Board.

Kenneth Kipnis, Ph.D., Professor of Philosophy at the University of Hawaii at Manoa, has written on legal philosophy and ethical issues in law, medicine, engineering, and other professions.

Financial assistance for developing the original Code was provided by NAEYC, the Wallace Alexander Gerbode Foundation, and the University of Hawaii.

Copyright © 1998 by the National Association for the Education of Young Children. Single copies of this brochure are 50¢ each; 100 copies are $10. **NAEYC order #503.**

An 11″ × 14″ companion poster for this brochure with the NAEYC Statement of Commitment is available from NAEYC for $2. **NAEYC order #450.**

Articles featuring an ethical dilemma or problem, and a variety of responses to it, often appear in *Young Children,* NAEYC's professional journal. These articles are designed for discussion by students and staff.

National Association for the Education
of Young Children
1509 16th Street, NW
Washington, DC 20036-1426
202-232-8777 800-424-2460 Fax: 202-328-1846
Website: http://www.naeyc.org
e-mail: naeyc@naeyc.org

Code of Ethical Conduct

Preamble

NAEYC recognizes that many daily decisions required of those who work with young children are of a moral and ethical nature. The NAEYC Code of Ethical Conduct offers guidelines for responsible behavior and sets forth a common basis for resolving the principle

Reprinted by permission of NAEYC

ethical dilemmas encountered in early childhood care and education. The primary focus is on daily practice with children and their families in programs for children from birth through 8 years of age, such as infant/toddler programs, preschools, child care centers, family child care homes, kindergartens, and primary classrooms. Many of the provisions also apply to specialists who do not work directly with children, including program administrators, parent and vocational educators, college professors, and child care licensing specialists.

Core Values

Standards of ethical behavior in early childhood care and education are based on commitment to core values that are deeply rooted in the history of our field. We have committed ourselves to

*   Appreciating childhood as a unique and valuable stage of the human life cycle
*   Basing our work with children on knowledge of child development
*   Appreciating and supporting the close ties between the child and family
*   Recognizing that children are best understood and supported in the context of family, culture, community, and society
*   Respecting the dignity, worth, and uniqueness of each individual (child, family member, and colleague)
*   Helping children and adults achieve their full potential in the context of relationships that are based on trust, respect, and positive regard

Conceptual Framework

The Code sets forth a conception of our professional responsibilities in four sections, each addressing an arena of professional relationships: (1) children, (2) families, (3) colleagues, and (4) community and society. Each section includes an introduction to the primary responsibilities of the early childhood practitioner in that arena, a set of ideals pointing in the direction of exemplary professional practice, and a set of principles defining practices that are required, prohibited, and permitted.

The ideals reflect the aspirations of practitioners. **The principles** are intended to guide conduct and assist practitioners in resolving ethical dilemmas encountered in the field. There is not necessarily a corresponding principle for each ideal. Both ideals and principles are intended to direct practitioners to those questions which, when responsibly answered, will provide the basis for conscientious decisionmaking. While the Code provides specific direction and suggestions for addressing some ethical dilemmas, many others will require the practitioner to combine the guidance of the Code with sound professional judgment.

The ideals and principles in this Code present a shared conception of professional responsibility that affirms our commitment to the core values of our field. The Code publicly acknowledges the responsibilities that we in the field have assumed and in so doing supports ethical behavior in our work. Practitioners who face ethical dilemmas are urged to seek guidance in the applicable parts of this Code and in the spirit that informs the whole.

Ethical Dilemmas Always Exist

Often, "the right answer"—the best ethical course of action to take—is not obvious. There may be no readily apparent, positive way to handle a situation. One important value may contradict another. When we are caught "on the horns of a dilemma," it is our professional responsibility to consult with all relevant parties in seeking the most ethical course of action to take.

Section I: Ethical Responsibilities to Children

Childhood is a unique and valuable stage in the life cycle. Our paramount responsibility is to provide safe, healthy, nurturing, and responsive settings for children. We are committed to supporting children's development, respecting individual differences, helping children learn to live and work cooperatively, and promoting health, self-awareness, competence, self-worth, and resiliency.

Ideals

I-1.1—To be familiar with the knowledge base of early childhood care and education and to keep current through continuing education and in-service training.

I-1.2—To base program practices upon current knowledge in the field of child development and related disciplines and upon particular knowledge of each child.

I-1.3—To recognize and respect the uniqueness and the potential of each child.

I-1.4—To appreciate the special vulnerability of children.

I-1.5—To create and maintain safe and healthy settings that foster children's social, emotional, intellectual, and physical development and that respect their dignity and their contributions.

I-1.6—To support the right of each child to play and learn in inclusive early childhood programs to the fullest extent consistent with the best interests of all involved. As with adults who are disabled in the larger community, children with disabilities are ideally served in the same settings in which they would participate if they did not have a disability.

I-1.7—To ensure that children with disabilities have access to appropriate and convenient support services and to advocate for the resources necessary to provide the most appropriate settings for all children.

Principles:

P-1.1—Above all, we shall not harm children. We shall not participate in practices that are disrespectful, degrading, dangerous, exploitative, intimidating, emotionally damaging, or physically harmful to children. *This principle has precedence over all others in this Code.*

P-1.2—We shall not participate in practices that discriminate against children by denying benefits, giving special advantages, or excluding them from programs or activities on the basis of their race, ethnicity, religion, sex, national origin, language, ability, or the status, behavior, or beliefs of their parents. (This principle does not apply to programs that have a lawful mandate to provide services to a particular population of children.)

P-1.3—We shall involve all of those with relevant knowledge (including staff and parents) in decisions concerning a child.

P-1.4—For every child we shall implement adaptations in teaching strategies, learning environment, and curricula, consult with the family, and seek recommendations from appropriate specialists to maximize the potential of the child to benefit from the program. If, after these efforts have been made to work with a child and family, the child does not appear to be benefiting from a program, or the child is seriously jeopardizing the ability of other children to benefit from the program, we shall communicate with the family and appropriate specialists to determine the child's current needs, identify the setting and services most suited to meeting these needs, and assist the family in placing the child in an appropriate setting.

P-1.5—We shall be familiar with the symptoms of child abuse, including physical, sexual, verbal, and emotional abuse, and neglect. We shall know and follow state laws and community procedures that protect children against abuse and neglect.

P-1.6—When we have reasonable cause to suspect child abuse or neglect, we shall report it to the appropriate community agency and follow up to ensure that appropriate action has been taken. When appropriate, parents or guardians will be informed that the referral has been made.

P-1.7—When another person tells us of a suspicion that a child is being abused or neglected, we shall assist that person in taking appropriate action to protect the child.

P-1.8—When a child protective agency fails to provide adequate protection for abused or neglected children, we acknowledge a collective ethical responsibility to work toward improvement of these services.

P-1.9—When we become aware of a practice or situation that endangers the health or safety of children, but has not been previously known to do so, we have an ethical responsibility to inform those who can remedy the situation and who can protect children from similar danger.

Section II: Ethical Responsibilities to Families

Families are of primary importance in children's development. (The term *family* may include others, besides parents, who are responsibly involved with the child.) Because the family and the early childhood practitioner have a common interest in the child's welfare, we acknowledge a primary responsibility to bring about collaboration between the home and school in ways that enhance the child's development.

Ideals

I-2.1—To develop relationships of mutual trust with families we serve.

I-2.2—To acknowledge and build upon strengths and competencies as we support families in their task of nurturing children.

I-2.3—To respect the dignity of each family and its culture, language, customs, and beliefs.

I-2.4—To respect families' childrearing values and their right to make decisions for their children.

I-2.5—To interpret each child's progress to parents within the framework of a developmental perspective and to help families understand and appreciate the value of developmentally appropriate early childhood practices.

I-2.6—To help family members improve their understanding of their children and to enhance their skills as parents.

I-2.7—To participate in building support networks for families by providing them with opportunities to interact with program staff, other families, community resources, and professional services.

Principles:

P-2.1—We shall not deny family members access to their child's classroom or program setting.

P-2.2—We shall inform families of program philosophy, policies, and personnel qualifications, and explain why we teach as we do—which should be in accordance with our ethical responsibilities to children (see Section I).

P-2.3—We shall inform families of and, when appropriate, involve them in policy decisions.

P-2.4—We shall involve families in significant decisions affecting their child.

P-2.5—We shall inform the family of accidents involving their child, of risks such as exposures to contagious disease that may result in infection, and of occurrences that might result in emotional stress.

P-2.6—To improve the quality of early childhood care and education, we shall cooperate with qualified child development researchers. Families shall be fully informed of any proposed research projects involving their children and shall have the opportunity to give or withhold consent without penalty. We shall not permit or participate in research that could in any way hinder the education, development, or well-being of children.

P-2.7—We shall not engage in or support exploitation of families. We shall not use our relationship with a family for private advantage or personal gain, or enter into relationships with family members that might impair our effectiveness in working with children.

P-2.8—We shall develop written policies for the protection of confidentiality and the disclosure of children's records. These policy documents shall be made available to all program personnel and families. Disclosure of children's records beyond family members, program personnel, and consultants having an obligation of confidentiality shall require familial consent (except in cases of abuse or neglect).

P-2.9—We shall maintain confidentiality and shall respect the family's right to privacy, refraining from disclosure of confidential information and intrusion into family life. However, when we have reason to believe that a child's welfare is at risk, it is permissible to share confidential information with agencies and individuals who may be able to intervene in the child's interest.

P-2.10—In cases where family members are in conflict, we shall work openly, sharing our observations of the child, to help all parties involved make informed decisions. We shall refrain from becoming an advocate for one party.

P-2.11—We shall be familiar with and appropriately use community resources and professional services that support families. After a referral has been made, we shall follow up to ensure that services have been appropriately provided.

Section III: Ethical Responsibilities to Colleagues

In a caring, cooperative workplace, human dignity is respected, professional satisfaction is promoted, and positive relationships are modeled. Based upon our core values, our primary responsibility in this arena is to establish and maintain settings and relationships that support productive work and meet professional needs. The same ideals that apply to children are inherent in our responsibilities to adults.

A—Responsibilities to Co-Workers

Ideals:

I-3A.1—To establish and maintain relationships of respect, trust, and cooperation with co-workers.

I-3A.2—To share resources and information with co-workers.

I-3A.3—To support co-workers in meeting their professional needs and in their professional development.

I-3A.4—To accord co-workers due recognition of professional achievement.

Principles:

P-3A.1—When we have a concern about the professional behavior of a co-worker, we shall first let that person know of our concern, in a way that shows respect for personal dignity and for the diversity to be found among staff members, and then attempt to resolve the matter collegially.

P-3A.2—We shall exercise care in expressing views regarding the personal attributes or professional conduct of co-workers. Statements should be based on firsthand knowledge and relevant to the interests of children and programs.

B—Responsibilities to Employers

Ideals:

I-3B.1—To assist the program in providing the highest quality of service.

I-3B.2—To do nothing that diminishes the reputation of the program in which we work unless it is violating laws and regulations designed to protect children or the provisions of this Code.

Principles:

P-3B.1—When we do not agree with program policies, we shall first attempt to effect change through constructive action within the organization.

P-3B.2—We shall speak or act on behalf of an organization only when authorized. We shall take care to acknowledge when we are speaking for the organization and when we are expressing a personal judgment.

P-3B.3—We shall not violate laws or regulations designed to protect children and shall take appropriate action consistent with this Code when aware of such violations.

C—Responsibilities to Employees

Ideals:

I-3C.1—To promote policies and working conditions that foster mutual respect, competence, well-being, and positive self-esteem in staff members.

I-3C.2—To create a climate of trust and candor that will enable staff to speak and act in the best interests of children, families, and the field of early childhood care and education.

I-3C.3—To strive to secure equitable compensation (salary and benefits) for those who work with or on behalf of young children.

Principles:

P-3C.1—In decisions concerning children and programs, we shall appropriately utilize the education, training, experience, and expertise of staff members.

P-3C.2—We shall provide staff members with safe and supportive working conditions that permit them to carry out their responsibilities, timely and nonthreatening evaluation procedures, written grievance procedures, constructive feedback, and opportunities for continuing professional development and advancement.

P-3C.3—We shall develop and maintain comprehensive written personnel policies that define program standards and, when applicable, that specify the extent to which employees are accountable for their conduct outside the workplace. These policies shall be given to new staff members and shall be available for review by all staff members.

P-3C.4—Employees who do not meet program standards shall be informed of areas of concern and, when possible, assisted in improving their performance.

P-3C.5—Employees who are dismissed shall be informed of the reasons for their termination. When a dismissal is for cause, justification must be based on evidence of inadequate or inappropriate behavior that is accurately documented, current, and available for the employee to review.

P-3C.6—In making evaluations and recommendations, judgments shall be based on fact and relevant to the interests of children and programs.

P-3C.7—Hiring and promotion shall be based solely on a person's record of accomplishment and ability to carry out the responsibilities of the position.

P-3C.8—In hiring, promotion, and provision of training, we shall not participate in any form of discrimination based on race, ethnicity, religion, gender, national origin, culture, disability, age, or sexual preference. We shall be familiar with and observe laws and regulations that pertain to employment discrimination.

Section IV: Ethical Responsibilities to Community and Society

Early childhood programs operate within a context of an immediate community made up of families and other institutions concerned with children's welfare. Our responsibilities to the community are to provide programs that meet its needs, to cooperate with agencies and professions that share responsibility for children, and to develop needed programs that are not currently available. Because the larger society has a measure of responsibility for the welfare and protection of children, and because of our specialized expertise in child development, we acknowledge an obligation to serve as a voice for children everywhere.

Ideals:

I-4.1—To provide the community with high-quality (age and individually appropriate, and culturally and socially sensitive) education/care programs and services.

I-4.2—To promote cooperation among agencies and interdisciplinary collaboration among professions concerned with the welfare of young children, their families, and their teachers.

I-4.3—To work, through education, research, and advocacy, toward an environmentally safe world in which all children receive adequate health care, food, and shelter, are nurtured, and live free from violence.

I-4.4—To work, through education, research, and advocacy, toward a society in which all young children have access to high-quality education/care programs.

I-4.5—To promote knowledge and understanding of young children and their needs. To work toward greater social acknowledgment of children's rights and greater social acceptance of responsibility for their well-being.

I-4.6—To support policies and laws that promote the well-being of children and families, and to oppose those that impair their well-being. To participate in developing policies and laws that are needed, and to cooperate with other individuals and groups in these efforts.

I-4.7—To further the professional development of the field of early childhood care and education and to strengthen its commitment to realizing its core values as reflected in this Code.

Principles:

P-4.1—We shall communicate openly and truthfully about the nature and extent of services that we provide.

P-4.2—We shall not accept or continue to work in positions for which we are personally unsuited or professionally unqualified. We shall not offer services that we do not have the competence, qualifications, or resources to provide.

P-4.3—We shall be objective and accurate in reporting the knowledge upon which we base our program practices.

P-4.4—We shall cooperate with other professionals who work with children and their families.

P-4.5—We shall not hire or recommend for employment any person whose competence, qualifications, or character makes him or her unsuited for the position.

P-4.6—We shall report the unethical or incompetent behavior of a colleague to a supervisor when informal resolution is not effective.

P-4.7—We shall be familiar with laws and regulations that serve to protect the children in our programs.

P-4.8—We shall not participate in practices which are in violation of laws and regulations that protect the children in our programs.

P-4.9—When we have evidence that an early childhood program is violating laws or regulations protecting children, we shall report it to persons responsible for the program. If compliance is not accomplished within a reasonable time, we will report the violation to appropriate authorities who can be expected to remedy the situation.

P-4.10—When we have evidence that an agency or a professional charged with providing services to children, families, or teachers is failing to meet its obligations, we acknowledge a collective ethical responsibility to report the problem to appropriate authorities or to the public.

P-4.11—When a program violates or requires its employees to violate this Code, it is permissible, after fair assessment of the evidence, to disclose the identity of that program.

Statement of Commitment

As an individual who works with young children, I commit myself to furthering the values of early childhood education as they are reflected in the NAEYC Code of Ethical Conduct.

To the best of my ability I will

- Ensure that programs for young children are based on current knowledge of child development and early childhood education.
- Respect and support families in their task of nurturing children.
- Respect colleagues in early childhood education and support them in maintaining the NAEYC Code of Ethical Conduct.
- Serve as an advocate for children, their families, and their teachers in community and society.
- Maintain high standards of professional conduct.
- Recognize how personal values, opinions, and biases can affect professional judgment.
- Be open to new ideas and be willing to learn from the suggestions of others.
- Continue to learn, grow, and contribute as a professional.
- Honor the ideals and principles of the NAEYC Code of Ethical Conduct.

The Statement of Commitment expresses those basic personal commitments that individuals must make in order to align themselves with the profession's responsibilities as set forth in the NAEYC Code of Ethical Conduct.

Leader's Resource 3–2

HOLIDAY CELEBRATIONS

Bridgetown Children's Center

The staff and coordinator of the Bridgetown Children's Center met to discuss developmentally appropriate ways of celebrating holidays in our three-year-old classrooms. We agreed that our priorities are as follows:

1. Meeting each child's needs will be our first priority.
2. We will be sensitive to the interests and wishes of parents and community.
3. We will inform parents and all staff of our plans and our rationale for what we do. We will welcome dialogue on any issues parents or staff may have about our decisions.

Some of the factors we took into consideration as we developed our policies and procedures are:

1. The classroom will provide a calm time and place—a respite from the hustle and bustle and aggression-producing stress of holidays for young children.
2. Classroom routines will be maintained and we will minimize any kinds of interruptions to those routines for special celebrations or parties.
3. In their planning, teachers will avoid attention to a holiday that is a long way off, keeping in mind the child's conception of time.
4. Teachers will plan developmentally appropriate ways to celebrate holidays. For example, they may provide holiday related materials for children's creative use such as red and green paper at Christmas time, or red, white and blue for July 4th. They may use pastel poster paints for spring and Easter, and red or pink during February.
5. Children will have time to talk about what is important to them, i.e., if children bring up the topic of a holiday, they will be encouraged to talk about it from their perspective. Teachers, however, will avoid overemphasis on any of the holidays.
6. Teachers will respond to children's questions honestly and will respect families' points of view on issues such as Santa Claus and religious beliefs.
7. When holidays are discussed, alternative views will also be addressed appropriately. Teachers will try to be sensitive to the fact that families celebrate different holidays in various ways, or in some cases, not at all.

We are eager to share the joys of holidays with young children. By following reasonable guidelines, we hope to ensure that holidays will be pleasurable and child-centered rather than stress producing.

Leader's Resource 3–3

HELPFUL HINTS *AND DON'TS*

Wear comfortable clothing—

- **dress to sit on the floor with children**
- **dress so you can go outside every day with children**
- *no tube tops, short shorts, torn jeans, dangling earrings, or long chains*
- *no adult chairs may be used in the classroom, muscle room, or outdoors*
- *no hats may be worn in the classroom (unless participating in dramatic play with children)*

Maintain a well-groomed, neat, and clean professional appearance—

- **keep hair controlled and tied back**
- **maintain clean, short fingernails**
- *no hair hanging over your face or into the faces of children*
- *no long nails which may interfere with use of fingerpaint, Play Dough®, diapering, or handling small manipulatives*
- *no perfumes or strongly scented body lotions or hair products*
- *no earrings in body piercings other than small earrings in ear lobes*

Eat and drink what is available for the children at snack time and mealtime

- **sit with children at mealtime and eat only what is served to them**
- **speak with your immediate supervisor if you have special dietary requirements**
- *no coffee, tea, sodas, or chewing gum in the classroom*
- *no smoking, alcohol or illegal drugs permitted on the premises*

Prepare to make or receive personal calls, receive messages, and use cell phones or pagers only when on break or outside working hours.

- **messages will be taken at the front desk and held for you**
- **emergencies will be reported to you immediately**
- **calls from parents will be put through to the classroom if they are urgent—otherwise messages will be delivered in writing and left in your mailbox**
- **you have a personal locked space where you can leave your cell phone, pager, purse, and any other personal belongings**
- *no classroom staff may carry a cell phone, pager, or purse while caring for children either in the classroom or on the playground*

Arrange to see personal friends or family at break or outside working hours.

- *no unauthorized visitors will be permitted in the building or on the premises and no personal visitors may interrupt your working day*

Visits and socializing with other staff and colleagues may occur in the staff lounge at break times or outside working hours for both of you.

- **messages from other staff may be left in your mailbox**
- *no visiting or discussion of personal business during the work day with other classroom staff*

Come to work awake, healthy, and prepared to work.

- **take sick days if you are ill**
- *no sleeping in the classroom at any time*
- *do not come to work if you are too ill to care for the children and unable to move about, sit on the floor, go outside, lift children, and handle all classroom responsibilities*
- *abuse of sick leave and personal leave will result in disciplinary action*

Sign in and out each day and if you leave the building during break time. If you have an emergency, notify the appropriate person that you will be late or will leave early.

- *failure to report to work on time or leaving early will be recorded and disciplinary action will be taken*

Treat all staff, parents, and children respectfully and courteously.

- *no discourteous or disrespectful language or actions, including profanity or physical or verbal threats will be tolerated*

Engage in practices which meet licensing regulations, NAEYC Accreditation Standards and NAEYC Code of Ethics at all times as you work with children, families, and center staff.

Report all accidents involving on-the-job injury or damage to self, others, or center property.

Transporting children to and from the center (outside the work day) requires written permission from a parent or guardian and must be approved by the director.

- *no employee may transport a child in the program from the center during work hours or within the child's day at the center*

Follow expectations in the Personnel Policies and Staff Handbook and feel free to discuss questions with the director or your immediate supervisor.

References

Bredekamp, S. & Copple, C. (Eds). (1997). *Developmentally appropriate practice in early childhood programs* (Rev. ed.). Washington, DC: NAEYC.

Colvin, G. (1999). *The ultimate manager* in FORTUNE.com.

Caruso, J. J. & Fawcett, T. (1999). *Supervision in early childhood education: A developmental perspective* (2nd ed.). New York: Teachers College Press.

Lee, G. V. (Spring 1991). Instructional leadership as collaborative sense-making. *Theory Into Practice,* Vol. XXX, 83–90.

Neugebauer, R. (1998). When friction flares—Dealing with staff conflict. In Neugebauer, R. & Neugebauer, B. (Eds.), *The art of leadership: Managing early childhood organizations.* Redmond, Wash.: Exchange Press, 236–238.

Read, K., Gardner, P. & Mahler, B. (1993). *Early childhood programs: Human relationships and learning.* Harcourt, Brace, Jovanovich.

Sciarra, D. J. & Dorsey, A. G. (1998). *Developing and administering a child care center* (4th ed.). New York: Delmar.

CHAPTER 4

Making the Supervisory Program Work

The leader who has the responsibility for supervision in a program also must understand what makes the supervisory program work effectively. In most small centers, the director is also the person who supervises classroom staff and other personnel. However, in larger organizations there are often educational coordinators who work with classroom staff, whereas other staff may be supervised by an office manager or a site manager. For the purposes of this section, the focus will be on the supervisor of classroom teachers.

Basic Assumptions

Some basic assumptions or principles apply when working with all staff. It is important to understand the characteristics of the adult learner, and to individualize the approach to supervision based on the needs and interest of each staff member. In the case of teachers, the goal of supervision is to foster independence so they can become independent learners who can assume responsibility for their own professional development. Supervisors who understand the developmental levels of those they supervise will be better able to find the most suitable ways to help teachers become both competent and independent.

Roles must be clear to everyone involved in the supervisory process. The supervisor is responsible for offering help and support to the teacher, who in turn is expected to commit to the mission of the program and work to provide quality services to children and families. Supervisors create a climate of mutual respect which allows teachers to practice, take risks, and question. The challenge for supervisors is to find ways to lead and support and, at the same time, recognize the reality for both the teacher and the supervisor that at some point, the role of the latter shifts to that of evaluator. Separating the supportive, nurturing, teaching function in supervision from the evaluative function always has the potential for creating tension and conflict for both teacher and supervisor, which is why it is so important for the supervisor to build a relationship of mutual trust and respect with each individual teacher.

Supervisors in early childhood education are often directors or staff persons who are trained and experienced in working with children and who took on leadership roles when those opportunities arose. However, they often have had little or no training in how to set up and implement an effective supervisory program. They know about child development and learning, but now they are also expected to understand how adults learn and develop.

The interpersonal skills they have learned and used with children and families apply to their supervisory activities with teachers. In order to meet the needs and interests of each teacher, supervisors must individualize their approaches based on their knowledge of the stages of teacher development. Teachers at different developmental levels will require qualitatively different supervisory strategies. For example, when working with a first-year teacher who is in what Katz (1977) calls Stage I—the Survival Stage—a supervisor needs to offer a great deal of reassurance and support. Sometimes it helps to offer direct instructions in specific skill areas such as managing a transition or redirection. At the other end of Katz' continuum, the Stage IV teacher—the Maturity Stage—may be ready to assume some responsibility for supervising other staff, write for the center's newsletter, and present at conferences. In the latter case, the supervisor models for this mature teacher who is preparing to take on a leadership role in the center and in the community.

Some would say that every encounter the supervisor has with a teacher is a supervisory or learning encounter. Thus, a brief meeting in the hallway, a casual visit to the classroom, planned observations, and conferences are all supervisory opportunities. Each encounter provides a unique opportunity to build and strengthen a trusting relationship with the teacher. It also offers the supervisor a chance to model good communication skills and give support.

Letitia has fifteen years experience as a classroom teacher and was reluctant to accept the position of director of the franchised center where she had been a lead teacher for five years. Although she was an exemplary toddler teacher, she was not sure she wanted the responsibility of a leadership position. As she reflected on what troubled her about this shift in roles, she realized that she was unsure about supervising and evaluating her adult peers. Conflict was something that bothered her. With the children, she felt secure about handling conflict and problem-solving because she knew many effective ways to deal with conflict in the classroom. But could she confront or handle conflict between and among adults? Were the strategies the same? Would adults respond to careful listening and support, followed by opportunities to offer solutions? How and when would she set limits for unacceptable classroom management strategies or inappropriate encounters with parents? She decided that she would have to talk with other administrators in the corporate structure, visit the corporate website, read literature on adult learners and supervision of adults, and give the matter a lot of thought before she could accept this promotion.

The Adult Learner

The goal of supervision is to promote independence in teachers so they will be intrinsically motivated to grow professionally and personally. As a supervisor, the hope is that the staff member or adult learner will become more self-confident and self-motivated. Understanding the adult learner enables supervisors to more effectively challenge and give support to their teachers. "As supervisors and teachers work together, each brings to the encounter an accumulated set of experiences, perceptions, beliefs and values that make them who they are, shape their behavior, and influence supervisory outcomes. These include early childhood experiences, cultural perspectives, images of supervisors, previous work experience, assumptions about people, and views about how individuals learn" (Caruso & Fawcett, 1999, p. 56). The adult learner brings many impressions and beliefs from previous experiences, all of which impact the supervisor-teacher relationship. To devalue these earlier experiences is, in a sense, a rejection of the person. Depending on their nature, these life experiences can be the foundation for new learning or can create psychological barriers which block learning (Alexander, 1999).

Adult Developmental Levels

It is helpful to view adults from a developmental perspective. When thinking about the best ways to build trust and promote independence, not only with the children in your care but also with staff, it is useful to consider their developmental levels. Some young teachers will be involved in finding equilibrium relative to their sense of personal identity when they join your staff. They are searching for a sense of who they are and what they will be. Dealing with this role confusion drains some of their energy that may be needed to handle the tasks and challenges of teaching. This situation demands patience and restraint on your part, as you seek to establish a trusting relationship with these young teachers.

Teachers who move from the self-absorption of the identity crisis to seeking the adventures of pairing and intimacy will be less self-absorbed but more "other absorbed." Teachers who are working through either identity or intimacy issues can still have a commitment to children, but until they move to what Erikson (1963) calls generativity, their energies are divided between their internal personal struggles and their desire to be an excellent teacher.

Generative adults are those whose energies are more other-directed. At this stage of development, their self-directed energies can lead to reflection, self-knowledge, and self-evaluation, but they are also ready to use their energies and find satisfaction from assuming leadership roles and taking responsibility for guiding and mentoring the next generation (Erikson, 1963; Sheehy, 1976). They can take direction well but are also able to lead.

Approaches to Supervision of Adults

Supervision can be completely collaborative or very directive, or fall anywhere between those extremes. Selecting the appropriate approach will depend not only on the situation and developmental levels of the individuals you supervise, but also on their previous experiences.

Past experiences with authority will surely affect the way a teacher responds to a supervisor. What kind of encounters with power figures has this teacher had? Because the supervisor is a significant power figure for teachers, the images brought to the present work site will be colored by the actions, gender, attitudes, and style of previous authority figures at home and in school or in other work environments. If family experience involved a domineering parent, or if school environments were authoritarian and previous work experience involved a dictatorial boss, then it will be more difficult to create a facilitative, collaborative relationship that supports independence. Those who have viewed power figures as controlling and authoritarian are more likely to be somewhat resistant and defensive and may mistrust your attempts to be a supportive and nurturing leader and teacher. On the other hand, those teachers who, because of different experiences, feel confident about their skills and view authority figures as helpers and partners will adapt quickly to a collaborative teacher-supervisor relationship.

REFLECTIONS

What feelings are conjured up when you face a person who, for you, represents power and authority? Reflect on how these feelings might relate to your memories of experiences with power figures such as parents, teachers, coaches, bosses, or police officers.

Ideally, the collaborative orientation for supervision is the most effective way to encourage adult learners to analyze their own practices, solve problems, and take responsibility for their learning. When the teacher-supervisor team is working well, they plan together, decide where to focus their inquiries, and determine what coaching is needed to enrich the teacher's practice. The supervisor is expected to have a solid knowledge base in early childhood education and know details about the center program, but does not have to have all the answers. Together the teacher and supervisor plan, discuss, and solve problems. If the teacher has concerns about puzzling behaviors of a particular child, then the teacher should observe and record the child's behaviors to establish the basis for discussion about the child. The supervisor clarifies expectations based on knowledge of child development and offers alternative explanations for the behavior based on experience in similar situations. Together, the team analyzes and determines how to find out more about what is going on with the child and what to do in the meantime.

More directive supervisory approaches are needed in situations where adults are disinclined to or show no interest in adjusting their practices or increasing their knowledge base, or when they are so inexperienced that they want to improve but are confused and unable to identify problems. Adult learners need guidance. Trial and error is not only time consuming but can be detrimental to children (Alexander, 1999). For those teachers who are disinclined to show interest in improving their practice or have an "attitude" which interferes with progress, the supervisor must define the expectations, set up a plan for meeting those expectations, and establish a timeline for meeting the expectations, and at the same time offer support and resources to do so. Outcomes in this latter scenario will depend on how well the teacher meets expectations within the agreed upon timelines.

It is important to remember that discussions about expectations must focus on concrete observable behaviors, especially when dealing with recalcitrant staff. Setting up an expectation to "change your attitude" is too vague and will only create more stress in the relationship between supervisor and supervisee. Deal with the behaviors around which the uncooperative attitude manifests itself. Asking teachers to stay late because parents are late picking up children is a realistic expectation. Approaching a resistant staff member about staying is likely to elicit a refusal accompanied by numerous reasons why it is not possible to comply with the request to stay late. The supervisor who takes a moment to reflect after the flood of excuses from the staff member, could comment calmly, "It seems you have a particular need to leave on time today." This would help diffuse the intensity of the emotion and set the stage for a more reasonable discussion of the expectation. Attacking the "attitude" only serves to intensify the emotion. It goes without saying that the supervisor must meet with this person the next day when both can take time to discuss the incident as well as other expectations related to this job. However, it is important that they deal with specific behaviors, rather than attitudes.

When working with young teachers who want to do well but need help in identifying areas in which they need help, a more directive approach can build teacher confidence, which in turn helps such teachers become more self-directed (Caruso & Fawcett, 1999). A frustrated but eager teacher who cannot understand why the toddlers in her room will not put their coats on when she announces "Time to go outside" will welcome suggestions about giving warnings, going to each child and initiating eye contact by stooping down, and offering a hand to a few while moving toward the coat cubbies; soon the "herding" phenomenon takes over and everyone comes for coats. The teacher feels a real sense of accomplishment because she was able to manage the transition with minimal hassle. That's when the supervisor can go on the playground and tuck a little note in her coat pocket: "YOU DID IT!" Adult learners respond to immediate encouragement and reinforcement.

LEADER'S CORNER

When I became a supervisor I tried to reflect on those who had supervised me. I recalled supervisors from various jobs I had while in college as well as those during my student teaching days. What were the things that really made me feel *good?* The first things that came to mind were the ways my student teaching supervisor would smile, give a reassuring touch on the shoulder, and give me a little note as he left the room. "Your question to Jamie about the Jello was wonderful" or "Damion is beginning to enjoy having you read to him." I recall one time when his note said, "You were so good when you were using active listening with Levita. We'll be talking more about that in class next week. Be ready to role play that incident in class."

Director/Supervisor—
church sponsored center

You may want to adjust your approach as you work with teachers who are at different levels of development. Those who are most inexperienced may need somewhat more directive strategies. The goal is to build their level of self-confidence because when they are more self-confident, they will trust themselves enough to join in a more collaborative process. Keep in mind that there is a tendency to "over-manage" those who are not doing well. These individuals need support and encouragement, but they also need time to work things through.

Adults Are Active Learners

For adult learners, it is important not only to consider their previous experiences and where they are in their personal and professional development, but also to remember that they, not unlike children, are active learners. They must be able to relate to the material and ideas presented to them and must be actively involved with it. When you model good listening skills while helping a teacher with a difficult situation you are helping that teacher experience effective communication skills in a relevant and reality-based situation. For example, consider a situation where you and a teacher are dealing with a situation concerning an irate parent. The teacher describes the situation and becomes defensive, trying to justify the fact that she shouted at the parent who was furious upon hearing that her son Jamie had been bitten at school.

Teacher:	"She stormed in and screamed that I should have stopped Ben from biting Jamie, and that I was probably not watching. So I told her that she wasn't there, so she didn't see it and, besides, Jamie has been known to bite other children at school."
Supervisor:	"You and she were both really upset. Sounds like you felt her accusations were not justified."
Teacher:	"No, they were not. She should be telling Jamie to stop biting at school, and maybe he wouldn't get bitten so often."
Supervisor:	"You want Mom to take more responsibility for what happened to Ben."

As you listen and respond reflectively, the teacher will gradually calm down and both of you will be able to discuss the incident more objectively. In the process, you have modeled what you hope this teacher will eventually learn to do in the future when confronted with an angry and seemingly unreasonable parent. The two of you may decide to take some time over the next few weeks to talk about encounters with parents and planned parent conferences as well. Role playing is an excellent strategy to use with most adult learners and could be very useful as you help teachers communicate and interact with parents. By suggesting that the teacher play the role of the parent and you, the supervisor, take the role of the teacher, you can use active listening techniques that will demonstrate what can be done to help the parent calm down and at the same time feel valued. Capturing opportunities like this, where the coaching is relevant and applicable to a real situation in the near future, is effective with the adult learner.

Adult learners must be convinced that what they are learning is relevant to their life and essential to their present position, so that they can personally validate the value of the learning (Pellicer & Anderson, 1995). Mature adult learners are more likely to be intrinsically motivated than their less mature counterparts. Thus, legitimate use of power and extrinsic rewards can sometimes be useful in moving an immature learner toward higher levels of competence. Eventually, the discerning supervisor will be able to gradually withdraw extrinsic motivation and allow intrinsic motivational forces to prevail. Often, teachers themselves will begin to define what they need: "I want to be better able to handle the transition from lunch to nap." Or they will tell you about how their successes bring them internal satisfaction: "I get so much satisfaction when I see how I have helped Jimmy's dad feel good about the way he is now able to handle and respond to Jimmy's difficult separation outbursts."

As teachers grow in self-confidence and come to trust themselves as problem-solvers, they become more independent. Supervisors can create environments in which teachers come to trust themselves as independent problem-solvers. Supervisors should reflect on the question of what their teachers do when confronted with a challenge. What choices do they make? Do they choose the joys and anxieties of growth and progression? In a trusting, supportive environment, hopefully that will be their choice, and they will move along the developmental path from novice to accomplished teacher. When this happens, children and families are the beneficiaries of being part of an organization that "grows its own staff."

Inevitably there will be some teachers you encounter who, despite all your efforts, choose the safety net of acceptance of the status quo or, worse yet, of regression. For whatever reasons, they are not motivated or are unable to grow and mature into accomplished teachers. They do not serve children, families, or the organization well and the administrators will be forced to deal with them accordingly.

Development of Teachers and Supervisors

Teachers and supervisors who make a commitment to the profession and are interested in their own professional development move through stages of development, each with its own unique identifying characteristic. There are novice supervisors just as there are novice teachers. Both focus on personal concerns and are anxious about living up to expectations. They go through a series of changes in how they view themselves and how they judge their job performance. The next section describes the characteristics of the levels of supervisor development followed by a discussion of teacher development.

Developmental Levels—Supervisors

Supervision is a new role for many master teachers, directors, or other leaders who are responsible for staff supervision. It is a new opportunity and challenge for them to grow and develop as they meet the demands of their new position.

New Supervisors

New supervisors, like new teachers, are at the survival stage in their new role. They will be better able to serve their staff if they have insight into where they are in their own development as a supervisor. Katz (1977) and others have noted how apprehensive and self-focused teachers are in their first year of teaching. Brock and Grady (1997) describe beginning teachers as "terrified," a term which applies to supervisors as well. They ask themselves, "Can I do this job?" "What will my supervisees think of me?" "Do I know enough to do this?"

New supervisors also may be uncomfortable in this position of authority and fear they will use their power unwisely. Unlike teachers, many of whom have been in teacher training programs, very few supervisors have had special supervisorial or management training. In early childhood education, people move up the career ladder, sometimes because they are capable and experienced, but other times owing to staffing shortages or problems—no one else is available to fill a leadership position and one becomes a director and supervisor essentially by default. Whatever the case may be, new supervisors often have had little or no training for the job. In larger organizations, preparing new supervisors by offering coaching and mentoring from within is effective, but that option is rarely available in smaller centers. More often than not, the new supervisor is in a "learn as you go" situation. These novices need and should have help and support during these first "terrifying" experiences in the supervisory role. Support can come from other center administrators, except perhaps at a small center where the director is administrator, manager, leader, supervisor, and "jack of all trades." Colleagues from other centers, board members, center parents, and friends or relatives can also be called on to offer support to the new supervisor. As a new supervisor, you must make your needs known and reach out to colleagues for guidance.

Teachers expect supervisors to be knowledgeable about child development, curriculum, and classroom management and to have an in-depth understanding of the center program. Therefore, in anticipation of becoming a supervisor, updating your knowledge of child development and curriculum and reviewing all center documents will be time well-spent in preparation for the challenges of this new position.

Teachers also expect their supervisors to be good communicators and to be sensitive to what each brings to the situation, including experience, culture, and personal attitudes and values. Such sensitivity is the basis for a trusting teacher-supervisor collaborative team that is built on mutual respect and appreciation for what each brings to the relationship.

Novice supervisors are likely to feel a level of discomfort about dealing with confrontations with staff. As in all new roles and relationships, gaining confidence in your abilities is a gradual process of building relationships with those who are essential to successfully fulfilling the expectations of that role. Just as new teachers deal with self-doubt and insecurities about handling daily dilemmas with parents and children or questions about the program and curriculum, a supervisor will have similar questions. Now that you are in a different position in the organizational structure, it will be important to understand the internal politics and lines of communication within the organizational structure as well as the special needs and problems currently of concern within the center community. It is essential to have a clear sense of and a commitment to the common culture of the center community.

If questions or issues arise which you are unable to answer immediately, you can take this opportunity to admit that fact and offer to find resources that will be helpful to both you and your supervisees. In this way, you model what you hope they will do when faced with a problem or question. No one has all the answers but resources are available, and the two of you can work together to find answers and solve problems. You are making it clear that both parties are now teachers and learners.

New supervisors, like many leaders in decision-making positions, must sooner or later face the dilemma of shifting from co-learner and coach to evaluator. The evaluator is, by definition and responsibility, in a superordinate role. Although teachers know at the outset that the supervisor will eventually be an evaluator, they still find it unsettling to have this support person evaluating performance. If the relationship is built on a foundation of trust and respect and the supervisor has maintained the fine line between being a collaborator and co-learner, *not* a buddy, then the way is paved for a smooth shift to evaluator when appropriate. The supervisor continues to be a support person who can objectively observe, reflect, and evaluate.

Experienced Supervisors

Experienced supervisors are similar to experienced teachers who are less focused on self and more able to direct their energies to the classroom and the children. They continue to recognize problems but still may be unsure about how to solve them. They are consolidating their supervising experiences and are able to step back a bit to see how they are doing. They are able to look beyond their personal needs and concerns and be more responsive to the needs and concerns of their supervisees. These experienced leaders are often more accepting of the power of their leadership role, even though they continue to be ambivalent about it. They are also continuing to work out that fine line between being a supportive colleague and a professional companion, not a personal confidante or counselor.

As supervisors strive to improve their practice, they will risk reaching out to their teachers and administrators to get feedback about how they are doing. When they ask for information about their performance and reach the point where they can really *hear* what their teachers are saying to them, they move toward a greater realization of their own strengths and weaknesses and, more important, they now have a clearer picture of the unique qualities of each teacher they supervise. That, of course, enables supervisors to better individualize their supervisory strategies for each teacher.

Experienced supervisors may be more relaxed and less anxious but they continue to need a great deal of support from their peers. Because they give so much to teachers, they may feel drained and need frequent "refueling." They are hungry for words of encouragement from peers, parents, and friends. However, they begin to feel pride and satisfaction as they watch their teachers make progress and assume more responsibility for their own professional growth.

Accomplished Supervisors

Accomplished teachers (and supervisors) are those who possess ". . . the characteristics of mature professionals: self-knowledge, self-confidence, in-depth understanding of the problems and issues associated with their work, and the skills necessary to do an effective job" (Caruso & Fawcett, 1999, p. 80). One of the outstanding characteristics of accomplished supervisors and teachers is that they know and evaluate themselves. They are able to step back and really see how they interact with others, how they come across to others, and how effective they have become as a communicator, a coach, and an evaluator. They realize when they have been too directive and have overwhelmed a teacher, but by the same token, they understand when, where, and with whom they must be more directive in order to help a developing teacher meet expectations. Although they continue to face the conflict associated with their dual role of supportive supervisor and evaluator, the reality is that they are responsible for helping teachers improve their practice and meet the expectations which are the basis for the evaluation process. This is not to say that the major focus of supervision is to prepare teachers for each coming evaluation. It does mean that teachers who are coached and helped to engage in excellent practice, which in turn offers high-quality experiences for families and children, will be well-prepared for periodic evaluations.

These accomplished professionals receive tremendous stimulation and satisfaction from their work, and they seek challenges and take risks. They are also ready to participate in professional meetings and conferences, offer training, serve on committees and boards where they can share their expertise and, in some cases, write for professional journals, AEYC newsletters, and other publications. As they further their own professional development through reading, training, and advanced course work, they move beyond generativity, which is the next to last stage of Erikson's Eight Stages of Man (Erikson, 1963), and progress to the level of wisdom. They become the "elders" of the profession and play a vital role in the field of early childhood education, not only because they work well with their staff, but also because they make things better for families and children.

Developmental Levels—Teachers

Teachers also go through stages of development (Katz, 1977) which parallel those of supervisors. In fact, discussion of teacher development has been part of the early childhood literature for some time, whereas information about the development of supervisors had not been addressed until fairly recently. Although the roles are different, the feelings and reactions of the novice teacher and supervisor are similar. Further, both contribute more and more to their profession as they mature and reach the level of accomplishment where they are ready to begin to coach and teach others.

New Teachers

New teachers may or may not have had previous special postsecondary training in early childhood education. Regulations differ across the states and in some places a high school diploma serves as an entry-level credential for a teacher or an assistant teacher in a child care center. Therefore, new teachers bring a wide range of skill levels to the classroom. Whether or not they have had training in early childhood or a related field usually makes a difference in how they work with children and how their supervisor will work with them.

Some new teachers are entering the profession directly from the college classroom, while others may be returning to work later in life or making a career change. Those who come directly from high school may have had some vocational training or may even have a Child Development Associate credential (CDA). In any case, all new teachers bring different experiences to this new setting and their new position, and all experience a change in personal identity as well as a major change in their interpersonal support network (Brock & Grady, 1997). The supervisor plays a key role in helping them explore and find their way in the interpersonal network of their new job.

Novice teachers, like novice supervisors, are both exhilarated and terrified. Their first year is the survival year, when they feel strange and uncomfortable in their new role in an unfamiliar environment and, even if they are fairly well-trained, they are not yet working from a fully formed and integrated knowledge base. They may feel lonely and isolated from the familiar and unsure about how to do the job they were hired to do. Their previous experiences with children—as a parent, babysitter, nanny, family home care provider, or even as a student teacher—were never quite so awesome as this new responsibility which accompanies the label "teacher."

During the first stressful months, even new teachers who have some training may block out much of that training and fall back on what they recall their teachers did, or how their parents handled them or their siblings. Some new teachers bring a distorted image of what is expected of them, or they feel a bit "heady" about their new position of authority. Sometimes this leads to the notion that they must be "teacher" and "teach" these children and make them behave. Other well-trained and highly motivated beginners are inclined to want to use all their wonderful curriculum ideas and teacher-made materials in their first few months of teaching, thereby overwhelming the children with the constant change in focus and the rapid rotation of materials. Because they are self-absorbed, they miss what the children are really interested in, and thus sometimes fail to offer a rich, emerging curriculum. Their frenzied pace is stressful for the children, and some of these new teachers suffer from early burn out. Supervisors must schedule large blocks of time with novice teachers in order to give them ongoing support and offer them the educational leadership they need during this critical stage in their professional development.

> "New teachers need daily or even hourly support: therefore, the supervisor must plan to spend some time each day not only observing but also teaching with the new teacher. If a new teacher is also recently trained, that teacher will be developing a personal teaching style and will profit from the example set by an experienced supervisor. It is very important for a supervisor to work beside a new teacher with children in the classroom. This supervisory procedure creates a rich learning environment for the new teacher and often provides a more favorable transition for the children and families who know the supervisor but are not yet well acquainted with the new teacher. As a supervisor, you must make sure to remove yourself gradually so that the new teacher can build a relationship with the children and families and begin to manage the classroom without your constant support. What you are doing, in effect, is providing hourly or daily support during the initial trust-building period but stepping back when the new teacher is able to function autonomously. However, stay nearby because your ongoing support is still important when things do not go well" (Sciarra & Dorsey, 1998, p. 382).

New teachers may be ready to take some small steps in expanding their knowledge base through guided reading and by attending training sessions. It is a good time to introduce such teachers to the professional organizations in the community and offer opportunities to attend training sessions. Although it may sound like too much hand-holding, in some cases it helps if the supervisor attends the meetings or training with the new teacher. This enables the supervisor to introduce new staff to colleagues from other centers, and if both attend a training together, they can build on that information when they are back in the classroom.

Experienced Teachers

Experienced teachers consolidate their gains from their first years of teaching and become more comfortable in their "teacher" role. Once they have enjoyed successes in planning for the children and managing a group of children, they begin to feel more competent and self-assured. They may still lose sleep when faced with confrontations with parents or other classroom staff, but are now able to discuss troubling situations with their supervisor, who will assist them in dealing with these conflict situations. By this time, they have practiced good communication skills and have done some role playing, so they have strategies to use with both parents and their classroom assistants.

Experienced teachers are less self-conscious and less self-absorbed and can begin to focus on children and plan creatively in response to their interests. These teachers integrate past experiences with new learning and blend the two into their practice. They can begin to reflect on their practice, analyze, self-evaluate, and be comfortable with their level of self-knowledge. They become more open to searching for better ways to provide quality services to the children and families (Brown & Manning, 2000).

Experienced teachers continue to profit from supervisors' support and, in a mutually trusting relationship, will be receptive to suggestions and ideas offered by the latter. Encouragement and constructive criticism are always excellent motivating factors, and these teachers are ready for growth and expansion in new directions. As they integrate and incorporate material learned in the past, they reach out and pull new learnings into their daily practice. For example, active listening skills may be so much a part of their style of interacting with children that they no longer have to think about how to phrase their responses when confronted with a conflict between two children. Now they are learning how to encourage children to generate solutions and bring closure to the incident in such a way that both children feel like winners.

Once experienced teachers and their supervisors are comfortable with their teaching styles, they can direct more of their attention to intellectually challenging professional growth activities. The supervisor, as a resource person, provides articles and books to read, offers internet resources, suggests course work and available training opportunities, and encourages teachers to attend professional meetings and perhaps even volunteer to serve on a committee.

"While experienced teachers are perfecting their teaching skills under the guidance of the supervisor, they should also be developing self-evaluation skills. With encouragement and help from a supervisor, experienced teachers feel secure enough to step back and evaluate their teaching. They can begin to ask themselves some of the questions a supervisor has been asking them and engage in some self-searching about their methodology. For example, 'How can I help Carlos? He seems to be morose and distressed each day, and I cannot seem to find ways to help him become productively engaged.' Another teacher might ask, 'How can I adjust my questioning techniques for all the children in order to help them become better problem solvers? I heard you mention Rheta deVries. Maybe you could give me something she has written on that topic.' " (Sciarra & Dorsey, 1998, p. 383)

Accomplished Teachers

Accomplished teachers, sometimes called *mature* teachers, *informed* teachers, or *influential* teachers, are those who have made a professional commitment to the field of early childhood education. They are self-reliant, competent, and self-motivated.

"The accomplished, long-term teacher is still perfecting teaching and self-evaluation skills and revising curriculum. However, having reached a new level of mastery, this teacher is ready to develop supervisory skills. While working with the teachers, the supervisor has not only exemplified teaching and self-evaluation skill, but supervisory skill as well. In working with accomplished teachers, the supervisor now turns to coaching them in supervisory skills. This teacher is preparing to assume responsibility for supervision of assistants, aides, and, in some situations, student teachers. To serve in this capacity, the teacher will need instruction and support to develop the necessary skills for fulfilling supervisory responsibilities. The supervisor is still observing and having conferences on a regular basis, giving attention to teaching strategies and self-evaluation. However, the new thrust is directed to this teacher's interaction with and supervision of other adults in the classroom." (Sciarra & Dorsey, 1998, p. 383)

Although in many cases lead teachers are expected to supervise other classroom staff, unless these lead teachers are accomplished and self-confident, they may find supervision of assistants a frustrating and overwhelming task. It is important that they be reflective about their practice and their personal growth and open to learning from mentors in the field. As they find ways to incorporate feedback from supervisors who model effective coaching and teaching strategies, they will in turn expand their developing self-knowledge (Brown & Manning, 2000). As these teachers grow and develop, with the support and vigilance of their supervisors, they should eventually feel comfortable taking responsibility for supervising other staff.

Summary

Effective supervisory programs are based on an understanding of the adult learner and of the personal and professional developmental levels of both teachers and supervisors. Adult learners bring many strengths and a wealth of information from their training and their life experiences that affect their performance with children and families as well as with other staff. When supervisors understand the adult learner and the developmental levels of the teachers with whom they work, they are better able to individualize their supervisory approach. Supervisors offer support as teachers grow and develop from novice to experienced and ultimately to accomplished teachers. Their collaborative working relationship offers a forum for questioning, problem-solving, and clarifying expectations.

Class Assignments

1. Write a brief essay describing your unique needs as an adult learner.
   - As an adult learner, what do you expect of your mentors in school, and on the job?
   - How would you describe what motivates you to learn?
   - How do you communicate your unique needs as a learner to your teachers, supervisors, mentors, or others?
2. Read one article from a journal, book or a website on "adult learners." Write a short paper covering the following:
   - List three things you learned about adult learners from this reading (use examples that did not appear in this chapter).
   - Write two or three paragraphs describing how this information would affect how you would work with a new classroom assistant who is assigned to the classroom where you are the lead teacher.

Class Exercises

1. Divide into groups of four or five and discuss what you see as the characteristics of adult learners (see Working Paper 4–1).
    a. How are adult learners similar to and different from children learners?
    b. What do adults expect from their mentors, teachers, or supervisors?
    c. Summarize the ideas discussed in each group and present to the class.
2. Role play the following scenario:

    An experienced teacher is participating in an interview of a prospective employee who, if hired, will be this teacher's classroom assistant. The director has requested that the teacher ask the applicant about her previous experience with supervisors in other work settings or while student teaching. The candidate will answer based on what her life experience has been with supervisors at previous work or school sites.
    a. After the interview, the experienced teacher and the director discuss the interview. How will this information affect how this teacher may supervise the applicant?
    b. What additional information does the experienced teacher need in order to be a more effective coach for the prospective assistant teacher?

Working Paper 4–1

Summarize the results of the class discussion about the characteristics of adult learners. Use this form to record the work of your group. These ideas are to be presented to the class and contribute to the summary of characteristics the class agrees on.

1. Compare adult learners to children as learners.

    -   How are they alike?

    -   How are they different?

2. What do adults expect from a supervisor or a mentor?

    -   For example, what questions and issues do they want to discuss? What information do they expect to get? What do they feel should happen at their meetings?

References

Alexander, N. P. (1999). Understanding adults as learners. *Child Care Information Exchange, 11,* 82-84.

Brock, B. L., & Grady, M. L. (1997). *From first year to first rate: Principles guiding beginning teachers.* California: Corwin Press.

Brown, N. H., & Manning, J. P. (2000). Core knowledge for directors. In M. L. Culkin (ed.), *Managing quality in young children's programs: The leader's role.* New York: Teachers College Press.

Caruso, J. J., & Fawcett, M. T. (1999). *Supervision in early childhood education: A developmental perspective.* New York: Teachers College Press.

Erikson, E. (1963). *Childhood and society* (2nd ed.). New York: W. W. Norton.

Katz, L. G. (1977). *Talks with teachers.* Washington, DC: NAEYC.

Pellicer, L. O., & Anderson, L. W. (1995). *Handbook for teacher leaders.* California: Corwin Press.

Sciarra, D. J., & Dorsey, A. G. (1998). *Developing and administering a child care center.* New York: Delmar.

Sheehy, G. (1976). *Passages: Predictable crises of adult life.* New York: E. P. Dutton.

CHAPTER 5

The Orientation Program: Starting the Relationship

A well-planned, individualized orientation program provides the ideal opportunity for the supervisor to set the stage for open communication and model good practice. During this program, the teacher has time to observe, read, ask questions, and learn about the program. Teachers and supervisors meet to discuss the program, share information, and clarify expectations. Setting up and implementing an orientation program for new staff may be one of the first major changes a new leader or director will make when coming into an administrative position.

An effective supervisory program begins with a carefully planned and individualized orientation program for all new hires. As discussed in Chapter 3, it is essential that all classroom staff and other new staff participate in an orientation program that is individualized and adjusted according to the position being filled. The program gives the new employee time to become familiar with the center culture, provides an opportunity to be introduced into the interpersonal network, and gives the new staff a great deal of information which will help them understand what is expected of them.

Gaining an understanding of the culture and sharing in the program values, norms, and attitudes requires much more than reading the program documents. Day-to-day experiences with colleagues and exposure to rituals and taboos are a few ways that new staff can begin to understand the common culture of their new environment. The experiences new staff have during their orientation will help them understand "what we do here and how we do it."

Felippe is the program administrator for an organization with six full-day center programs and a total of forty full-time classroom staff. Like many administrators, Felippe deals with a great deal of staff turnover as well as site directors who struggle with staff members who fail to live up to expectations. When he met with site directors to discuss what steps could be taken to alleviate these problems, he realized that orientation for new staff is done differently in each of the six centers. Several directors were uneasy about what they should expect from classroom staff, and all site directors were asking for guidelines for supervision of staff and for orienting new staff. Because Felippe had several big projects on the "back burner," such as building a new center at one site and piloting a zero-to-three environment at another site, he decided to hire a special projects coordinator *to help him at corporate headquarters. Her first assignment was to develop an Orientation Plan for use in all six centers. The job also includes follow-up on the success of the orientation program, and she is expected to gather data on staff turnover, director and staff satisfaction, and parent reaction when the new staff orientation plan is in place.*

Centers should have a staff orientation plan in place for every new-hire and ancillary staff, including aides, volunteers, and student teachers. For a consulting psychologist or speech therapist, the orientation plan may be a brief meeting with the director. At that time the director can describe the program and the population served, give a tour of the building, and introduce the specialist or consultant to the educational coordinator or classroom teacher who will be the contact person from then on. For new lead teachers or assistant teachers, orientation may last a week or more, but the essentials could be consolidated into a two- or three-day plan if necessary. The comprehensive orientation program includes observations in all classrooms, attendance at a planning session in one room, regular meetings with the director and other supervisory personnel, attendance at a parent meeting, involvement in a board meeting, and other related activities.

In the face of a staff crisis, where a person is needed immediately to meet required ratios or fill a vacancy resulting from an unexpected resignation, an orientation program concentrated into the first weeks on the job may be totally unrealistic. However, such a program is time and money well-spent in the long run. The new hires learn what to expect and what is expected of them. They come to feel at home and a valued part of the center community. They begin to know some of the families and children, and they begin to feel secure and trusting. An orientation program should involve all new staff, including cooks, bus drivers, business managers, receptionists, and custodians.

Larger centers may have an assistant director or educational leader who is responsible for orienting all new staff and volunteers. In smaller centers, it is usually the director who is responsible for staff orientation and, subsequently, supervision of those staff members.

REFLECTIONS

Think about your first days on a new job. Reflect on what words describe how you felt. Did you feel confident, fearful, lonely? Did you feel welcome? Did you feel challenged and pleased about this new opportunity, or did you feel overwhelmed?

Orientation of New Staff

Although it is more economical to orient groups of new staff, it is probably more realistic to plan an individualized orientation program because with the exception of start-up programs, most centers rarely have more than one or two new employees at any one time. An individualized plan can be readily adapted for small group use.

Depending on the size of the organization and whether or not there is an overarching corporate structure, new staff may spend the first day or two filling out paperwork related to payroll and benefits or collecting health records and attending new employee trainings. In order to meet state licensing requirements, new classroom staff may be required to attend training in first aid training, cardiopulmonary resuscitation (CPR), and communicable diseases before they can be in the classroom. It also takes time to introduce new people to all the staff and give them a tour of the facility so they know where the bathroom is and where supplies are stored.

The majority of the first couple of days is spent handling important paperwork and attending meetings. Some time must be spent reviewing program documents so the new employee understands the structure of the organization and other personnel information contained in those documents. The employee must know who is in charge of what, where to get needed signatures, where to send forms, and where to obtain keys or parking passes.

Assigning a "buddy" to each new staff person on the first or second day is a procedure that seems to work well. This assigned buddy can be anyone on the staff who enjoys helping others, is empathetic, and has something in common with the new employee. It may be a wonderful way to enrich the role of the cook, because he becomes that special person who answers the new teacher's questions about how things work at the center. The cook will know where the business manager's office is because that is where employees pick up their check, and he can also tell the new teacher how much must be put into the coffee fund each week. He will also know the community and can help the newcomer find the post office or the dry cleaner and details about the public transportation in the area. What a great way to make both the new teacher and the cook feel valued and welcome!

Teachers and assistant teachers will focus on classroom observations, with special attention to their assigned classroom during their orientation program. Other staff, whether bus driver, business manager, or receptionist, must also spend some time observing in various classrooms in addition to their on-the-job training for their particular position.

Classroom observations will be more meaningful if the observers are given some guidelines about how and what to observe. Those who have never been in a preschool classroom before may have no idea about where to sit or what to say to a child who approaches boldly and, with hands on hips, asks "What are you doing here?" When the new office manager or the cook are being prepared for their classroom visits, it helps to offer suggestions about what to say to a child who is concerned about their presence: "My name is Eric, and I am going to be working at your school. I came to watch you play today." Also, providing a few written questions for each observation will help observers focus their attention on selected specifics, and give them reason to tell the children "I am writing down what I want to remember about your room" (Sample Observations Guides, Leader's Resources 5–1, 5–2 and 5–3). When time permits, the experience can be further enriched by having the director or supervisor join the new staff person and do a "guided" observation. The center administrator or whoever is handling this new employee's orientation (in the case of the cook, the nutrition coordinator), will be this person's supervisor and thus the person to model appropriate observation procedures. Observers should knock first, enter quietly, and move quickly to a place that will not interfere with children's play, and then sit on a child's chair or a designated visitor's chair to watch the activity. When the supervisor and staff person observe together, they can compare notes and reactions to the classroom events, and highlight those events exemplifying the philosophy and mission of the program.

Orientation of Classroom Teachers

The classroom teacher orientation, like the orientation of all staff, introduces the teacher to the culture, the organizational mission and structure, the center program, and the expectations for the classroom curriculum and pedagogical practices. Teacher orientation is usually considerably longer than that of office staff or other center staff such as custodians, cooks, bus drivers, or volunteers and student teachers. A comprehensive teacher orientation program requires a fairly large block of time for both the newly hired teacher and that teacher's assigned immediate supervisor, but it is essentially the foundation of an effective supervisory program.

Quality orientation programs are intense, time-consuming, and costly to the organization because two staff members—the new teacher and the assigned supervisor—will be involved in the process together for as much as a week or more. They will be observing, meeting, discussing, and planning the best ways to execute the individualized program fashioned to the job responsibilities for this particular teacher.

Both directors and teachers know the importance of orienting children and families to the program. They recognize the importance of doing a gradual intake process with each child accompanied by a familiar adult, usually a parent. They know that the child must feel at ease with the new surroundings and new people before she can comfortably benefit from the classroom experience. At the same time, the parent is learning about the teacher, the program, and the other children in the group. Both parent and child begin to understand what is expected and what to expect and, most important, they begin to develop a trusting relationship with the teacher as well as other center staff so they feel valued and a part of the center community. This process is both time-consuming and expensive, but it is necessary for the well-being of the child and the family.

So it is with new teachers—intense and expensive, but necessary for everyone involved. When teachers are given time to understand their position in this new organization and know what is expected of them, they will function more effectively and are more likely to make a commitment to the program and its leaders whom they have come to trust. The ultimate goal is better staff retention, lower turnover, and fewer changes for children and families.

To achieve some flexibility in individualizing the orientation program, it is helpful to set it up in a sequence of steps or phases, thus giving individuals involved choices about the scheduling and duration of each phase of the process. Ultimately a timetable for each phase must be set up so there is time for tours of the facility, doing the required paperwork, meeting all staff, observing in all classrooms, reading and reviewing all program documents, conferencing with the supervisor to assess progress, and planning the next phase. (See Chapter 3 for a list of documents, and Leader's Resources 3–1, 3–2, and 3–3 and Leader's Resource 5–5 for sample documents.)

Phases of the Classroom Teacher Orientation Program

Setting up a teacher orientation in steps or phases that include all the activities in the program offers the flexibility of being able to select segments from the complete program which meet the needs of the particular teacher involved as well as a realistic time table for this teacher and the supervisor. An orientation checklist that includes a plan for this teacher's orientation can be set up so that both the teacher and the supervisor can check off tasks completed and note what the next step will be.

Orientation is an ongoing process lasting from a few weeks to several months, depending on the employee's experience and the complexity of the organization. In the case of a new teacher, the first days of employment can be spent reviewing documents and observing in classrooms. It is essential that a minimum of two days be set aside when the new teacher is on the payroll but not counted in ratio. It is preferable to set aside four or five days of the first week to work through the first four phases of an orientation program such as the one described below. The process will go on for the next weeks and months, with ongoing support from the immediate supervisor and the assigned buddy. It is also helpful to assign a peer mentor, an experienced or accomplished teacher, who can offer additional help with curriculum planning and classroom management issues. These assigned support people can serve as a safety net for the new teacher, who may bring rich experiences but must find the best way to blend them into a new setting.

The sequence of phases suggested here is an example of one way to organize a teacher orientation program. This sequence includes much of what is necessary for a comprehensive program, but it can be adapted and changed in length and content, depending on the organization's size and program. It can also be adapted in length and content for other staff positions. Samples of documents listed here and a sample timetable can be found in Leader's Resources 5–4 and 5–5.

The Orientation Plan must include classroom observations, overview and review of program documents, and ample time to meet with the supervisor, the assigned buddy, and the assigned mentor. Creative leaders find ways to make these first stressful days more interesting and relaxing. The use of videos that explain the program and introduce administrators, or using slides and recordings as a way to see other teachers and children in classrooms before observing, are alternative ways to communicate new information. Offering snacks and beverages for some of the time spent in meetings or reading documents in the staff lounge is another way to help new staff feel welcome. This is a special time for learning and also an important time for beginning to work together and blend into the culture of this new community.

Phase I

- Meet with director (if that person is not the immediate supervisor)
- Tour the building and complete building checklist
- Meet all office and classroom staff
- Assign and meet your "buddy"
- Read Personnel Policies and review with supervisor (sample in Leader's Resource 5–5)
- Read Program Philosophy and Program Mission and Vision statements
- Take home Parent Handbook
- Read *Guides to Speech and Action* (Read, 1993)
- Read "Helpful Hints and Don'ts" (Leader's Resources 3–3 and 5–5)

Phase II

- Begin classroom observations, completing observation guides that are to be used as a basis for discussion with the supervisor (sample observation guides in Leader's Resources 5–1, 5–2, 5–3)
- Discuss *Guides to Speech and Action* and relate to classroom observation.
- Discuss "Helpful Hints and Don'ts"
- Review Personnel Policies with director or office staff responsible for answering personnel questions
- Review Parent Handbook
- Read Employee Handbook

Phase III

- Continue classroom observations, now focusing on assigned classroom
- Meet with director and supervisor together to discuss progress, reactions to the program up to now, and to get answers to questions
- Read files for children in assigned classroom

Phase IV

- Begin to interact with children in assigned classroom on a regular schedule
- Attend a staff meeting
- Attend a parent meeting (if possible)
- Read selected articles from *Young Children, Parent's Magazine, Child Care Information Exchange,* or from a website (reading is selected jointly with the supervisor)
- Revisit *Guides to Speech and Action*
- Read and review selected sections of NAEYC's Developmentally Appropriate Practice (DAP) (Bredekamp & Copple, 1997)

Phase V

- Review Employee Handbook
- Review Parent Handbook
- Complete review of records for children in assigned classroom and discuss children and families with supervisor

Phase VI

- Discuss Building and Procedures Checklist (sample in Leader's Resource 5–5)
- Go over Performance Appraisal tool—how it will be used to assess and evaluate performance (samples in Leader's Resources 5–5, 6–1, 6–2, and 6–5)
- Read and discuss Grievance Procedures (sample in Leader's Resource 5–5)
- Review Staff Handbook
- Review progress in this orientation period and how the first assessment and evaluation will be handled
- Review how all conflicts and issues will be handled and, hopefully, resolved

Some parts of the orientation can continue well into the teacher's first weeks on the job and must be arranged to fit the teacher's scheduled hours in the assigned classroom. This time can be more productive and less stressful if classroom time can be reduced to four or five hours per day, leaving time to read documents and relevant literature, meet with the supervisor on a daily basis, and make some of the home visits.

LEADER'S CORNER

As I look back on my experience supervising staff, I think about what is most important to new classroom staff when they come on the job. I carefully go over building policies and personnel policies so they know what is in those documents that are in their orientation packets. I also make absolutely certain that we review the performance appraisal process and all the documents used to evaluate performance because I am aware of how anxious teachers are about that piece of the supervisory process.

Understanding Expectations

Much of what has been said about program culture and program description in Chapter 3 and orientation of new staff in this chapter relates to helping staff members understand what is expected of them. Teachers and leaders in early childhood education realize how important it is for children to understand what is expected of them. Knowing what to expect and what is expected of them helps children feel more confident and secure. If there is to be an orderly, safe environment, then adults as well as children must understand "what we do here and how we do it." When a daily predictable routine is established where grouptime follows outside time and lunch comes after group, children know what to expect and soon adjust to what is expected of them, which gives them a safe, secure feeling. Likewise, new staff also find security and feel they can trust themselves and others when they know what is expected of them.

Defining expectations for all staff at all levels is an ongoing process that extends beyond the staff orientation and probationary period. As teachers develop professionally, more is expected of them, just as they expect more of themselves. After basic expectations are communicated during the orientation process through reading and discussion of all program documents, classroom observations, and frequent conferencing with the supervisor and other center staff, there will be meetings and various memos and documents to update staff on any changes which could affect expectations.

Of course, the ongoing supervision cycle and evaluation (see Chapter 6)—observations, conferences, goal setting, and taking time to review change and progress—will always include time for classroom staff to question and discuss expectations. The range of issues discussed might include expectations about future training and course work, adjustments in classroom management strategies, playground dress codes for summer, or calls to parents about home visits.

There are always center memos or group meetings where staff read or hear about changes in expectations or elaboration and reiteration of those already established. This information may be:

- memos and updated copies of handbooks or other documents
- staff meetings and staff retreats
- attendance at parent meetings
- minutes from board meetings
- staff newsletters
- parent newsletters
- the Center's Web site

These materials or experiences are available to everyone on the center staff and some are also available to parents. In the case of classroom staff, meetings and regular conferences with a supervisor further personalize expectations to fit individuals and their job responsibilities. If a discussion occurs at a parent meeting about policies and developmentally appropriate practices for celebration of holidays at the center and each parent has received written guidelines about suitable snacks or acceptable outfits for Halloween, then teachers must be informed about what was said and receive copies of the written guidelines. However, a given teacher may want to know exactly how to handle the annoyed parent who rushes in the next day and announces, "I bought Sammy a special fur-covered monster outfit for Halloween, and there is no way I'll be able to stop him from wearing it to school that day." Supervisors and teachers, in anticipation of such a reaction from a parent following the parent meeting, need to work together to plan who will handle these situations and what the procedures will be. In most cases, the advice will be to defer to the director or someone in administration who usually handles these special issues with parents. Unless teachers and class assistants understand what kinds of situations with parents to handle in the classroom and when to defer to someone else, they are unsure and feel they are "put on the spot."

Expectations at all levels affect how people do their jobs. Teachers have to know what is expected of them in the classroom in terms of planning and implementing curriculum and classroom management. They also need a clear understanding of what additional course or training is expected, what their responsibilities are for setting up or cleaning storage areas, outside spaces and large muscle rooms, and all the expectations in connection with record keeping and working with families. When teachers understand what is expected of them, they feel more in control of the situation and are better able to work successfully with children and families as well as peers. Most importantly for our purposes, they are better able to work collaboratively with their supervisor whose goal for them is to have them become independent, accomplished teachers.

Summary

A well-planned and carefully executed orientation program provides a sound basis for the supervision and evaluation of staff. In most cases, it is the director who plans and implements the orientation for new teachers and other center staff. However, it is best if each new staff person's supervisor participates in the orientation process, so their relationship begins as they go through that process together.

During orientation and throughout the supervisory process, the teacher and the supervisor are building a relationship based on trust and mutual respect. Their collaborative working relationship offers a forum for asking questions, problem-solving, and clarifying expectations.

Class Assignments

1. Describe an orientation program you have experienced (for a new job, at school or university, at a club or summer camp).
   - Summarize the orientation procedures and the information you received.
   - Evaluate the program
     - How was it helpful?
     - What should have been added?
     - What could have been eliminated?
     - Reflect on how you felt about the experiences during the orientation process.
2. Design a three-day orientation program for a new business manager for Felippe's organization (see page 90). Questions to consider:
   - Should visits to all six sites be scheduled?
   - Which program documents should be reviewed?
   - Who should be assigned as a "buddy" and who might be the best person to become a mentor for this new person?

Class Exercises

1. Role play a discussion among three center directors and two accomplished teachers. One of the directors must assume responsibility for convening the meeting and starting the discussion. Use Working Paper 5 1 to guide this discussion.
   a. Directors' Roles: All three directors are planning to set up an orientation program for the new teachers they hire. They have all thought about how time consuming and expensive such a program would be. However, all are beginning to feel that they must do something more to help their teachers understand their program, its philosophy, and its mission, and to get a clearer understanding of what is expected of them. Director No. 1 decided to call the group together to discuss the matter, and they all agreed that it would be helpful to have input from a couple of excellent teachers in their community.
   b. Teachers' Roles: The two teachers both know that they were invited to this meeting to discuss teacher orientation programs. They are also aware that these three directors see them as accomplished teachers, and they both have participated in an orientation in the centers where they teach.

   The directors want to come away from this meeting with some ideas about the advantages and disadvantages of a teacher orientation program as well as some of the elements of the orientation program the two teachers experienced.
2. Using Classroom Assignment No. 2, select two students to role play the first conference between Felipe (program administrator) and the new business manager. Felipe is to explain the orientation plan to this new staff member and answer questions about it. Use the Orientation Plan developed by the student who agrees to take the role of Felipe.

Working Paper 5–1

The following questions are meant to guide the discussion among the directors and teachers about what constitutes an effective orientation program and of its value to teachers.

1. What should be included in a teacher orientation program?
   - What information should be included?

   - What activities should be scheduled for teachers and supervisors?

2. How can the program be individualized so it works for teachers at different levels of development?

3. How would you adjust the orientation for a new teacher who had little or no experience with children from diverse ethnic backgrounds.

4. What are the advantages to such adjustments? Why should it be done?

Leader's Resource 5–1

SAMPLE OBSERVATION GUIDE

Nonclassroom staff

Date _____   Observer _____

Time _____   Teacher _____

Instructions for Observing

- Knock and enter quietly. The teacher and the children know you are coming.
- Sit on a child's chair in a place the teacher suggests and do not move about unless children go the playground or large muscle room. Follow the children. The teacher will tell you where to sit. You may be asked to sit on the floor or on the edge of the sandbox because there will be no adult chairs in these spaces.
- If a child approaches and speaks to you, answer quietly, but avoid engaging the child in conversation when you are observing.
- If a child asks who you are and what you are doing, offer a simple explanation such as, "I will be the new cook at your school and I wanted to see what you do in your classrooms in the morning."
- Spend the full time assigned to this part of your orientation program.
- Take notes on this form so you are prepared to talk about your observation with your supervisor.

1. What did you notice first as you entered this classroom?

2. What was different than you expected? Were there things that surprised you?

3. How would you describe the way the teacher talks to the children?

   a. Give an example of how the teacher greeted a child as she entered the room.

   b. Give a specific example of how the teacher encouraged a child to help or cooperate.

4. What kinds of things are the children doing? What are they playing with?

Leader's Resource 5-2

SAMPLE OBSERVATION GUIDE

Classroom staff—first observation

Date _____   Observer _____

Time _____   Teacher _____

Instructions for Observing

- Knock and enter quietly. The teacher and the children know that you are coming.
- Sit on a child's chair in a place the teacher suggests and do not move about unless the children leave to go to the playground or large muscle room. Follow the children. The teacher will tell you where to sit. It may be on the floor because there will be no adult chairs in these spaces.
- If a child approaches and speaks to you, answer quietly, but avoid engaging the child in conversation when you are observing.
- If a child asks who you are and what you are doing, answer honestly and simply: "I am going to be a teacher in your school (or in your room) and I want to see what you do in this classroom in the morning."
- Spend the full time assigned to this part of your orientation program.
- Take notes on this form so you are prepared to talk about your observation with your supervisor.

1. What did you notice first when you entered the classroom today?

2. What centers are set up for the children? List the materials available in one of those areas.

3. How would you describe the activity level and the feeling/tone of this group today?

4. Using exact quotes, indicate how this teacher talks to the children (when asking for help or cooperation, when transitioning children, etc.). List five samples of teacher "talk."

5. What is the guidance philosophy in this classroom? Give three examples to support your decision about the guidance policy.

6. How is this classroom setting alike and how is it different from those you have seen as a student, a parent, or a teacher in another center?

Leader's Resource 5–3

SAMPLE OBSERVATION GUIDE

Classroom staff—all subsequent observations

Date _____   Observer _____

Time _____   Teacher _____

Follow "Instructions for Observing" from Leader's Resource 5–2. Focus of today's observation is _____. (i.e., transitions; social interactions of children, a particular child, a particular teacher, grouptime; interactions between teacher and assistant teacher)

Focus of today's observation is *transitions*.

1. What was the first thing you noticed about initial transition of the children into the classroom today? Describe in detail the transition of one child and parent, providing enough detail so a person who was not in the room will know how it looked and what happened.

2. Choose either transition to outside or transition to group and describe how it was done. What did the teacher do and say? How did the children respond? How long did it take?

3. Putting yourself in the position of the teacher, how would you have included your assistant teacher in this process? Or as an assistant teacher, how would you have assisted the teacher in the transition?

4. What do you see as the critical elements in facilitating a smooth transition for young children?

Leader's Resource 5–4

SAMPLE ORIENTATION SCHEDULE

Lead Teacher Position

This four-day orientation is during the first week of employment and begins on Tuesday of that week, leaving Monday to complete necessary paper work and collect all records needed to set up your personnel file. (Samples of many of the items mentioned in this schedule can be found in Leader's Resource 5–5.)

Day One

9:00–10:30 A.M.

- Meet with director (or supervisor if different from director)
- Meet all staff and tour the building
- Receive some of the documents which describe the program:
  a) Handbooks (staff and parent)
  b) Personnel Policies–Guidelines for Working in the Classroom
  c) NAEYC'S Developmentally Appropriate Practice (DAP) in Early Childhood Programs
  d) *Guides to Speech and Action,* by Katherine Read
- Discuss sign in and sign out procedures
- Discuss plan for the orientation process
- Discuss work schedule for this first week
- Receive a copy of the letter sent to families about new teacher coming
- Meet your "buddy"

10:30–11:00 A.M.

- Start to read documents
- Lunch with buddy if possible

1:00–3:00 P.M.

- Meet with director (or supervisor)
- Go over the documents received this morning
- Discuss philosophy and personnel policies and review "Helpful Hints and Don'ts" list
- Get questions answered

3:00–5:00 P.M.

- Explore teacher's resources shelf (books, journals, etc.)
- Read *Guides to Speech and Action* and selected sections of NAEYC's Developmentally Appropriate Practice (DAP)
- Read one article on classroom management or curriculum from the journals available in the staff lounge on the teacher's resource shelf.

Day Two

The focus today is on classroom observations. The new teacher will observe in all the classrooms, using the Observation Guides provided (Leader's Resources 5–2 and 5–3).

8:30–9:30 A.M.

- Observe infant area

9:30–11:00 A.M.

- Observe toddler area

11:00 A.M.–Noon

- Consolidate notes and prepare for conference with the director (or supervisor)

Noon–1:00 P.M.

- Lunch with buddy, if possible

1:00–3:30 P.M.

- Discuss observations with director using the notes from the Observation Guides
- Discuss materials read previous afternoon.

3:30–4:30 P.M.

- Explore storage areas—check out resources for preparation of teacher-made materials, check classroom materials available (manipulatives, puzzles, books, art materials, prop boxes, etc). Make notes on availability and comment on adequacy or what you might enjoy having if it seems not to be there.

5:00 P.M.

- Attend after-hours staff meeting (flex-time will be scheduled)

Day Three

Focus on classroom observations in this teacher's assigned classroom.

8:30 A.M.–12:30 P.M.

- Observe in assigned classroom for at least two hours this morning and be sure to observe transition into lunch and the lunch—eat lunch with the children if it seems comfortable for the children and the teacher currently in charge, and sit in on group-time if there is one.

1:00–2:30 P.M.

- Read the files of children in assigned classroom

2:00–4:30 P.M.

- Participate in assigned classroom and meet parents as children are picked up

Day Four

8:30–11:30 A.M.

- Participate in assigned classroom and meet parents as they arrive with children

11:30 A.M.–1:00 P.M.

- Lunch and meet with director (or supervisor) to discuss other staff in the assigned room, as well as the children and families

1:00–2:30 P.M.

- Use time as needed to complete reading of files, work out next week's schedule, get questions answered, etc.

2:30–3:30 P.M.

- Participate in assigned classroom
- Leave early today (to make up for day you stayed late to attend staff meeting)

Leader's Resource 5–5

ROARK LEARNING CENTER, INC.

Sample Orientation Plan
(Associate Teacher)

History

Roark Learning Center, Inc. (RLC, Inc.) is a non-profit corporation that operates six child care programs in the greater Cincinnati area. All of the sites are part of a collaborative pilot project with Cincinnati Public Schools and the Hamilton County Office of Education offering Head Start enhancement services. The centers provide quality child care for children ages three months through eleven years. RLC, Inc. began contracting with the United Way & Community Chest in 1983 and became a United Way agency in 1991. The corporation became the first non-profit agency in Cincinnati to have all of its sites accredited by the National Association for the Education of Young Children.

Mission

The mission of Roark Learning Center, Inc. is to develop and operate model professional early childhood programs that meet the diverse needs of the children and families in the communities we serve.

Vision

Roark Learning Center, Inc. develops premier early childhood and childcare programs, creating new models that meet the needs of our diverse families and changing communities. We will be proactive in uncovering needs for additional and innovative programs, and in designing and implementing such programs. We will lead in replicating our successful models in our own organization and among other area centers. Our programs will set the standard of excellence for all other programs in the communities we serve.

We will be in the forefront of accomplishing universal accessibility for all children and their families who need early childhood programs. We will value and include the diversity of families and individuals in our communities, and welcome people of different cultures, economic opportunities, and abilities. Our programs will partner with families, support them and encourage their active involvement in our programs.

Roark Learning Center, Inc. will be the leading place for early childhood professionals, with our staff always among the best-educated and trained child care professionals in the community. We will be their recognized center for training opportunities. Our staff will share their talents in mentoring, teaching and helping their peers, student interns and caregivers from other centers. We will encourage and support our own staff's ongoing personal and professional development. We will provide salaries, benefits and working conditions for our staff that reflect their education and training and the critical work they do, and are an example for other centers.

We will enhance our relationships with current funders and develop relationships with new funding sources, including businesses. Business relationships will also provide us with access to families in need of the programs we provide. Our initiative in cre-

Reprinted by Permission from Roark Learning Centers, Cincinnati, Ohio

Cincinnati Learning Center: Organizational Chart

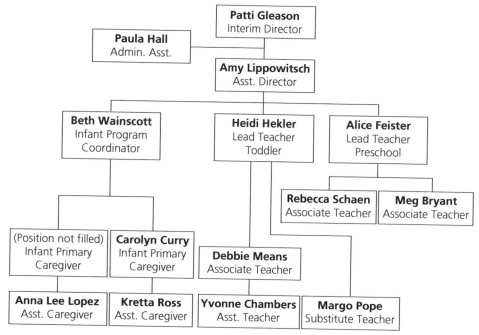

1 Infant Classroom (9 children; 3:1 ratio), 1 Toddler Classroom (10 children; 5:1 ratio), 1 Preschool Classroom (18 children; 9:1 ratio).

ating and supporting these relationships, together with our effective use of our funding, will assure that our vision and our mission drive our actions.

We will extend our vision to other centers, their staffs, our families, our funders and the communities we serve.

Program Goals

I. Organization

Roark Learning Center, Inc.

II. Sponsorship

This organization is a nonprofit, nonsectarian, interracial and nonpolitical institution founded by Eila and Dale Roark. Roark Learning Center, Inc. is managed by a Board of Directors comprised of community professionals, parents and educational specialists. No part of its earnings shall fall to the benefit of any member or individual. All funds earned by the school shall be reinvested in the program.

III. Purpose

A. The purpose of this program shall be to provide a full-day preschool, infant, and toddler program that will benefit the child, the parent, and the community.

B. To obtain funding from federal and local sources to subsidize low income families who need child care.

IV. Goals
  A. For the Child:
    1. To provide opportunities for children of diverse backgrounds and abilities a setting conducive to the development of wholesome social relationships.
    2. To provide appropriate play experiences that contribute to the developmental needs of each child.
    3. To provided opportunities for meaningful play that is based on the child's individual needs, interests, special needs and abilities, and that will build important foundations for future reading skills and other academic pursuits.
    4. To provide a setting where the development of independence can be fully enhanced.
    5. To provide opportunities where children can develop self-help skills.
    6. To provide a wholesome atmosphere in which the positive self-esteem of each child will avail.
    7. To provide enriched experiences in which children can learn to appreciate his aesthetic surroundings.
    8. To provide an enriched environment where each child can develop to his full capacity, intellectually, emotionally, socially, and physically.
    9. To provide an environment enriched with opportunities to enhance language development.
    10. Through subsidized child care, provide all children an equal opportunity to succeed in school through early childhood education.
  B. For the Families:
    1. To provide opportunities to meet with and work with other parents and teachers who have as their common concern the interests and needs of the child.
    2. To provide care for the child while the family pursues their own work and interests.
    3. To provide opportunities to grow in the understanding of child development through a planned educational program.
    4. To provide funding to make a quality early childhood program available to parents who are working or in training who otherwise could not afford it.
  C. For the Community:
    1. To help meet the needs of the community for an early childhood education facility.
    2. To contribute to the wholesome growth and development of the future citizens of the community.
    3. To provide a setting where a diverse group of people can come together for a common interest.
    4. To provide the community with subsidized child care that enables citizens to become viable community members by pursuing their careers and education.

Philosophy

The philosophy of our child care center provides a basis for the types of activities available for the children and the kind of care they will receive in our center. Our core belief is that growth is a sequential and orderly process, and that each child has a personal pace and a unique way of developing physically, emotionally, socially, and cognitively. It is the role of the teacher to build on those things children are able to do in each of the growth areas by creating a rich environment and encouraging children to play. Classroom environments are designed to reflect the needs of the children at their individual developmental levels. The work of Piaget and Erikson provides the theoretical framework around which the curriculum is planned.

We support the rights and responsibilities of parents and the development and well-being of families. The family is our foundation and our starting point for developing services and program content. Together with the family, the child is our focus. We believe that only through partnership with the family can the goals for our children be realized. A strong, trusting relationship between the family and our program is the foundation for achieving common goals in the best interest of our children. Together the staff and parents create the best program for our children and families.

We have strong views and values about quality care and education. Our centers are required to meet the National Association for the Education of Young Children (NAEYC) accreditation standards. The NAEYC guidelines for Developmentally Appropriate Practice are the basis for the programs' day to day pedagogical practice.

NAEYC Guidelines for Developmentally Appropriate Practice

- Provides for all areas of a child's development: physical, emotional, social, and cognitive through an integrated approach. Any activity that stimulates one dimension of development affects other dimensions as well.
- Is based on teachers' observations and recordings of each child's special interests and developmental progress.
- Emphasizes learning as an interactive process. Teachers prepare the environment for children to learn through active exploration and interaction with adults, other children, and materials.
- Provides learning activities and materials that are concrete, real, and relevant to the lives of young children.
- Provides for a wider range of developmental interests and abilities than the chronological age range of the group would suggest. Adults are prepared to meet the needs of children who exhibit unusual interests and skills outside the normal developmental range.
- Provides a variety of activities and materials: teachers increase the difficulty, complexity, and challenge of an activity as children are involved with it and as children develop understanding and skills.

Discipline

Our goal is to create a positive climate which promotes self-discipline. A positive approach to discipline increases a child's self-esteem, helps children feel valued and enables them to engage in positive, cooperative interactions. Children are encouraged to take responsibility and initiative as they interact with other children and engage in problem solving.

It is the responsibility of the teacher to use guidance strategies to help children express feelings of anger and frustration in socially constructive ways. Teachers who are most effective in helping children manage anger and aggression are those who model constructive management of their own frustration, anger, and self-regulatory skills. Positive strategies in setting limits and establishing boundaries are utilized with children. As teachers develop relationships with children, they begin to have insights into what each child seeks to accomplish. As children strive to achieve their goals, redirection, support and encouragement are provided.

When limits have to be set for children who are hurting themselves or other children, the teacher first intervenes to prevent further harm. After supporting both of the children involved, the teacher helps the aggressive child make amends/reparation, always keeping in mind that children of this age are at the earliest stage of conscience development.

Children are shown positive alternatives and are helped to see how their actions affect others in an environment in which adults are fair and consistent. They feel successful and in control. They are better able to solve problems and enjoy relationships as they become more self-disciplined.

Roark Learning Center, Inc.

5 Phase Orientation Plan

Phase 1

1 Orientation to building and agency
(History, Mission, Vision, Program Goals, Philosophy, Job
Description)
Observe in classroom for 1 hour _____
Complete Classroom Observation Guide _____
2 Meet with Director to discuss Classroom Observation Guide _____
3 Spend remaining time in classroom with children and staff _____
4 Take Parent Handbook home to read _____

Phase 2

1 Interact with the children for 3 hours in the classroom _____
2 Meet with the Lead Teacher to discuss strengths and weaknesses _____
3 Receive a copy of Read's Guides to Speech and Action

Phase 3

1 Interact with children in the classroom
2 Meet with the Director to discuss Read's Guides _____
3 Receive a copy of Don'ts and Do's List _____
4 Review Read's Guides _____

Phase 4

1 Interact with the children in the classroom _____
2 Meet with the Director to discuss progress, answer questions, etc. _____
3 Review Personnel Policies _____

Employee Name:

The Building and Procedures

_____ building security/lock/code

_____ staff restrooms

_____ pop machine/cafeteria
_____ copy machine
_____ phone system

_____ Director's office/mailbox

_____ paper supplies

_____ exits/fire extinguishers

_____ first aid kits/medicine kit
_____ personnel paperwork/insurance pkt.

_____ corporate offices
_____ job description/personnel policies
_____ performance appraisal

_____ trainings
_____ sign in/out staff

_____ sick days/staff roster
_____ snow days/holiday staffing

_____ breaks/planning time
_____ ratios
_____ staff meetings

_____ Family-centered practices

_____ parent meetings/parent conferences

_____ confidentiality
_____ funding/tuition/tuition box
_____ late pick-up procedure/form
_____ greeting children and families
_____ daily report/feedback to parents
_____ classroom job list/naptime responsibilities
_____ children's files
_____ emergency contacts (children)
_____ sign in/out (children)
_____ opening/closing procedures
_____ food preparation procedures
_____ playground rules
_____ illness policy/medication form (children)
_____ incident forms (children)
_____ medical/dental emergency plans
_____ emergency numbers
_____ fire/tornado procedures
_____ Accreditation booklet

Phase 5

1. Interact with children in the classroom   _____
2. Meet with Director to discuss progress, answer questions, etc.   _____
3. Discuss Observation Guide and Building Checklist   _____
4. Discuss Performance Appraisal tool   _____
5. Set 3 goals to work toward in the first 3 months of employment   _____
6. Set date for bi-weekly meeting to discuss progress and check in   _____

_____   _____
Signature of Staff   *Date*   *Signature of Director*   *Date*

Job Description—Associate Teacher

Description:

The Associate Teacher actively participates in planning and implementing the curriculum, working with parents, and assessing the needs of individual children under the guidance of the Lead Teacher.

Accountability:

The Associate Teacher reports to the Lead Teacher.

Minimum Qualifications:

Must possess a high school diploma. Must be at least 18 years of age and be able to model self after the Lead Teacher. He/she must be in the process of meeting the requirements of the city and state licensing agencies. This person must have a warm and friendly personality, be sensitive to the feelings and needs of others and be able to relate well to children. In addition, he/she must be willing to fulfill his/her responsibilities in accordance with the center's educational philosophy. It is expected that after one year of employment that if the candidate has not completed a CDA he/she will begin the process.

Responsibilities:

To establish and maintain a safe and healthy environment

1. Assist in establishing and maintaining an environment for children which is clean, safe, stimulating and which is appropriate for each child's developmental level.
2. Assist the Lead Teacher with the appearance, decor, and learning environment of the classroom.
3. Assume an equal share of the housekeeping responsibilities of the staff.
4. Promote healthy eating practices through participating in family style meals and planning and implementing nutritional activities.
5. Meet and maintain licensing requirements for ratio.
6. Assume the role of leadership in absence of the Lead Teacher.

To advance physical and intellectual competence

1. Interact with children in accordance with developmentally appropriate practices as established by NAEYC guidelines.
2. Ability to manage classroom through positive redirection, problem solving, setting appropriate limits, and active listening.
3. Support Lead Teacher in development and implementation of lesson plans.

Job Description—Associate Teacher

To support social and emotional development and provide positive guidance

1. Treat each child, parent, family member, and co-worker with dignity and respect.
2. Consider the individual child in relationship to his/her culture and socio-economic background.
3. Help each child to become aware of his role as an integral member of a group.

To establish positive and productive relationships with families

1. Communicate parent questions and concerns to Lead Teacher and or Director.
2. Communicate your concerns about a child's development to the Lead Teacher and or Director.
3. Help families feel welcome in the environment, greet parent and child at arrival and departure times.
4. Assist with home visits.
5. Offer support to teaching team relaying observations.

To ensure a well-run, purposeful program responsive to participant needs

1. Maintain daily schedules posted in each room.
2. Assist in implementation of daily, weekly, and monthly plans under the guidance of the Lead Teacher.
3. Assist in observations and documentation of individual progress through anecdotal notes, development checklist, portfolio assessments, and other designed screenings.

To maintain a commitment to professionalism

1. Upon hire, each employee must begin training to meet state requirements. This training must include first aid, communicable disease, and child abuse recognition and prevention, CPR as well as other child development topics as required by your director.
2. Attend all staff meetings, parent meetings, and other mandatory or required inservices.
3. Promote agency's code of ethics.
4. Keep open communication with the Lead and assistant teacher at all times.
5. Maintain professional attitude and loyalty to the program at all times.
6. Maintain confidentiality regarding staff, families, and children at all times.
7. Relate to families in a positive and respectful manner.

ROARK LEARNING CENTER, INC.

Performance Appraisal Procedures

1. Frequency of Appraisals

   Performance appraisals will be completed every six months. It is the responsibility of the Director to evaluate staff members with the aid of the Assistant Director and Infant Program Coordinator. All appraisals will be shared with the staff member and then become part of the personnel file.

2. Purpose of Appraisals

   The primary purpose of the appraisal is to create a mutual understanding between the Director and each member of the staff of what is expected and how they both view the best way to move toward fulfilling those expectations.

   Semi-annual appraisals will be used as a basis for continued employment, opportunities for mobility, and where appropriate, salary increase.

3. Basis for Appraisals

   Staff members will be appraised based upon their knowledge of the position as detailed in the job description, quality of skill demonstrated in fulfilling the job, interest and initiative, dependability, a commitment toward establishing goals, personal and professional growth, attendance and punctuality, and the ability to work effectively in cooperation with other staff members.

4. Appraisal Procedure

   Each staff member will be notified as to when his or her appraisal will take place. The Director and staff member will each complete a performance appraisal, which will be discussed at their meeting. This will also include a discussion around the meeting of goals set at previous appraisals. The staff member will be provided the opportunity to express agreement or disagreement. Together, the Director and staff member will design goals for moving forward. The appraisals and any corresponding notes from the discussion will become part of the staff member's personnel record.

Performance Appraisal—Associate Teacher

Name: _____

Date: _____

	seldom	sometimes	frequently	always	Comments

To establish and maintain a safe and healthy learning environment

1. Establishes and maintains an environment for children, which is clean, safe, stimulating and appropriate for each child's developmental level.

2. Assists the lead teacher in maintaining the appearance, decor, and learning environment of the classroom.

3. Assumes an equal share of the joint housekeeping responsibilities.

4. Promotes healthy eating practices.

5. Meets and maintains licensing requirements for ratio.

6. Assumes the role of leadership in the absence of the Lead Teacher.

To advance physical and intellectual competence

1. Interacts with children in accordance with developmentally appropriate practices as established by the National Association for the Education of Young Children.

2. Manages classroom through positive redirection, problem solving, setting appropriate limits, and active listening.

3. Supports the Lead Teacher in the development and implementation of the lesson plans.

To support social and emotional development and provide positive guidance

1. Treats each child, parent, and co-worker with dignity and respect.

2. Considers the individual child in relationship to his/her culture

3. Helps each child to become aware of his/her role as of the group.

Adapted from Bloom, P. J., Sheerer, M., & Britz. J. (1991). *Blueprint for Action: Achieving Center-Based Change Through Staff Development.* New Horizons, P.O. 863. Lake Forest, IL. 60045. Reprinted with permission.

Name: _____

Date: _____

	seldom	sometimes	frequently	always	Comments

To establish positive and productive relationships

1. Communicates parent questions and concerns to Lead Teacher and/or Director.
2. Communicates any concerns about the child's development/behavior to the Lead Teacher and or Director.
3. Helps families feel welcome in the environment, greets parents and child at arrival and departure times.
4. Assists with home visits.
5. Offers support to teaching team relaying observations.

To ensure a well-run, purposeful program responsive to participants needs.

1. Maintains daily schedule as posted in the classroom.
2. Assists in implementation of daily, weekly, and monthly plans under the guidance of the Lead Teacher.
3. Assists in observations and documentation of individual progress through anecdotal notes, development checklist, portfolio assessments, and other designed screenings.

Adapted from Bloom, P. J., Sheerer, M., & Britz. J. (1991). *Blueprint for Action: Achieving Center-Based Change Through Staff Development*, New Horizons, P.O. Box 863, Lake Forest, IL. 60045. Reprinted with permission.

Name: _____

Date: _____

	seldom	sometimes	frequently	always	Comments

To maintain commitment to professionalism

1. First aid, Communicable disease, child abuse recognition and prevention, CPR as well as other child development topics completed as required.
2. Attends all staff meetings, parent meetings and other mandatory or required inservices.
3. Follows agencies code of ethics.
4. Keeps open communication with the Lead and Assistant Teacher at all times.
5. Maintains professional attitude and loyalty to the program at all times.
6. Maintains confidentiality regarding children, families, and staff as stated in the employee handbook.
7. Relates to children and families in positive and respectful manner.
8. Punctual in meeting daily work schedule.
9. Follows attendance and punctuality policy of the center as stated in the employee handbook.
10. Maintains professional appearance at all times as stated in the employee handbook.

Additional Comments:

Name of supervisor _____

Adapted from Bloom, P. J., Sheerer, M., & Britz, J. (1991). *Blueprint for Action: Achieving Center-Based Change Through Staff Development*, New Horizons, P.O. 863, Lake Forest, IL. 60045. Reprinted with permission.

Goal Blueprint

Name _____

Supervisor _____

Date _____

Areas in need of growth

1. _____
   _____
   _____

activities	time needed	resources needed
1.		
2.		

2. _____
   _____
   _____

activities	time needed	resources needed
1.		
2.		

3. _____

_____

_____

_____

activities	time needed	resources needed
1.		
2.		

_____ Teacher

_____ Supervisor

Adapted from Bloom, P. J., Sheerer, M., & Britz, J. (1991). *Blueprint for Action: Achieving Center-Based Change Through Staff Development,* New Horizons, P.O. Box 863, Lake Forest, IL 60045, Reprinted with permission.

Professional Career Standards Toddler/Preschool

Professional Level	Education	Experience
Professional Level 1	High School Degree	Experienced Preferred.
Professional Level 2	High School Degree Completed all mandatory training to meet licensing requirements	A minimum of 3 months.
Professional Level 3	High School Degree with 45 hours of training (based on ODHS licensing requirements) or currently enrolled in college for education or related field having course work that will meet 45 hours	A minimum of six months experience and a proven ability to supervise children.
Professional Level 4	CDA Associate-Masters in ECE	2 years of experience 0-2 years of experience
Professional Level 5	Associate-Masters in ECE	2-4 years of experience A proven knowledge of child development and a team leader.
Professional Level 6	Associate-Masters in ECE	4 years of experience Provided outreach to the community and has proven themselves as a mentor to others.

ROARK LEARNING CENTER, INC.
Personnel Policies and Procedures

Notice

This is not a contract of employment. Your employment with Roark Learning Center, Inc. (RLC) is an employment-at-will relationship. Any individual may voluntarily leave employment or may be terminated by RLC at any time for any reason or without reason. Any oral or written statement or promises to the contrary are hereby expressly disavowed and should not be relied upon by any prospective or existing employee. Statement in this handbook, specifically including but not limited to those concerning discipline or reasons for discharge are only general guidelines used by RLC. RLC may take disciplinary action other than that outlined herein in a particular case and may discipline or discharge an employee for reasons not listed in this handbook.

In addition, certain employee benefit plans are defined in legal documents such as insurance certificates or plan documents. Such legal documents are controlling. Should there be any conflict between this handbook and the certificate, plan, or other formal document, the formal document governs and not the informal descriptions contained in this handbook or in any other description or notice provided by RLC.

This handbook and/or any policy or provision contained herein may be revised, modified, altered or revoked by RLC at any time with or without notice.

Administration of Personnel Policies

It is the responsibility of the Executive Director and the Board of Roark Learning Center, Inc. (RLC) to review and submit revisions of the Personnel Policies each year. Any additions to and or deletions from the policies must be approved by the Board before going into effect.

I. Employment

Equal Employment Opportunity

Roark Learning Center, Inc. recognizes our employees as one of our greatest assets. We are committed to provide equal employment opportunities for all, without regard to race, color, religion, national origin, age, gender, marital status, sexual orientation, and/or disability.

These opportunities include, but are not limited to, recruitment, hiring, training, promotion, compensation, benefits and all other terms and conditions of employment.

Employee Status

Full-time employees have a basic schedule between thirty-five (35) and forty (40) hours per week. Part-time employees have a basic schedule between twenty-four (24) and thirty-four (34) hours per week. Employees working a permanent schedule of 30 hours or more are eligible for health and life insurance.

Promotions and Transfers

Upon notification from an employee of his/her interest in another position or transfer to another location, the Director over the position or location will determine the eligibility for promotion and/or transfer. The employee must meet the following criteria to be eligible:

- Minimum of six (6) months in current position
- Current job performance is satisfactory, meeting expectations or above
- No pending corrective counseling or disciplinary warnings in effect
- Recommended for the position by the current Director

Once the above criteria has been met, the employee can be interviewed for the open position or transfer opportunity. The receiving Director will make final determination on the promotion and/or transfer.

Attendance and Punctuality

RLC employees are expected to be on the job, on time, on a regular basis. Our work schedules are based upon the understanding that all employees will be at work and at their work stations on time. We recognize that on occasion it may be necessary for an employee to be tardy or absent from work due to illness or personal problems; however, absence or tardiness can hamper or prevent others from performing their jobs properly. Repeated or chronic tardiness will subject an employee to discipline (up to and including discharge) at the discretion of RLC.

If you are unable to come to work on a scheduled or regular work day, you must give notice to your supervisor or director as soon as you are aware that you will be absent. If your absence is due to illness, injury, or other personal reasons, you must call in as soon as possible. If you know that you will be absent for more than one day, you must advise your supervisor or director of that fact and the expected duration of your absence. Otherwise, you or someone on your behalf must call each day of your absence.

Subject to the provisions of the Family/Medical Leave Act, the Americans with Disabilities Act, or other applicable laws, any employee who is absent more than 15 days in a calendar year, whether for reasons of illness, injury, personal reasons or otherwise, will be subject to discharge. In the case of serious illness or injury, unpaid leave may be granted at the discretion of the Director; however, no such leave will exceed 30 days and any employee who is absent for more than 30 days for any reason shall be subject to discharge.

No Solicitation

In order to avoid interruption of your work and to protect you from unnecessary annoyance, solicitation and/or distribution of literature on RLC premises is limited to the following rules:

Non-employees of RLC have no right to distribute materials or solicit our associates on RLC property at any time.

Employee to employee solicitation or distribution or acceptance of literature by employees is prohibited during work hours. Work time does not include time before or after an employees scheduled work hours, meal periods, or paid break periods. This policy includes solicitation and distribution of literature for all purposes, such as lotteries, raffles, charitable or political organizations and the like. Any exceptions to this policy must be made by the Executive Director of RLC.

Reference Inquiries

Any and all reference inquiries about current or past employees must be forwarded to the Executive Director. This is the only person authorized to share employee reference information with anyone outside the company. A signed release must be provided by current or ex-employees for reference information to be shared with another party.

Probationary Periods

Your first ninety (90) days of employment are considered a probationary period. During your first ninety (90) days your Director will provide information regarding your job duties and responsibilities. You will also receive feedback on your job performance throughout this period. If any performance problems develop during the probationary period, you may be placed on counseling. The decision as to whether you continue employment will be made by your Director within or at the conclusion of your probationary period.

Throughout your employment at RLC you will be expected to fulfill your assigned job responsibilities and follow our policies and procedures. If you are not able to meet our standard or follow our policies and procedures, your employment may be terminated.

Business Expenses

The following conditions must be met for employees to receive reimbursement for any company business expense:

- Approval is granted by the Director, Assistant Director, or a supervisor.
- An original receipt must be submitted.

Dress Code

All employees are encouraged to wear comfortable clothing. A professional appearance must be maintained at all times. The following shall be observed:

- Jeans should be in good condition.
- Halter tops, tube tops, or other revealing clothing should not be worn.
- Uphold the standards of good hygiene (clean hair, clothing, etc.).
- Hiking shorts or sun dresses are examples of appropriate summer wear.

No Smoking

In an effort to provide a healthy, comfortable, smoke-free environment for all of our employees and children, smoking in all areas of our facilities is prohibited.

Drug and Alcohol Policy

RLC strongly supports the creation of a drug-free society as well as a safe drug-free and alcohol-free workplace. Accordingly, we have developed a Company Policy on Drug and Alcohol Abuse. We trust that all RLC employees will accept this policy in the spirit in which it has been developed, and will help us work to reach our common goal of a drug-free and alcohol-free workplace.

If you are taking prescription medication, it is your responsibility to obtain a doctor's permission to work. If you have any doubt as to whether you can safely work, notify your supervisor immediately.

Persons believing themselves to be disabled by an addiction to drugs or alcohol must notify RLC immediately. Such self-identification must occur before any adverse performance or job consequences are suffered or become apparent; failure to so notify RLC will make accommodation of an employee's claimed disability difficult or impossible.

Tests

RLC, Inc. reserves the right to test for illegal drugs and/or alcohol:

- upon hire, and/or transfer to new location
- when an employee is involved in a workplace accident, or off-site accident while performing work for RLC
- when there is suspicion or probable cause
- when an employee returns from a leave of absence
- as required by RLC contract agreement or government regulations
- as mandated by RLC (including random testing).

Searches

RLC reserves the right to search any person entering any center or other RLC property and to search property, equipment, and storage areas for illegal drugs, drug paraphernalia, unauthorized controlled substances, alcohol or other intoxicants. This shall include but is not limited to clothing, personal effects, vehicles, buildings, offices, parking lots, desks, cabinets, lockers, closets, lunch boxes/bags, and/or equipment.

Penalties for Refusal

Any RLC employee who refuses to submit to a diagnostic test or a search as permitted by law will be subject to disciplinary action up to and including discharge. Any employee refusing to submit to a search will be denied access and be asked to immediately leave any center, work site or other RLC property.

Penalties

a) Possession of alcohol, drugs, or drug paraphernalia in any center or other RLC property or work site:
First offense: Termination

b) Distribution of alcohol, drugs, or drug paraphernalia in any center or other RLC property or work site:
First offense: Termination

c) Use of illegal drugs, unauthorized controlled substances, or alcohol during working hours in any center or other RLC property or work site, or being under the influence of drugs and/or alcohol during working hours or in any center or other RLC property:
First offense: Termination

The drug and alcohol abuse policy will also include random testing. RLC reserves the right to begin this procedure anytime.

II. Compensation

Compensation Program

RLC compensation program is competitive within the early childhood education profession and the local markets within which we conduct business. Increases to compensation will be based on the individual employee's performance and the overall performance of the company.

Exempt employees are paid a base salary, which is agreed upon at the time of hire. Compensatory time will be granted to exempt employees for any work performed over forty (40) hours in a week. The accrued compensatory hours must be used within the following twelve (12) months and cannot be carried over beyond twelve (12) months after they have been earned.

Overtime

Exempt employees are not eligible for overtime pay. Non-exempt employees are eligible for overtime pay for hours worked beyond forty (40) hours in a week. Pay for overtime is included in the semimonthly payroll. Overtime must be authorized in advance by the Director.

Split Shift

Employees will earn an extra two dollars ($2.00) per hour for working a split shift when it is not a standard or regular work schedule.

Performance Appraisal

Employees are evaluated on an annual basis. Details regarding these procedures are included in the Orientation Manual.

Position Descriptions

Job descriptions are reviewed with the employee at the time of hire and a copy of their job description will be maintained in their personnel file. Job descriptions can be revised by the Director with the approval of the Program Administrator.

Hours of Work

Employee's hours will be set upon hiring. Schedules will change according to enrollment and all teachers are required to sign in and out each day. If an employee should be late for any reason, he/she must call the center to notify staff as early as possible. Employees are required to attend all staff meetings and are expected to attend parent meetings when scheduled, along with any activities to improve parent-teacher relationships. When staff meetings are scheduled after shift hours, non-exempt employees will be compensated for this time in accordance with applicable wage/hour laws. All employees are required to have time sheets signed and approved by their supervisor or Center Director.

Pay Periods

Employees are paid on a semimonthly basis, on the 15th of the month and the last day of the month. If the 15th or last day of the month falls on a holiday or weekend day, pay will be issued on the last workday before the holiday or weekend.

III. Benefits

Family Medical Leave

Pursuant to the Family and Medical Leave Act of 1997, employees may be entitled to up to twelve (12) weeks of unpaid leave per year under certain circumstances as set forth in the Act. During leave taken under the terms of the Act, medical insurance and certain other benefits in which the affected employee is a participant will be maintained on the same basis as for active employees. While the employee does not continue in "active service" for purposes of accruing vacation, retirement or other benefits related to length of service, leave taken pursuant to the Family and Medical Leave Act does not constitute a "break in service" for such purposes. At the completion of leave taken pursuant to the Act, the employee will be restored to his or her former position or, if necessary and appropriate in light of the needs of RLC and at RLC's sole discretion, to a position substantially similar in terms of pay, benefits, and conditions of employment.

Under the Family/Medical Leave Act, employees who have been employed by RLC for at least twelve (12) months and who have been credited with 1250 hours of active service during the year immediately preceding the requested leave period are eligible for this leave.

The Act provides that eligible employees may take up to twelve (12) work weeks of leave during any twelve (12) month period for one or more of the following: (1) birth of a child of the employee, in order to care for such child; (2) placement of a child with the employee, either through adoption or foster care; (3) to care for the employee's spouse, child or parent with a serious health condition; (4) a serious health condition of the employee that makes it impossible for the employee to perform the functions of his or her employment.

Leave taken pursuant to the Act will be offset by paid or unpaid leave otherwise available to the employee, i.e., accrued vacation, personal, medical and/or sick leave must be used as the first part of the twelve (12) week maximum leave period.

In the event of the birth or placement of child, the employee's entitlement to leave to care for such child expires twelve (12) months after such birth or placement. Further, if a husband and wife are both employed by RLC the maximum leave for both spouses combined will be twelve (12) weeks in any given year for the birth or placement of a child or the care of a parent with a serious health condition.

Under the Act, any employee requesting leave must give RLC thirty (30) days advance notice if the need for the leave is foreseeable. Otherwise, notice is required as soon as practicable. An expected date of return shall be determined prior to the commencement of any leave, and may be extended for good cause but in no event past the maximum leave period allowed by the Act. If the leave is requested because of serious health condition, RLC may require certification signed by a bona fide health care provider and may request a second opinion at RLC expense. RLC may also require recertification on a reasonable periodic basis. During any such leave, the employee shall be required to check in with his or her supervisor on Monday of each week to determine the employee's status and to discuss possible changes in the employee's expected date of return.

While the employee is on leave under the Act, RLC will continue group health coverage on the same basis as though the employee continued to be in active service. If the employee fails to return to work after the leave period has expired for reason other than a continuing serious health condition or other circumstances beyond the employee's control, RLC will be entitled to recover from the employee the cost of any health coverage provided during the leave period. Employee copayments or contribution for such coverage will be required to keep coverage in force during leave under the Act.

Consult with your supervisor or the Director for more details about the terms and procedures applicable to leaves under the Family and Medical Leave Act.

Vacation

The eligibility for paid vacation is based on the status of employment and length of continuous service.

Upon hiring each full-time employee will receive two (2) vacation days to be used in his/her first year of employment. Upon hiring each full-time employee will accrue one (1) vacation day for every fifty-two (52) days worked to be used in the following year. After one year of employment, vacation days are accrued at one (1) for every thirty-seven (37) days worked, also to be used in the following year. Vacation days must be used each year or be forfeited. The following chart outlines how vacation days are accrued for full-time employees.

Period	Vacation Days
0-12 Months	2 days
after 1st anniversary	5 days
after 2nd anniversary	7 days

Part-time employees will be given two (2) vacation days per year after their first full year of service. Management personnel will be given vacation that will accrue at a rate of one (1) day per every twenty-six (26) days worked.

Requests for vacation time must be approved in advance by the director, who will take into consideration the employees' length of service. No deductions from pay will be made for vacation or holiday closings.

Holidays

All employees are paid for the following holidays: New Year's Day, Martin Luther King Day, July 4th, Labor Day, Thanksgiving Day, and Christmas Day, when these fall on a regular work day (Monday through Friday).

Personal Days

After thirty (30) days of employment each full-time employee will receive one personal day each month. These days will be scheduled by the Director or scheduler no more than three (3) months before, and no less than one (1) month before. The center reserves the right under special circumstances to reschedule personal days. These days are not accrued vacation and none will be due to staff who resign or are terminated. An employee may save up to three (3) personal days per year to be used as vacation. They must be used within the same year. If, due to a staffing shortage, an employee elects to forfeit a personal day within twenty-four (24) hours of their scheduled day off, and they come in to work, they will be paid time and a half for the hours worked.

Sick Days

Upon hiring, each full-time employee immediately receives two (2) sick days, and will then start accruing sick days for their first year of employment. Sick days are accrued at a rate of one (1) sick day for every fifty-two (52) days worked, with a maximum of five (5) sick days per year. These must be used within their anniversary year as sick days or vacation days.

Overview of Time off

Benefit	Full-Time	Part-Time
Vacation: 0-12 months	2 days	0 days
Vacation: First anniversary	5 days	2 days
Vacation: Second anniversary	7 days	2 days
Personal days:	12 days	0 days
Sick days:	5 days	0 days
Holidays:	7 days	7 days

Jury Duty

You will be excused from work on any work day during which you are subpoenaed to serve on a jury or as a witness in any Federal, State, County, or Municipal Court, provided you give prior notice to your supervisor or director.

If you are subpoenaed to serve on a jury and you report for such service, you will be paid the difference between the number of straight time hours you would have otherwise worked (not more than eight [8] hours per day) times your rate of pay and the pay received for jury service.

Employees released prior to noon must return to work for the balance of the regular work day. **You will not receive more than three (3) days of jury service pay in any calendar year.**

Snow Days

Employees are expected to report to work on days when the centers are closed due to snow. Any employee in attendance on a snow day will receive split shift pay for the hours that they work. If the employee does not report they are required to take a vacation or personal day, or take it without pay (part-time employees only).

Health Insurance

RLC offers quality health-care plans to eligible employees to ease the burden of costs associated with illness. Should an employee choose coverage to include other family members, all costs above the employee's cost will be the obligation of the employee through payroll deduction. (Single standard plan costs are paid by RLC.)

The design of our health care plans is guided by:

* a commitment to make cost-efficient health care possible;
* an expectation that employees are responsible for personal health as a function of lifestyle, prevention, dietary habits, and self-care, taking responsible precautions to ensure good health;
* a cooperative effort to work toward influencing external factors to control health-care costs;
* a review of health-care plans on a continual basis to satisfy the needs of RLC and its employees.

Life Insurance

RLC provides eligible employees with financial protection through term life insurance for their families in the event of the employee's death.

All eligible employees are to be enrolled within thirty (30) days of employment.

The plan provides each employee with coverage of $35,000. Plan coverage is provided at no cost to the employee.

Retirement Savings Plan

Full-time employees may be eligible to participate in a pre-tax 403 (b) retirement funding plan. See your director for further information about this benefit.

Tuition Reduction

Center employees may be granted a reduced tuition rate as follows:

All full-time employees: 20% tuition reduction.

Reduced tuition slots are limited based upon available accommodations and management's discretion.

COBRA

RLC reserves the right to treat any such leave as a triggering event under the Comprehensive Omnibus Budget Reconciliation Act (COBRA) and to notify the employee of his/her right to continue any group health insurance coverage at the employee's cost for the duration of such leave.

Subject to the provisions of the Americans with Disabilities Act, the Family and Medical Leave Act, or other applicable state or federal laws, time spent on leave of absence shall not be counted as actual service time for purposes of calculating such items as vacation or sick time accrual, or any other fringe benefits. Further, an employee on leave of absence may not engage in any form of gainful employment or occupation without prior written approval from the Director. Violation of this policy will result in cancellation of the leave and termination of employment.

IV. Standards of Conduct

Performance Development Requirements

Regardless of their previous education or experience, employees will be expected to continue studies of and training in early childhood education practices in order to keep abreast of new developments in the field. This continued study and training may take place on the employees' own time outside of regular working hours, and as recommended by the director. Methods employed may include, but are not limited to, in-service training classes at the center, attendance at a recommended professional conference or meeting, membership in a professional organization and attendance at its monthly meetings, and/or enrollment in pertinent courses offered by local colleges and universities.

Child Development Training

Each non-degreed (ECE) employee must complete a minimum of fifteen (15) hours of child development training each year. Also, associate teachers must be enrolled in a Child Development Associate (CDA) credential program after one year of employment. Each degreed employee must complete a total of six (6) hours of annual training, four (4) of which will be child development topics. These requirements may be waived by the Director if the employee is taking a university credit course of one (1) to three (3) hours.

Inservice Training

Two (2) days each year, typically on Good Friday and the Friday after Thanksgiving, the center will be closed for inservice training. The inservice days will consist of training and individual time for planning, goal setting, etc. Every employee must attend. If someone misses due to illness they must make this time up on a Saturday and replacement training will be at their own expense. This inservice must be made up with thirty (30) days of it being offered/scheduled.

Children and Closing

It is the closing employees' responsibility to confirm that all children have been picked up before leaving the building. Two employees must always be present when a child is in the center. In the event that a child is not picked up at the closing of the center, the remaining employees will follow these guidelines:

a. If attempts to reach parent at work and home are unsuccessful, call emergency contact number.

b. If attempts to contact emergency contacts are unsuccessful, contact the director immediately.

c. YOU ARE A PROFESSIONAL: AT NO TIME MAY YOU TRANSPORT A CHILD OR LEAVE A CHILD UNATTENDED.

Harassment

It is RLC's policy to maintain a working and learning environment free from all forms of sexual harassment or intimidation. This policy pertains to employees, supervisors, students, parents, suppliers and other non-employees. Unwelcome sexual advances, request for sexual favors and other verbal or physical conduct of a sexual nature are serious violations of our policy and will not be condoned or permitted. Not only is sexual harassment a violation of our policy, but it may violate Title VII of the Civil Rights Act and other federal and state laws.

If you are subjected to sexual harassment or intimidation you should contact your supervisor, any other supervisor, or any member of management with whom you feel comfortable, for immediate help. All complaints of sexual harassment will be promptly and confidentially investigated and appropriate action will be taken against anyone found to have violated this policy. No employee who reports unlawful harassment or who assists in any investigation by RLC will be subjected to retaliation of any sort, and such retaliation will not be tolerated and is itself a violation of RLC policy. Submission to such unwanted conduct will never constitute a condition of employment. Any employee violating this policy will be subject to disciplinary action up to and including termination; sexual harassment of RLC employees by parents may result in the child being dismissed from the center, harassment by suppliers or other outside parties may result in termination of business relationships with RLC and will also be addressed in accordance with applicable state and federal laws.

Confidentiality

Records of all children are confidential and only staff and referral agencies may have access. A file may not leave the Director's office without approval. **An employee may be dismissed for discussing children outside of the school, staff, or referral agencies.**

Corrective Counseling

RLC recognizes that on occasion it may be necessary to discuss specific areas of an employee's performance or conduct that are below the expected standards. These discussions are designed to help the employee correct whatever problem may exist. The corrective counseling may range from a verbal discussion to written warnings to termination.

Termination of Employment

Certain circumstances, depending on the seriousness of the offense, may result in a final written warning, suspension or a termination without any prior notice or corrective counseling.

Certain types of conduct are offensive to our employees and children and cannot be permitted. The following examples illustrate some (but not all) types of conduct that may result in immediate dismissal without warning:

- theft or embezzlement of property or money belonging to RLC, its employees or the children
- falsification of any company records, such as employee records, timekeeping records, activity reports, etc.
- possession, sale, distribution or use of illegal drugs
- possession, sale, distribution or use of alcohol while on work time or company property
- severe insubordination, direct refusal to comply with legitimate request from a supervisor
- misuse or unauthorized removal of company, employee, or children's records, or confidential information of any nature
- possession or storing of firearms, weapons, ammunition, or explosives on company property
- unauthorized use, blatant misuse or destruction of company, employee or children's property
- flagrant discourtesy to a child, parent, or employee. This includes, but is not limited to, fighting, or inciting a fight, using obscene or abusive language, or threatening an employee, parent, or child
- violation of the company harassment policy
- reckless conduct resulting in injury or harm
- immoral, indecent or illegal conduct reflecting negatively on the company or violating the rights of the employees or children

Resignation

If you choose to resign your employment, it is requested that you submit a written two-week notice.

Open Door Policy

An open door philosophy is an essential part of maintaining strong communication and a positive work environment. We are interested in knowing our employees' ideas, questions, suggestions, problems or concerns.

In most instances, your immediate supervisor is the person best qualified to solve a problem or answer a question and you are encouraged to communicate your concerns and suggestions to them.

However, there may be times when you wish to discuss a concern or problem with someone other than your immediate supervisor. You are encouraged to bring these matters to any other member of the management.

Outside Employment

While employed at RLC you may decide to seek employment outside of your regular working hours at your center. RLC has no objections to this type of work, provided it does not interfere with your assignments and responsibilities at RLC. Furthermore, you cannot be employed by a competitor of RLC that would create a conflict of interest in your employment.

Recruitment

Applications are always to be accepted and filed. The center works with the University of Cincinnati and local vocational schools to provide placements for students in teacher training programs. When a position becomes available within the corporation, employees are notified and can be considered for the position if qualified.

Employee's Acknowledgement

I have received and read the Roark Learning Center, Inc. Personnel Policies and Procedures Handbook. I expect to be guided by the rules and policies contained therein. I further understand and agree that my employment with Roark Learning Center, Inc. is at will and may be terminated by me or Roark Learning Center, Inc. at any time for any reason or without reason. I understand that nothing in the Personnel Policies and Procedures Handbook or in any oral statement or representation by any employee or representative of Roark Learning Center, Inc. shall be deemed to create a contract of employment or any other modification of the at-will employment relationship. I also understand that any or all of the provisions contained in the Personnel Policies and Procedures Handbook may be modified, amended, or eliminated by Roark Learning Center, Inc. at any time with or without notice.

_____   _____

Employee Signature   Date

_____

Employee Social Security Number

_____   _____

Center Director Signature   Date

Grievance Procedure

RLC, Inc. acknowledges that circumstances may arise about which an employee may desire to seek formal assistance in resolving questions or concerns about employment. RLC wishes to provide all employees with considerate supervision and fair treatment. To that end, the following grievance procedure has been adopted to resolve such questions or concerns.

1. Every employee question or complaint should first be discussed with the director within three (3) days of the occurrence of the cause of the grievance. (If the director is the cause of the grievance, the employee may begin at Step 2.) It is hoped that a satisfactory resolution of the grievance can promptly be reached between the employee and the director. In any event, what the director proposes shall be given in writing to the employee with a copy sent to the Program Administrator and the Human Resources Director.
2. If the employee is not satisfied with the resolution of the grievance proposed by the director, the employee may appeal his or her grievance in writing to the Program Administrator and the Human Resources Director. They will jointly render a written decision within ten (10) working days after the filing of the appeal.
3. The decision of the Program Administrator and the Human Resources Director shall be final and binding on all parties and not subject to any further appeal. They shall keep the Executive Director and the President of the Board informed of personnel concerns involving grievances.
4. In the case of a grievance either against or by the Program Administrator or Human Resources Director, the Executive Director shall hear and review evidence presented by the grievance; in the case of a grievance either against or by the Executive Director, the President of the Board shall hear and review evidence presented by the grievance; if deemed necessary by the President of the Board, he/she shall appoint a committee of the Board to hear the grievance. If this committee fails to satisfy the parties involved; an appeal may be made in writing to the President for a hearing before the entire Board. Decisions by the Board will be final.

The Program Administrator, Human Resources Director, and Executive Director shall maintain an "open door policy," in which any employee may, in private, present a grievance or other agency concern.

Positive Discipline

How do young children learn self-control, self-help, ways to get along with others, and family and school procedures? Such learning occurs when parents and teachers of infants, toddlers, or preschoolers are continuously involved in setting limits, encouraging desired behaviors, and making decisions about managing children.

When making these decisions, caregivers often ask themselves these questions: Am I disciplining in a way that hurts or helps this child's self-esteem? Will my discipline help the child develop self-control? This digest suggests methods and language that can be used in handling common situations involving young children.

Methods of Discipline That Promote Self-Worth

1. Show that you recognize and accept the reason the child is doing what, in your judgment, is the wrong thing:

    "You want to play with the truck but . . ."

    "You want me to stay with you but . . .

    This validates the legitimacy of the child's desires and illustrates that you are an understanding person. It also is honest from the outset: The adult is wiser, in charge, not afraid to be the leader, and occasionally has priorities other than those of the child.

2. State the "but":

    "You want to play with the truck, *but Jerisa is using it right now.*"

    "You want me to stay with you, *but right now I need to (go out, help Jill, serve lunch, etc.).*"

    This lets the child know that others have needs, too. It teaches perspective taking, and may lead the child to develop the ability to put himself in other people's shoes. It will also gain you the child's respect, for it shows you are fair. And it will make the child feel safe; you are able to keep him safe.

3. Offer a solution:

    "Soon you can play with the truck."

    One-year-olds can begin to understand "just a minute" and will wait patiently if we always follow through 60 seconds later. Two- and three-year-olds can learn to understand, "I'll tell you when it's your turn," if we always follow through within two or three minutes. This helps children learn how to delay gratification but does not thwart their short-term understanding of time.

4. Often, it's helpful to say something indicating your confidence in the child's ability and willingness to learn:

    "When you get older I know you will (whatever it is you expect)."

    "Next time you can (restate what is expected in a positive manner)."

    This affirms your faith in the child, lets her know that you assume she has the capacity to grow and mature, and transmits your belief in her good intentions.

5. In some situations, after firmly stating what is not to be done, you can demonstrate how we do it, or a better way:

    "That hurts. Be gentle. Pat my face gently." (Demonstrate)

    "You can use the pieces in the puzzle. Let's put them in their place together." (Offer help)

    This sets firm limits, yet helps the child feel that you two are a team, not enemies.

6. Toddlers are not easy to distract, but frequently they can be redirected to something that is similar but OK. Carry or lead the child by the hand saying,

    "That's the gerbil's paper. Here's your paper."

    "Peter has that toy. Here's a toy for you."

    This endorses the child's right to choose what she will do, yet begins to teach that others have rights, too.

7. Avoid accusation. Even with babies, communicate in respectful tones and words. This prevents a lowering of the child's self-image and promotes his tendency to cooperate.

8. For every no, offer two acceptable choices:

    "No! Rosie cannot bite Esther. Rosie can bite the rubber duck or the cracker."

"No Jackie. That book is for teachers. You can have this book or this book."
This encourages the child's independence and emerging decision-making skills, but sets boundaries. Children should never be allowed to hurt each other. It's bad for the self-image of the one who hurts and the one who is hurt.

9. If children have enough language, help them express their feelings, including anger, and their wishes. Help them think about alternatives and solutions to problems. Adults should never fear children's anger.

10. Establish firm limits and standards as needed. Until a child is 1 ½ or almost 2 years old, adults are completely responsible for his safety and comfort, and for creating the conditions that encourage good behavior. After this age, while adults are still responsible for the child's safety, they increasingly, though extremely gradually, begin to transfer responsibility for behaving acceptably to the child. They start expecting the child to become aware of other's feelings. They begin to expect the child to think simple cause/effect thoughts (provided the child is guided quietly through the thinking process). This is teaching the rudiments of self-discipline.

11. To avoid confusion when talking to very young children, give clear, simple directions in a firm, friendly voice. This will ensure that children are not overwhelmed with a blizzard of words and refuse to comply as a result.

12. Remember that the job of a toddler, and to some extent the job of all young children, is to taste, touch, smell, squeeze, tote, poke, pour, sort, explore, and test. At times toddlers are greedy, at times grandiose. They do not share well; they need time to experience ownership before they are expected to share. They need to assert themselves ("No," "I can't," "I won't," and "Do it myself"). They need to separate to a degree from their parents, that is, to individuate. One way they do this is to say no and not to do what is asked; another is to do what is not wanted.

If adults understand children in this age range, they will create circumstances and develop attitudes that permit and promote development. Self-discipline is better learned through guidance than through punishment. It's better learned through a "We are a team, I am the leader, it's my job to help you grow up" approach than through a "me against you" approach.

Creating a Positive Climate Promotes Self-Discipline

Creating a positive climate for the very young involves:

- spending lots of leisurely time with an infant or child;
- sharing important activities and meaningful play;
- listening and answering as an equal, not as an instructor (for example, using labeling words when a toddler points inquiringly toward something, or discussing whatever topic the 2-year-old is trying to tell you about);
- complimenting the child's efforts: "William is feeding himself!" "Juana is putting on her shoe!" (even if what you are seeing is only clumsy stabs in the right direction); and
- smiling, touching, caressing, kissing, cuddling, holding, rocking, hugging.

Adapted from the ERIC Clearinghouse on Elementary and Early Childhood Education—University of Illinois at Urbana-Champaign.

Harmful, Negative Disciplinary Methods

Criticizing, discouraging, creating obstacle and barriers, blaming, shaming, using sarcastic or cruel humor, or using physical punishment are some negative disciplinary methods used with young children. Often saying, "Stop that!" "Don't do it that way!" or "You never . . ." is harmful to children's self-esteem. Such discipline techniques as removal from the group, or isolation in a time-out chair or a corner, may have negative consequences for the child.

Any adult might occasionally do any of these things. Doing any or all of them more than once in a while means that a negative approach to discipline has become a habit and urgently needs to be altered before the child experiences low self-esteem as a permanent part of her personality.

Good Approaches to Discipline

- Increase a child's self-esteem,
- Allow her to feel valued,
- Encourage her to feel cooperative,
- Enable her to learn gradually the many skills involved in taking some responsibly for what happens to her,
- Motivate her to change her strategy rather than to blame others,
- Help her to take initiative, relate successfully to others, and solve problems.

Adapted from the ERIC Clearinghouse on Elementary and Early Childhood Education—University of Illinois at Urbana-Champaign.

ROARK LEARNING CENTER, INC.

Don'ts and Do's
Guidelines for Working in the Classroom

Don'ts	Do's
Don't ignore the parents or children as they arrive or leave the center	Do greet children and families as they arrive and acknowledge them when they leave
Don't discuss the children or their families with anyone other than the Director or the Lead Teacher	Do discuss your concerns about the children with the Director and the Lead Teacher who will talk with the family if necessary
Don't bring your outside problems to work	Do come to work ready to be productive
Don't arrive at the exact time you are scheduled to be at work	Do come to work early enough to put away personal belongings and be ready to start working on time
Don't call in sick at the last possible moment	Do let the scheduling person know the night before you are scheduled to work or as early as you can
Don't leave the building a mess	Do stay to clean up; you will be paid for your time
Don't transport a child in your personal vehicle	Do follow the center's guidelines for handling emergencies or late pick-up
Don't leave the room without communicating with the other teachers	Do tell others where you are going and check ratios before leaving
Don't gossip about your co-workers	Do follow the proper grievance procedures if there is a conflict
Don't divert your attention from the children (i.e., accepting or making personal calls, sleeping, reading personal books or magazines, etc.)	Do use your break time for these activities
Don't argue with a child	Do state your intentions in a positive manner and redirect if needed
Don't be insensitive to the children (i.e., laughing at, teasing, or making fun of)	Do respect the children as people and they will respect you
Don't call a child by a "cute" name (i.e., sweetie, honey, baby)	Do call the child by her given name
Don't play favorites with the children	Do treat all children with equal respect

Don't let your biases show	Do treat all children with equal respect regardless of their race, age or sex
Don't sit with your back to the children	Do position yourself so you can monitor all areas
Don't tower over a child when speaking with them	Do bend down to the child's eye level
Don't constantly stay in one area	Do move from area to area as needed, making sure you've spent time with each child
Don't yell across the room to a child	Do walk over to a child and state your request in a quiet voice
Don't leave any child unattended	Do supervise all children at all times
Don't exceed ratio	Do be aware of how many children you have at all times and call for assistance if you go over ratio
Don't send the children on errands by themselves	Do call someone to help if necessary
Don't make models for the children (i.e., drawing pictures or building structures)	Do foster the children's creativity by allowing them to think of their own ideas
Don't do too much for the children	Do foster independence by allowing the children to do what they are able to by themselves
Don't put the word "OK" on the end of each request	Do state requests in a positive manner; saying the word "okay?" implies that the child is being given a choice
Don't use a loud or disruptive voice	Do talk in a quiet, low key voice unless there is an emergency
Don't use physical discipline (i.e., pulling, pushing, grabbing shaking, shoving, spanking, hand slapping, etc.)	Do use problem solving skills and/or redirect the child verbally Call for help if you need it
Don't be inconsistent in your classroom management strategies	Do be consistent with the other teachers as you work together to carry out the program philosophy
Don't sit on tables or shelves	Do be a good model and sit on the floor or on a child-sized chair
Don't stand over the children during mealtimes	Do sit down with the children and taste all the foods just as we ask of the children
Don't serve food with dirty hands	Do wash your hands before touching any foods

Don't set food on dirty tables	Do clean all tables with a bleach/water solution
Don't touch any body fluids including soiled clothing without a barrier	Do use latex gloves or plastic bags as a barrier
Don't play on the children's outdoor equipment	Do stand with the children at the equipment and be available to them at all times
Don't sit in the muscle room or outside (do not keep adult size chairs in these areas)	Do circulate around to facilitate learning and prevent accidents
Don't wear clothing that will expose your body inappropriately (i.e., halter tops, short shorts, midriffs, tube tops)	Do wear clothing in good repair that will reflect your professionalism
Don't wear hats or clothing that bear slogans of an adult nature (i.e., beer labels, slang or sarcastic slogans, drug paraphernalia, etc.)	Do wear clothing in good repair that will reflect your professionalism
Don't carry cell phones, purses, or listen to radios in the classroom	Do use your break time to use these items (developmentally appropriate children's music may be played in the classroom)
Don't eat candy or chew gum in the classroom or offer candy to the children at any time	Do eat the meals and snacks provided by the center with the children

References

Bredekamp, S., & Copple, C. (Eds.). (1997). *Developmentally appropriate practice in early childhood programs* (Rev. ed.). Washington, DC: NAEYC.

Read, K., Gardner, P., & Mahler, B. (1993). *Early childhood programs: Human relationships and learning.* Florida: Harcourt, Brace, Jovanovich.

CHAPTER 6

The Supervision Process

Supervision and evaluation, along with staff development are the dimensions of the staff enhancement program which form the framework for improving and maintaining effective programs for families and children. When teachers and supervisors, who are often also directors, work together as colleagues and focus on meeting the needs of the children and parents, staff feel more competent and program quality improves. While supervisory and evaluative procedures differ in purpose and somewhat in procedure, the overarching goal of both is to support and improve staff performance. This, in turn, improves quality of service to children and families and creates a rich, rewarding environment for all staff.

Connection: Supervision and Evaluation

Paula, who is the administrator in charge of educational programming in the five WonderWorld centers, initiated a supervisory/evaluation cycle for these centers about a year ago. She recognized the importance of offering support to the five site directors as they began to implement the cycle at their respective centers. They were responsible for supervising and evaluating classroom staff. The directors were most concerned about being in two seemingly conflicting roles, namely that of supportive, helpful supervisor and that of evaluator. Paula, with the help of one of her directors who felt comfortable with this dual role, worked together with the others to help them see that this is all really part of the same process. She pointed out that the mentoring and coaching which she did during supervision was what prepared her teachers for evaluation and helped them understand that part of her job was to carry out both pieces of the process.

The primary purpose of supervision is to help and support teachers as they refine their practices and grow professionally and personally, whereas the focus of evaluation is making decisions about level of performance with children, families, and colleagues. Caruso points out that supervisors assist teachers in increasing the control, authority, and responsibility they have for their own teaching and professional development, whereas evaluation "sums up" the effectiveness of a staff member's performance against certain predetermined standards and, in some cases, can lead to pay raises or promotions (Caruso & Fawcett, 1999). Some supervisors, whether directors, educational coordinators, or lead classroom teachers supervising classroom assistants, feel uncomfortable about the dual role of supervision/evaluation and need special help in dealing with what seem to be conflicting roles.

The conflict over shifting from the role of supportive supervisor to objective evaluator has the potential for creating stress for both the teacher and the supervisor. However, it is helpful if one can look at both aspects as pieces of the same process. The supervision piece of the process involves observation and data collection followed by conferencing, and it is a collaborative effort where both teacher and supervisor contribute information and engage in dialogue. During this formative part of the cycle, the two players are both preparing for the regularly scheduled summative assessment which, in turn, sets the stage for the next supervision cycle.

Numerous observations with rich data collection by both the supervisor and the teacher, followed by a conference where the teacher takes the lead role in interpreting and analyzing the observation data and both individuals discuss what and how to adjust practices, prepare both for the evaluation step. That will be the time when the supervisor observes, gathers, and organizes data, only this time it is the supervisor who interprets the data and makes judgments about performance. Throughout the entire supervision/evaluation cycle, there is individualized goal setting and planning for training for each teacher. As a result, not only is there a formative supervisory process leading to a summative assessment, but also the basis for an individualized staff development plan folded into the package.

Isela is a director in a small center where she supervises four classroom teachers. A great deal of informal contact and observation occurs each day as she checks in with each teacher and occasionally helps out in the classroom. In addition, she does more formal observations on a regular basis. "I know my teachers very well—I can enumer-ate their strengths and where they need support and coaching. So when I am preparing for their evaluations, I feel very secure about talking about those things they do very well and how they have improved in places we have been working on over the past six months. Because we have worked together, my teachers are growing and becoming more confident, and I am quite comfortable about dealing with those behaviors which must change and improve during the next supervisory period.

The preparation for evaluation or summative assessment throughout the supervisory program also applies when classroom teachers are responsible for supervision of their assistants. In these situations, the classroom teacher does much of the data gathering and conferencing, being careful to offer assistants opportunities for input. At the same time, the teacher's supervisor who has been in the classroom, has sat in on planning meetings, and knows all staff very well, can support the teacher who is now also super-vising others in the room. It is very important that the director or the person who super-vises lead teachers knows all staff well because responsibility for the summative assess-ment of all staff usually falls to the one in that position.

In cases where lead teachers supervise assistants, the director gathers data for the per-formance assessment of these assistants, shares it with the teacher, and together they con-sider what should be communicated in the summative conference. In this, as in all cases, it is important to help the supervisees understand the components of the supervision/evalua-tion process and to appreciate how each contributes to their development as teachers.

Individualizing Supervision

"Life would be very easy for supervisors if they could read a book or take a course that would guarantee them one workable method of supervision that would almost always succeed" (Caruso & Fawcett, 1999, p. 4). You have been taught that it is very important to individualize your approaches to the children you work with, and in Chapter 5 there was frequent reference to individualizing your staff orientation program. Supervision is no different. Just as in the classroom or in orientation, it is important to adjust supervi-sory strategies based on both the personalities and the level of professional development of supervisees as well as their individual skills and abilities. In any case, the first step is to work on the relationship—to build trust and mutual respect with staff. As a supervi-sor, your first few encounters with all people you supervise must focus on building trust. It is a time for affirmation, a time for inquiring about interests and feelings about being with children, and a time for sharing some personal information to establish common ground.

Before making any formal observations of a new teacher, look for opportunities to offer encouragement and words of appreciation for things you notice about that teacher. Each encouraging note or comment paves the way to a more positive relationship.

- "Your smile is always so welcoming as you meet these new children and their par-ents."
- "I noticed at naptime how you used a soft, soothing voice with Brian."
- "Thanks for completing that accident form accurately. We need those for our files."
- "It was so helpful to find the room in such good shape this morning. I know you closed yesterday. The room was in great shape for the early arrivals this morning."

Sometimes there is a tendency to focus on teachers who are having difficulty or those who are new to the center, forgetting that even the strongest teachers need ongoing affirmation and support from their supervisors. They not only appreciate the attention, but they too face numerous problems in the course of any given day and in that regard are not any different from their less experienced colleagues. Accomplished teachers appreciate recognition for their expertise and are often eager to move forward as they develop their own supervisory skills with their staff. Teachers who are ready to supervise their assistants not only see their supervisor as a role model, but also as someone who will help them find ways to work with a teacher who may be resistant to change, or one who rarely contributes during planning meetings. On the other hand, their problem may be with an assistant who *does* contribute but the ideas are not age-appropriate or consistent with the program philosophy.

The teacher in a mixed age group at Eliza's center came to her with concerns about an assistant teacher who offered to bring in her new laptop computer to share with the children at grouptime. The teacher knew that bringing in a computer for grouptime would not be consistent with center philosophy, and it was not an appropriate grouptime activity because it would be too difficult for children to refrain from touching this "toy" which this young assistant wanted to show. She needed guidance from Eliza about what to say without squelching the assistant's enthusiasm and participation in future planning meetings. Eliza agreed to sit in with them on the next planning meeting and explain that, because it was a center policy not to have computers in the classroom for the children, showing a computer at grouptime was not consistent with center policy. They would also discuss the research and several recent books addressing the controversy about computers in early childhood classrooms.

There are always special challenges for supervisors when they are faced with being directive with a staff member on any issue because they feel that being directive is not supportive. More often than not, the supervisor wants to avoid conflict and confrontation. It is not easy to decide when and with whom to be directive and when to solve problems by using conflict-resolution strategies. Clearly, it depends on both the situation and the person involved. You would be very direct when a two-year-old child runs out of the room as the door opens to bring in the lunch cart. When safety is an issue, the response is direct. However, when that toddler and her friend are screaming and pulling on the same grocery cart in dramatic play, you would step between them and then try to help them solve the problem. The staff member who is often late and rarely calls needs to be confronted with her tardiness and be ready to agree to a plan to handle future possible tardiness. That same person, who may be new to the center and its philosophy, may fall into a practice of drawing pictures for the preschoolers, who beg and can be very persuasive. Approaching the teacher about this practice offers an opportunity for the supervisor to review a few documents from the orientation process, including Read's (1993) *Guides to Speech and Action* (see Chapter 5) so both can discuss what is viewed as good practice. The new staff person who enjoys drawing may be offered a chance to help another teacher make classroom charts or join a group of parents who are making items for a future fund-raiser. However, if this new staff person and her lead teacher are complaining to the supervisor about an inability to work together, it is time to bring them together to problem-solve.

Experienced staff, eager and cooperative teachers, as well as slow-to-warm up and reluctant teachers, all bring their special skills and talents, temperaments, and personalities to the classroom. Just as good teachers accommodate the diversity among children in their classrooms, so too must supervisors strive to respect and value differences in teachers and at the same time help them grow and develop their talents and skills while guarding the integrity of the center program. Keep in mind that when you are responsible for supervision of staff, you will inevitably have to spend time and energy dealing with conflict.

REFLECTIONS

> How do you feel about confrontation and conflict? Do you withdraw and avoid it like a turtle? Do you approach and attack like a shark? Do you watch and wait like an owl? Consider your style of dealing with conflict and confrontation. How might that affect your performance as a supervisor?

The Supervisory Cycle

The first step in the supervisory cycle is to learn about or do what Caruso & Fawcett (1999) call "discovering" how well a person is performing followed by some type of dialogue, which is usually done in a planned conference. At the close of the conference, time is set aside for goal setting and planning the beginning of the next cycle. This three-step process is individualized and is scheduled to repeat on a regular basis, interrupted at intervals in order to carry out a similar three-step procedure for the summative assessment (Table 6–1). The summative process is sometimes called performance evaluation or performance appraisal. Some organizations evaluate all staff once each year, whereas others may do that more often, depending on the schedule for pay increments and for opportunities to move up the career ladder.

When the teacher and supervisor prepare to go through the initial supervisory cycle, they should have had many opportunities to work together and discuss issues during the Orientation Program (see Chapter 5). Ideally, they have begun to build a relationship based on trust and mutual respect and are prepared to participate collaboratively in an ongoing supervisor/supervisee relationship.

The three steps in the supervisory cycle (discussed below) are meant to serve as a guideline or a framework for setting up programs in various types of centers and for different staff levels. In larger organizations, such as public school systems and Head Start, there are specific procedures and forms with precise timelines for supervisors to use in this process. Smaller centers also need forms and guidelines, but procedures and timelines may be more flexible.

The Discovery Step

Most encounters between a supervisor and supervisee (for this discussion, a teacher) can be viewed as part of the discovery process. They are learning about each other, not only from their earlier meetings during orientation but also from the most casual contacts, which may occur when the supervisor checks in with a morning greeting or comes to lunch with the children or for grouptime, or at scheduled times when the supervisor sits to the side to observe and record ongoing classroom events. As you, the supervisor,

Table 6–1 Supervisory Process

Summative Supervisory Cycle	Formative Supervisory Cycle
Discovery Step	
Supervisor observes supervisee - Evaluation tool - Performance appraisal	Supervisor observes supervisee - Anecdotal records - Narrative records - Checklists - Casual notes and comments
Conference Step	
Supervisor reviews previously set goals Supervisor presents findings based on the performance appraisal Supervisor and supervisee discuss results of the performance appraisal	Supervisor empowers supervisee - Nurturing and coaching - Sharing information and concerns
Planning and Goal-Setting Step	
Supervisor states the decisions based on the performance appraisal - Raise - Promotion - No change in status - Probation - Dismissal	Supervisor and supervisee set mutually agreed upon goals
Develop the action plan and put it in writing - Training - Course work - Reading - Conditions of the probationary period - Steps necessary to finalize dismissal	Develop the action plan and put it in writing - Readings - Training or course work - Observing peers or teachers in other programs
Set the time for the next summative conference	Set the time for the next formative conference

do your morning "pep" walk-through, find bits of evidence of creativity in a room or listen for special comments from a teacher. Put a little note in the teacher's pocket as you leave or put a note on her e-mail, "It was such a joy to hear you singing to Marcus today while you were changing his diaper."

During casual visits, the supervisor has an opportunity to get a feel for what is happening in the room or on the playground, and also has time to linger and interact with children. It is an ideal time to model appropriate interactions with both children and adults in this environment. These special times, planned or unplanned, when teachers and supervisors are working side by side not only strengthens their relationship but also enriches their conference discussion. Sharing an experience with a particularly challenging child or watching a delightful dramatic play sequence evolve provides a wealth of information for future discussions and planning.

When working with teachers in a particular classroom, it is important to sit in on their planning meetings from time to time. In fact, you may want to arrange a systematic way to join teachers for their planning times on a regular basis. Not only does this put you in a position to model ways for lead teachers to support their assistants, but it also gives you insight into dynamics of this team and how this communication network is working.

Notes from casual contacts are helpful in building your relationship with your teachers, but you will want to establish more formalized systems for collecting detailed information. Documentation can be done in a variety of ways. Open-ended anecdotal notes or running records give you somewhat more detailed information than do checklists or assessment tools. Videotaping, tape recording, or taking photos are also useful ways to gather information. Any or all of these ways can be used at different times and for various reasons.

Sample Anecdotal Note

Name: Jessie (lead teacher)   Time: 8:15 A.M.
Room: Toddler–Room 2   Date: 3/27/01
When I stopped in to say Good Morning, Jessica was talking with Ms. Peterson, who rushed by me in the hallway with her toddler, Jamie. Jamie was whimpering and clinging to Mom's pant leg. Jessie said, "Ms. Peterson, my assistant who closed last night left a note saying your baby sitter was 15 minutes late picking up Jamie—that is the second time this week." Ms. P. said she was aware of the problem. Jessie went on to ask that she please try to make adjustments, etc. Conversation lasted about 7 or 8 minutes.

If the teacher and supervisor have agreed to work on ways to help set limits with children or deal with conflict with parents, then anecdotal notes that capture the essence of an encounter between teacher and child, or teacher and parent, will provide helpful information for the next conference. Sometimes a running record from a grouptime or a transition can form the basis for discussion about developmentally appropriate content for those daily events.

Sample Running Record

Name: Andy T. (Assist. Teacher-Susan's room) Time: Grouptime
Room: Preschool Rm 3   Number of Children: 13
Date: 1/15/01
11:00 A.M.
Children are coming in from outside—Andy (A) is putting out carpet squares in a large circle. Susan helps children get coats hung up and directs them to go over to A. who waits in the story area. Five children come to sit on a carpet square. Jake, Colin, and Becky wander around and ignore Susan's attempts to have them join the circle. Greg and Tommy both want to sit next to A., but a child is already

sitting there. Mandy, Jessica, and Kiera are chatting over by the cubbies—they seem to be good friends.

11:20—

A. starts the song, "We're All At School Today"—Mandy, Jessica, and Kiera run over—Greg and Tommy still struggling for a spot next to A.. Susan sits opposite A. and Jake plops into her lap. Colin and Becky stroll and stand near Susan. The song ends and A. begins to read "Silly Sally"—he stops to ask Becky and Colin, "Colin and Becky, there is a carpet square here for both of you, come sit please." Both linger near Susan. A. makes a place for Greg on one side and says, "Tommy, you can sit next to me tomorrow, I'll make a note so I remember." Tommy pouts and whimpers his disappointment. A. responds, "You're disappointed, you will get a turn, we'll make a note together after grouptime—remind me to do that." Tommy stands nearby but does not sit down.

11:20—

Colin and Becky wander off to see what's for lunch. The three girls (M.,J.,K.) are now chatting about Jessica's birthday party. A. starts the story over. Now Tommy spits on Greg. Susan gets up to take Tommy aside, "You spit on Greg—I know you really want to sit next to A—you are not to spit on him. Let's write that note about tomorrow." A. starts to read "Silly Sally' for the third time now. As he starts to read, Greg calls, "I have to go potty." A. sends Greg to Susan for help as Tommy returns to the circle and sits in Greg's spot.

11:30—

A. finishes "Silly Sally" and starts transition to bathroom and lunch. A. calls each child's name as he shows the name card. Tables are set (floater sets the tables while children were outside). Transition to lunch goes well. Children, A., and Susan all at lunch by 11:30.

Running records paint a picture of an event and they can be used in discussion with the teacher later in the day or during the conference.

Checklists and other assessment tools cover a range of topics including interactions with children, interactions with families and other staff, room arrangement, handling routines and transition, curriculum, and other work-related responsibilities (see sample Staff Evaluation Form—Leader's Resource 6–1.)

Sometimes supervisors will use a section of the comprehensive checklist or evaluation tool. For example, when you and your teacher agree that it will be helpful to focus on the guidance techniques being used in the classroom, in addition to anecdotal notes, running records, or teacher report from observations, a brief checklist focused on guidance strategies is another way to gather information on that area of classroom practice. (see Sample Teacher Assessment/Guidance Techniques—Leader's Resource 6–2.) Evaluation tools are often used several times prior to the summative evaluation in order to get a picture of overall performance for both the supervisor and the supervisee before the actual evaluation is done.

Parents and peers can also provide information and insights into teacher performance as does the teacher's own self-evaluation. Parents usually are willing and often pleased to have the opportunity to fill out a brief questionnaire regarding their child's teacher. It goes without saying that teachers are always informed about this involvement of parents in the teacher evaluation process. (See Sample Parent Feedback Survey—Leader's Resource 6–3.) Encourage your teachers to save the cards and notes from parents throughout the year and to make them part of the material they share with their supervisor.

A system of peer observation and peer coaching is yet another way to gather information on staff. A peer partner is assigned for each staff member and that person becomes an additional support person. The "buddy" assigned during orientation may not be the same person who later becomes a peer partner. The peer partner can also be a buddy but is really a coach, a "sounding board" for new ideas, a helper when preparing new materials, and a support when needed. The peer partner may also participate in the ongoing assessment process by observing as well as doing some peer coaching. (Sample Peer Observation—Leader's Resource 6–4.)

Any and all information, whether from casual encounters or more formal methods, becomes part of the discovery step in the supervisory cycle. The information gathered forms the basis for the discussion at the supervisor/supervisee conference.

The Conference Step

Regularly scheduled conferences following classroom observations and collecting data from various sources is the next step in the supervisory cycle. Whether during the formative evaluation periods of the supervision process or after the regularly scheduled summative assessment, a planned conference provides the forum for discussion and decision-making. Just as the formative and summative evaluations are part of the total process, so are the formative and summative conferences, with each serving a unique purpose.

The Formative Conference

Regularly planned formative conferences provide time for discussing and integrating information pertaining to teaching practices, planning, curriculum, interactions with children, staff and parents, and issues of professionalism. Revisiting descriptive documents and expectations of staff can also be a part of the conference agenda. It is a time for reflection and sharing within a nurturing, supportive climate.

When the supervisor/teacher relationship is based on trust and caring, both parties bring knowledge and skills to the table for an open and frank discussion. Although the supervisor, by virtue of her position, is in a position of power in this collaborative relationship, appreciation for the teacher can be shown by inviting and accepting a presentation of issues and concerns while being helpful and in control without dominating the conference.

When dealing with staff, it is always wise to find ways to empower them. It is helpful to have the teacher help set the conference agenda, just as directors empower all staff by offering them an opportunity to participate in setting staff meeting agendas. This is especially true for conferences that are part of the formative assessment process. For example, if the teacher and supervisor have agreed that grouptime and transitions are areas of concern and should be observed, then they have essentially agreed that these should be the topics for the next conference.

However, if the teacher comes to that conference and immediately begins to talk about her assistant who failed to pick up on what was needed on the playground that day, the supervisor realizes that the most helpful thing to do for that moment is to listen. Allowing the teacher to ventilate frustration and then, together, reflect on the annoying event and reach a calm is sometimes enough to resolve the issue and move on. Remember to listen first as you lead up to defining the problem:

Caressa comes to her conference with her supervisor Danielle, plops down in the chair, and breathlessly blurts out: "I am so frustrated *with Marcus (her classroom assistant). I feel I can't trust him to keep the children safe on the playground!"*
Danielle: You're really upset—*something happened on the playground with Marcus this morning.*
Carissa: YES! It's crazy! He's tossing ball with two children out there and has his back to the swings and the playhouse!
Danielle: You were worried about the safety of the children.
Carissa: YES! And I have to keep running from one side of the space to the other to supervise them.
Danielle: It's tiring for you to keep running around our large playground, and you take your responsibility for keeping children safe very seriously.
Carissa: Yes (much calmer now), I do, and I don't like to be bossing him around all the time. I want to be able to get along with the other teachers in my room.
Danielle: This is really your first experience at giving an assistant directions and its seems you're not real comfortable about telling him what you expect him to do on the playground. What can we do to work this out?

Listening is an important element in good communication and when it is followed by carefully framed questions and helpful information, it can lead to productive shared problem-solving.

As mentioned previously in the formative assessment, the supervisor usually has the supervisee take the lead. That can happen only if the supervisor offers the opportunity by knowing how to frame questions and by being alert to nonverbal and verbal signals which open the way to defer to the supervisee during the conference. Sometimes, as in the situation just presented, Caressa was overwrought about a situation that had just happened that day, so she was given the lead and Danielle listened carefully and responded to her feelings. Think about the Sample Anecdote (page 149) where Jessie, the toddler teacher, was talking with a frazzled parent who had just rushed in with her whimpering toddler. It would be easy for the supervisor to start the conference by saying, "I made a note about Ms. P's arrival with Jamie and on occasions like that, it's best if you help Jamie separate from Mom—maybe stoop down and chat while Mom signs him in. Communicate the problem about pick-up on the previous day another way—by calling that evening, or by starting a journal system for each child where you and the parent communicate each day via the journal." Now *pause*—How can your teacher respond? Does Jessie feel uncomfortable? Defensive? Inadequate? Maybe all of the above? She may fall silent, or she may begin, "Yes, but," and then you are trapped into a round of "yes, buts." Jessie may say that she'll try to do as you ask next time. However, it is important to note that she was not given a chance to take the lead because you took the lead from her at the start.

An opening comment or question can empower your teacher to take the lead. In this case, you might say, "I was interested in the incident with Jamie and Ms. P. yesterday. In fact, I jotted it down so I would remember to ask you about it. Tell me what's happening there?" The outcome may be the same because there can still be discussion about alternatives for future handling of similar situations, but your teacher has a chance to tell her side of the story, which may give you more information and ideas about other ways to help. "Questioning is critical to accomplishing conference goals and in training supervisees to think through and analyze their behavior" (Caruso & Fawcett, 1999, p. 111).

In the example with Ms. P., the question was meant not only to shift the lead to the teacher, but also to get information about "What's happening here?" Questions can also be used to explore how the teacher communicates with classroom assistants:

> "How do you let Karen know that she is expected to put all the shelves in order and clean up the easel before she leaves in the evening?"

When you have concerns about handling a specific child, other questions are helpful:

> "What are you planning for Demarcus during the early morning to help him settle in and become engaged in some activity?"

If you want to explore or generate a discussion about curriculum, your question may be:

> "What have you and Andy been thinking about for dramatic play now that over half of your children will be five by the end of this month?"

When you want to hear how your teacher reacted to the particular situation with Andy at the grouptime described in the Sample Running Record (page 149), you may ask:

> "Was that a pretty typical grouptime, or were there extenuating circumstances on that day?"

This question about the grouptime can lead to some dialogue about related concerns and issues, such as:

- Perhaps there are too many children in the group, and that half the children could be outside while the other half have a grouptime.
- Several children seem to have special issues about space, whereas others seem disinterested in group.
- Grouptime activities should be planned so they are age-appropriate and relevant.
- Roles for staff in the room at grouptime should be defined and communicated to everyone involved.

A well-framed question or two can set the stage for a discussion that is informative and supportive for both the teacher and the supervisor.

All conferences should be set up for a specific length of time and, when at all possible, should begin promptly and end at the agreed upon time. Given the current staffing problems in most places, it may be difficult to get classroom coverage for the teacher. In addition, finding a quiet, comfortable space for an uninterrupted meeting is a problem in some facilities. Planning the meeting to coincide with naptime and offering a snack for the teacher can make it a pleasant time, and is almost always a treat for a weary teacher. In programs where flex-time is available, asking a teacher to stay late or arrive early may be an option.

It is up to the supervisor to keep track of the time and bring the conference to closure, making sure to leave time to summarize, indicate action plans for the coming days and weeks, and set the next conference date.

The Summative Evaluation Conference

The purpose of the summative conference is to present the supervisee with the results of the summative evaluation or performance appraisal. Now roles shift and the supervisor takes the lead in presenting the results of the assessment. Although most teachers feel somewhat anxious about being evaluated, their anxiety is likely to be reduced in situations where the teacher and supervisor have worked collaboratively over time and have agreed on what the performance expectations are. When that is the case, there should be no surprises at the summative conference.

In this conference, the supervisor presents a summary of the results of the performance appraisal and shares the documentation with the supervisee. It is helpful for each to have a copy of the final document, so both can follow as the supervisor points out strengths and sets the stage for planning and goal setting.

Devanna is a director in a church sponsored child care center with four classrooms and ten full-time staff. She is responsible for supervision and annual evaluation of all classroom staff. Devanna is a very warm, accepting person who has set a tone of respect and appreciation for all teachers, families, and children. Most of her employees are enthusiastic and relatively competent, and they all get along quite well together. She has one teacher, Julie, with whom she has much in common and they have shared experiences here as well as at a previous job site. They often discuss good books they have read or movies they have both seen.

Initially, Julie was a strong player and was well-liked by colleagues and parents, but late in her second year at this center her performance faltered. Her classroom became cluttered and messy, there was little or no "creative sparkle" in her planning, and she was not taking care of assigned responsibilities such as setting up the muscle room or taking her turn at straightening up the dramatic play dress-ups.

Parents were now complaining and Devanna, after gathering data and documenting the concerns, had to confront Julie with an number of things which had not improved, even after reminders, coaching, and conferencing about them. It was very difficult for Devanna because she really likes Julie, but because Devanna knows that this was expected of her and it was part of her job, she could no longer mollify her feedback.

When they reached the summative conference at the end of Julie's second year, Devanna had no choice. She began the conference by saying, "Julie, liking you makes my job easier and brightens my day, but I still have to hold you accountable for your work." It set the stage for sharing the difficult material. Julie was not surprised.

These conferences are always more difficult when the message holds more negatives than positives. That does not happen often because, in most effective supervisory programs, the ongoing support and the coaching and mentoring of a respected supervisor is enough to motivate and energize teachers to grow and improve their practice. These teachers then move toward greater independence and grow professionally. In those cases where the best of supervision and support does not have the desired effect, the supervisor must be the bearer of that message. In these situations, it is important to focus on the behaviors and not attack the person's values or self-worth (Caruso & Fawcett, 1999). Make certain you are working from information based on your own observations, not on hearsay, and consider the source of the problem. If the source is job related, then it is important to offer extra support to adjust job conditions, if possible, and set a specific time period for possible improvement. It may mean spending more time coaching and co-teaching, or perhaps reducing the paperwork load for a time so the teacher can focus more energy on the classroom. If the problem is personal, then listening or offering time to seek help may be helpful; however, you, as the supervisor, have little control over personal problems or family issues. It may be appropriate to offer help with finding outside resources that will provide help and professional support.

The Planning and Goal-Setting Step

The final step in the supervisory cycle is planning and goal-setting that leads to the period of "discovery" and the cycle begins again. It is up to the supervisor to plan for time at the end of each conference to discuss planning and goal setting. Planning can include everything from setting the time and focus of the next observation, to arranging to do some co-teaching, or attending a meeting together, or focusing on a topic for reading and study. The supervisor and teacher could decide to co-teach so they can try out a new transition strategy. Attending a meeting with an infant teacher on some of the new brain research could provide new common understandings on which to base discussions with other infant staff members. Reading some of Katz and Chard's work on the "project approach" can offer ideas for expanding and extending curriculum for the older fours in the classroom in a summer program (Katz & Chard, 1990). Clearly, some of the planning is for the short term, such as setting time for the next observation, whereas investigating a topic of interest will extend over time.

Goals, whether short-term or long-term, can be both personal and professional. An immediate goal for the classroom may be to gain a better understanding of a particularly challenging child. This becomes a goal for both the teacher and the supervisor, because both have a vested interest in making this child's day richer and more comfortable. All the stakeholders, including the child, the family, and the caregivers, can benefit from energy invested in achieving this goal. After setting goals, the next step is to articulate and record an agreed-upon plan to achieve the goals as stated. It is important to write down exactly what will be done and a timeline for doing it.

Often goals emerge in the course of the conference as a result of questions teachers ask or as supervisors' observations are reviewed. When a grouptime such as that described in the Sample Running Record (page 149) is reviewed, a discussion of strategies for planning and implementing grouptimes may be the focus for the next few weeks. The plan might be for the supervisor to observe again at grouptime while the teacher and assistant work out a system for dividing the group at that time of the day. A visit to another center to observe a grouptime may be helpful, or have a peer teacher or the supervisor co-teach during several grouptimes. In addition, the supervisor can find reading material which will be helpful for future discussions about content for a rich grouptime experience. Thus, the problem could be approached in a variety of ways involving both the teacher and the supervisor, each working toward their common goal—to enhance the grouptime experience for the children in this classroom.

Personal goals for teachers often involve career moves and professional development. For example, when a teacher reaches the top of the pay scale in her present position and needs an advanced credential to take the next step on the center's career ladder, goal setting and planning will focus on getting that next credential. An aide or floater may have a CDA, but based on licensing regulations, Head Start requirements or center standards, the next step to assistant teacher requires an Associate Degree in early childhood.

The goal, then, will be the Associate Degree, and the planning will involve obtaining funds, scheduling time off to take classes, and perhaps pairing up with a peer coach or mentor who, along with the supervisor, offers support and encouragement.

Procedures for achieving stated goals are spelled out in writing and are agreed on by both the teacher and the supervisor. Sometimes performance appraisal tools include a final section with space to write strategies for improvement and goals for the future. (See Sample Staff Evaluation Form—Leader' Resource 6–1, Performance Appraisal Lead Teacher—Leader's Resource 6–5.) It is also helpful to develop an action plan that breaks down the goals and objectives into specific steps to achieve expected outcomes. (See Staff Development Action Plans—Leader's Resource 5–6 and 5–7.) Action plans are developed collaboratively at the end of the conference. They are individualized and form the core of an individual staff development plan. (For further discussion of Staff Development see Sciarra & Dorsey, 1998.)

The discussion about changes in status and salary adjustments or, in some cases, the decision to move to probationary status or dismissal occurs at the end of the summative conference. If you are a director who also supervises staff, this final step at the conference, whether good news, bad news, or some combination thereof, is your responsibility. Depending on the size of the organization, it is wise to get advice and support from an administrator, board chairperson or board committee before final decisions are made in cases of reprimands or dismissals.

Delmyra has been a director for almost twenty years. She is passionate about her work and an inspiration to other directors and managers in her community. She says, "I know I am not a good manager, but I feel I can motivate and inspire others to be as passionate about this field as I am." She is the type of leader who finds her own inspiration by reading and listening to people like Stephen R. Covey (The Seven Habits of Highly Effective People) *and Tom Peters* (The Pursuit of WOW). *She often reflects on a sobering quote from Peters: "Firing is awful. You are screwing up people's lives in a big way, even if it honestly is for the long-term good. You are acknowledging that you did: (1) a rotten recruiting job, (2) a rotten development job, or (3) both. 'Both' is most likely the correct answer." (Peters, 1994, p. 24)*

Dismissal of an Employee

Center leaders, whether director, supervisor or educational coordinator, will at some point in their career face the unpleasant task of firing an employee. When a teacher is not performing at the expected level and support and training opportunities have failed, the decision to terminate must follow. "When opportunities for change have been exhausted, it's time to say goodbye. Keeping a teacher who performs poorly lowers morale and encourages resentment from teammates. Their continued employment sends the wrong message to staff who go over and above standards you have set for the center" (Khanagov, 1999, p. 35). Before taking this final step, there are a number of things to consider, not the least of which is to ensure that there is enough written documentation to support the decision. Keep in mind that dismissal decisions are not always for incompetence or disciplinary reasons. Sometimes enrollment is down or the agency is downsizing; however, whatever the reasons for the dismissal, there are a number of things to keep in mind, not only for your own protection, but for that of your employer as well.

Dismissal Guidelines (adapted from Caruso & Fawcett, 1999)

- Check personnel policies carefully to be sure all procedures have followed the adopted organizational guidelines.
- Get legal advice on questions about laws and statutes that may place restrictions on the planned actions.
- Have all the relevant facts in hand for the meeting with the employee involved.
- Allow time for the employee to offer explanations and ask questions.
- If dismissal is owing to downsizing or low enrollment and the employee has served the center well, explain what support will be available in the pursuit of another job.
- To minimize disruption to ongoing center activities, plan the dismissal for late in the day, perhaps on a Friday, and do it in a private, quiet space in the building.
- Make a record of all that transpired during this final conference and keep it with all the other paperwork and documentation for this employee.
- Be cautious about firing "on the spot," even if the wrongdoing is very serious. Put the employee on administrative leave and then investigate what happened, because hasty decisions can lead to costly mistakes that can precipitate legal action.

Documentation of all steps leading up to a dismissal and procedures throughout the process is critical for the protection of the center, its board, and all administrative staff. As a final step in this process, it is helpful to use a Resignation/Dismissal Employment Checklist (see Sample Resignation/Termination Checklist—Leader's Resource 6–8). This should be completed, signed, and dated before the employee leaves on the last day of employment. In the case of a resignation, this information, along with results of the exit interview, become a part of the employee's personnel file. It is filed with all the data collected prior to and during a dismissal.

LEADER'S CORNER

The most difficult part of my job is when I have to terminate an employee. I do not like to do it but sometimes I have to bite-the-bullet and do so. It is not only distasteful because it is always hurtful, but it is a lot of work. I have to be *so* sure that I have all the documentation in place to defend my actions should I have to do that for my board or, the worst scenario, in court.

Administrator, university affiliated child
care center

Dismissals are unsettling for everyone involved, including children and families in that classroom as well as all other staff. Even when it may be a relief for some, reactions will vary depending on the popularity of the person who has been dismissed. Teachers will be concerned about what will happen next. Will I be discharged? Will my work load increase? Whom can I trust now? Children will express their anxiety in various ways. They may ask repeatedly about the person who is gone. A child may fear "My other teachers may also disappear and then, who will take care of me?" Parents have concerns about all turnover because they realize that it is hard on their children. They are eager to know how quickly a replacement will come and who it will be.

Healing Staff after a Dismissal

The major damage of a dismissal can be erosion of trust in the leader by children, parents, and staff. On the other hand, if the former employee was an incompetent, uncooperative team member, then the dismissal can strengthen trust in a leader who is now seen as someone who will do what is necessary to maintain quality. In either case, it is important that both staff and families are notified immediately, so they do not hear about it through the "grapevine." How this notification is accomplished will depend on the established communication network for the center. Written notices placed in each family's mailbox on the day the dismissal occurred is one way to inform parents. A posted notice on the parent board may be too public and may create uneasiness among other staff. A brief staff meeting at the beginning of the next day will quickly get the word out to staff, but it may make for an uneasy day for all. Going from room to room to inform each individual staff member is more personal. Giving the other teachers a chance ask a question or two and providing a brief rationale for the decision may dilute their anxiety and help them feel supported.

Professionalism is imperative in sensitive situations like reprimands and dismissals. It is important that explanations given to all concerned be sincere and void of personal details. If you are the supervisor or manager who will be telling staff, think through what you will say and give each person essentially the same information. "This was a business decision. We are here to care for the children, and we have standards that we cannot compromise. This person decided that she could not meet those standards. I assure you we gathered a lot of information and considered all the facts before the decision was made. The person was treated fairly and respectfully" (Khanagov, 1999, p. 37). If this was a great person and a good friend of many, it is even more difficult to tell other staff that ". . . even a wonderful person can do a poor job in the classroom."

As a director, be prepared for a flood of negative comments from both staff and parents. Depending on the feelings about the person who is now gone, these comments will confirm the poor performer's faults or will be critical of the action of the administrators who were responsible for firing a friend. Remember that energy spent fueling the grapevine with negative comments lowers morale and diverts attention from the primary job of caring for children. You, as the director or supervisor, will have to use your influence to help the staff focus on working together to repair the damage. There will be lingering consequences, including many questions for you and some issues about loyalty to the center. Concerns about missing a friend and guilt about still being on staff when a team member is gone can also affect performance of those who remain. It is important to acknowledge what it means to lose a teammate and to help your staff build a new team, but never underestimate the impact that a termination has on the rest of the staff (Khanagov, 1999).

The board of directors of a child care facility which is part of a women's prison has been scrutinizing the staff turnover and current staffing crisis at the center. The director is the only person who has remained on the center staff continuously since the program's inception three years ago. The six classroom staff plus a family coordinator have completely turned over twice in that time. Three of the twelve who are gone were asked to leave and the remainder left for other reasons. Members of the board and the director have concerns about consistency and continuity of quality care for the children in the program. The board has been assured that salaries and benefits are competitive, but that entry level credentials and ongoing expectations exceed those of most programs in the community. The board chairperson is asking the director to evaluate the hiring process as well as the ongoing supervision and support system. In addition, an ad hoc board committee will look into retention and possible reasons for the high staff turnover. Board members want more information about why people are leaving the agency.

Exit Interviews

The turnover/retention dilemma currently plaguing the early childhood field is a serious problem. Some of the problem arises as a result of dismissals, as mentioned previously, but it is exacerbated by the reality that many staff leave for other reasons. There is constant movement of trained child care people as they go from program to program, return to school, relocate or, often, leave the field. Because turnover is so disruptive for other staff, families, and children, it is important that centers establish a database from former staff to track where they have gone and what they plan to do. In addition, it is helpful to talk to them in order to gain a better understanding of why they made the decision to leave. As a director, if you can get feedback that will help you understand the issues and concerns which led to a resignation, then you may be able to make adjustments and changes to reduce the turnover rate. One way to get information from former staff is to arrange for an exit interview.

The purpose of the exit interview is to gather information that will provide insights into the major reasons for leaving. These data can be a rich resource, not only for how to work with remaining staff, but for future hiring as well. Whether conducted by phone or in person, the exit interviewer should be knowledgeable about the program, but not directly involved with the former employee. In agencies with multiple sites, it could be a manager or administrator from another site. Board members, business managers, center public relations people or, in some cases, parents can make the call or visit for the interview. Selecting the interviewer is critical to the outcome of an exit interview. The goal is to have an honest and frank discussion about the former employee's view of the center and the job in an atmosphere of acceptance and objectivity. Careful listening and questioning while addressing the issues to be considered in the interview will encourage openness and put the interviewee at ease (see Sample Issues to Address at an Exit Interview—Leader's Resource 6–9).

Confidentiality is often an issue for employees, and some may refuse to participate in an exit interview. When the system is in place and one person is assigned to do the exit interviews, that person can compile data and pass them along to center leaders who are responsible for future hiring as well as current staff. Although it may be difficult to maintain anonymity, every effort should be made to protect those involved. The information should never be used in a way that could damage the professional reputation or future employment of those who participate in the exit interview process. It should be taken seriously as administrators and board members examine their staff retention records.

Evaluating Center Leaders

Who evaluates directors or supervisors? They spend their time evaluating their staff, but staff seldom have an opportunity to evaluate their supervisors or directors. "Make evaluations by subordinates a key component of all bosses' performance appraisals" (Peters,

1994, p. 1). The focus of the assessment by the "subordinate" should be the ". . . perception of the extent to which the supervisory and evaluative processes at the center pose restraints or opportunities for professional growth" (Bloom, Sheerer, & Britz, 1991, p. 197). At all levels, find ways to obtain feedback from staff about their immediate supervisor, whether a lead teacher, master teacher, educational coordinator, or director. In each case, this information becomes part of the supervisor's performance appraisal (see Sample Supervisory Behavior Questionnaire—Leader's Resource 6–10).

Center leaders are responsible for how well their center serves clients. Assessing parent satisfaction is one way to evaluate how well they and their staff are doing. The measure of how administrators respond to both negative and positive feedback from parents can be viewed as a benchmark of their qualifications to manage and lead. Note that the Parent Feedback Survey was mentioned earlier as part of the teacher appraisal process.

Self-Evaluation

"Supervisory conferences lay the groundwork for self-evaluation, for it is through conference dialogue that staff members practice reflecting, predicting, judging and suggesting alternatives to caregiving and teaching behaviors" (Caruso & Fawcett, 1999, p. 154). Throughout the collaborative supervisory process, teachers and their supervisors are reviewing their skills and practices, whether it be with each other, with other staff and team members, or with children and parents. One characteristic of an accomplished supervisor or teacher is the ability to step back, reflect, and self-evaluate performance. The corollary to this is that these competent professionals are also able to define what they need to further refine their practice and reach even higher levels of mastery. After they consider responses from staff, parents, and other center leaders about their performance, they evaluate themselves and formulate their personal staff development action plan.

When working with staff, you as the leader will find that some staff require structure to assist them in thinking about their progress. Some type of form should be developed to provide guidelines for self-evaluation (see Sample Staff Self-Evaluation Form—Leader's Resource 6–11). The purpose of a self-evaluation form is to help individuals focus on particular issues or areas of development as they reflect on what they do and what they like most about it.

- "What training experience or new idea excited you most during this past month?"
- "What has happened at work this month that has given you the most pleasure?"
- "What were the most stressful events at work during this month? How did you handle that stress?"
- "What strengths serve you well as you work with parents?"

Reviewing feelings and memories of what offers joy, disappointment, or anxiety enables your teachers to pinpoint interests and concerns, and facilitates planning for growth and satisfaction.

Supportive supervisors can help supervisees feel comfortable and free from threat, thus enabling them to be frank and realistic about self-assessment. Occasionally, supervisees will overrate or underrate themselves, which can create a dilemma for the supervisor. However, as teachers feel empowered by the confidence and trust in the supervisor/supervisee relationship, they are better able to judge themselves.

Summary

Supervision and evaluation are both pieces of the same process. Together, they lead to professional and personal growth of staff. Supervision is done by the director or other selected administrator in the program and, in some cases, lead teachers take responsibility for supervising other classroom staff. The supervisor/supervisee relationship must be built on mutual respect and trust, which is the basis for a collaborative, productive partnership.

The supervisory cycle begins with data collection or "discovery," followed by conferencing and planning. Ongoing, year-round data collection through casual and formalized observation, using various performance assessment tools, and input from peers and parents is a formative process that offers support and guidance for the participants. The conference, which follows data collection, provides a forum for dialogue about performance, concerns, and expectations. The conference ends with planning for future data collection and conferencing. Self-evaluation is also a valuable part of the total process for both supervisors and teachers.

The evaluative or summative aspect of supervision occurs on a regular basis and involves the same three-step process. However, it differs in that the supervisor is now drawing conclusions about performance and making decisions about raises, promotions, future expectations and, in extreme cases, termination. All members of the center community are affected by the departure of a staff member, and there is much healing to be done when staff turnover occurs.

Class Assignments

1. Read an article on supervision or evaluation from an early childhood, special education, or elementary school journal or a relevant website or a magazine. Write a one-page summary of the article. (You may use *Young Children, Exceptional Children, Child Care Information Exchange,* or their respective websites, or other journals or websites approved by your instructor.) Write several paragraphs about some experiences you have had at a work site (other than an educational setting) where you were supervised or evaluated. In writing, compare and contrast supervisory and evaluation practices in educational environments and business settings. Be prepared to discuss these comparisons in class.

2. Plan to do a one-hour observation of one of your classmates as she is working in a classroom with children.
   a. Write three anecdotal notes during the first half-hour of your observation and a narrative or running record for the last half-hour of your observation.
      - Arrange the observation with the director or cooperating teacher as well as with your classmate.
      - Get permission from the classmate you observe.
      - Be alert to all ethical and confidentiality issues.
      - Questions about confidentiality and ethics should be discussed with your instructor.
   b. Write out the opening comment and question you would use in a follow-up conference based on this observation.

Class Exercises

1. In groups of four, discuss the supervisory practices in educational environments and those in business settings. (See Class Assignment No. 1.)

    a. Using Working Paper 6–1, answer the following questions:
  - What are the basic elements of supervision and evaluation that are evident whether in educational or business settings?
  - How do they differ and why?

2. Using the running record of Andy and the grouptime experience in his classroom, role play a conference between a supervisor and a teacher. Following the pattern of one of the Action Plans in Leader's Resources 6–5 or 6–6, complete an action plan for Andy before the conference ends.

  - If you are in the role of the supervisor, think through what your opening statement and question will be.
  - If your role is Andy, realize that you are the assistant teacher in the setting and that you want to learn as much as possible while you are in this job.

3. In groups of two, role play the following scenario. Take fifteen minutes to discuss the transition problem presented and then together reflect on the questions posed for the teacher and the supervisor.

This is a formative conference between a supervisor and an experienced teacher. The teacher has been teaching a preschool group housed in a public school building for five years, and six months ago came to this YMCA-sponsored child care center located in an old house. The supervisor has observed transitions from free choice time to outside several times and has concerns about the regimentation and the noisy singing strategy used for these transitions. When she observed on Wednesday, things were very chaotic—children's behaviors escalated and some were on the verge of being out of control. The teacher was using various loud and directive strategies to have the children clean up and then line up for outside. The teacher was clearly frustrated and embarrassed because she was being observed, and finally, in desperation, she just opened the door and the children pushed past her and her assistant before either one of them could get to the playground.

The supervisor has issues about the disorganized chaos, about the regimentation about trying to get the children to clean-up and line-up, and about safety because the children were outside ahead of the adults.

The teacher is frustrated and embarrassed because she feels the children are not listening to her and she really wants to make a good impression on her supervisor.

At the conference, the supervisor's opening question is: "Tell me what you think was going on with the children on Wednesday around 10:00 when they were preparing to go outside?"

The teacher's response is: "Goodness! I don't know. They didn't listen at all. They don't like to clean up, and they are too fidgety to stand in line and wait until everyone is ready."

As the supervisor:

- Were you able to reflect your teacher's feelings?
- Did you define what you saw as the problem?
- Were you a helpful resource for your teacher?

As the teacher:

- Did you feel the director listened to you?
- Did you feel she understood your concerns?
- How were you included in the problem-solving process?
- Did you leave the conference feeling positive about what happened?

Working Paper 6–1

Comparing Supervision in Different Settings

1. List the basic elements of supervision/evaluation, whether in educational or business settings, based on your reading for Class Assignment No. 1.

    a. In what ways do supervisory processes differ in the two settings?

    b. Should there be differences here?

    c. Why do you think there may be differences in the practices in educational and in business settings?

Leader's Resource 6–1

SAMPLE PERFORMANCE APPRAISAL

Staff Evaluation Form

Employee _____ Evaluation period _____

KEY - How often observed:　F = Frequently　O = Occasionally　N = Never

General work habits	F O N
1. Arrives on time	— — —
2. Reliable in attendance	— — —
3. Responsible in job duties	— — —
4. Alert in health and safety matters	— — —
5. Follows center's philosophy	— — —
6. Open to new ideas	— — —
7. Flexible with assignments and schedule	— — —
8. Comes to work with a positive attitude	— — —
9. Looks for ways to improve the program	— — —
10. Gives ample notice for absences	— — —
11. Remains calm in a tense situation	— — —

• **Examples of behaviors observed:**

_____
_____
_____
_____

Attitude and skills with children	F O N
1. Friendly, warm, and affectionate	— — —
2. Bends low for child-level interactions	— — —
3. Uses a modulated, appropriate voice	— — —
4. Shows respect for individuals	— — —
5. Is aware of developmental levels/changes	— — —
6. Encourages independence/self-help	— — —
7. Promotes self-esteem in communications	— — —
8. Limits interventions in problem-solving	— — —
9. Avoids stereotyping and labeling	— — —
10. Reinforces positive behavior	— — —
11. Minimal use of time out	— — —
12. Regularly records observations of children	— — —

Attitude and skills with parents	F O N
1. Available and approachable with parents	— — —
2. Listens and responds well to parents	— — —
3. Is tactful with negative information	— — —
4. Maintains confidentiality	— — —
5. Seeks a partnership with parents	— — —
6. Regularly writes journal entries for parents	— — —
7. Holds parent conferences on schedule	— — —

• **Examples of behaviors observed:**

_____
_____
_____
_____
_____

Attitude and skills with class	F O N
1. Creates an inviting learning environment	— — —
2. Provides developmentally appropriate activities	— — —
3. Develops plans with goals from observations	— — —
4. Provides materials for all key experiences	— — —
5. Provides an appropriate role model	— — —
6. Anticipates problems and redirects	— — —
7. Is flexible, responsive to child interests	— — —
8. Is prepared for day's activities	— — —
9. Handles transitions well	— — —

• **Examples of behaviors observed:**

_____
_____
_____

Attitude and skills with co-workers   F   O   N

1. Is friendly and respectful with others   — — —
2. Strives to assume a fair share of work   — — —
3. Offers, shares ideas and materials   — — —
4. Communicates directly, avoids gossip   — — —
5. Approaches criticism with learning attitude   — — —
6. Looks for ways to be helpful   — — —

- **Examples of behaviors observed:**

_____

_____

_____

_____

_____

- **Identified strengths and leadership for center:**

_____

_____

_____

_____

_____

_____

- **Goal or improvement sought for next period:**

_____

_____

_____

_____

_____

- **Agreed upon action plan to meet goal:**

1. _____

_____

_____

_____

Attitude and effort toward professional development   F   O   N

1. Takes job seriously, seeks improvement   — —
2. Participates in workshops, classes, groups   — — —
3. Reads, discusses handouts distributed   — — —
4. Sets goals for self in development   — — —

2. _____

_____

_____

_____

- **Examples of behaviors observed:**

_____

3. _____

_____

_____

_____

_____

_____

_____

- **Summary of discussion from evaluation conference:**

_____

_____

_____

_____

Employee _____

Date _____

Supervisor _____

Date _____

© Margie Carter 1990

From Child Care Information Exchange, P.O. Box 3249, Redmond, WA 98037, (800) 221-2864, childcareexchange.com. Reprinted by permission.

Leader's Resource 6–2

TEACHER ASSESSMENT

(Lead Teacher)

TEACHER CHILD CARE COMPETENCIES	NOT OBSERVED	SELDOM	USUALLY	ALWAYS	
A. GUIDANCE TECHNIQUES					DOCUMENTATION
Suggests words to children for expressing feelings.					
Accepts and responds to feelings expressed by the children.					
Establishes and carries out reasonable limits set for activities by self, another team member.					
Follows through with directions given to the child.					
Uses actions when necessary and does not persist in verbal direction which is proving ineffective.					
Is able to become involved with the children without dominating their play; remains in facilitating role.					
Accurately interprets and responds to non-verbal cues given by the children.					
Reinforces appropriate behavior by praising the behavior, not the child.					
Avoids calling attention to misbehavior by ignoring inappropriate behavior when feasible.					
Is aware of activities of entire group when dealing with only part of it; positions self in strategic location; looks up from involvement often.					
Uses non-verbal techniques to reinforce appropriate behavior.					
Redirects or channels disruptive play and talk into more acceptable outlets.					
Provides children dual choices acceptable to adult and to child; agrees to child's decision.					
Mediates communication between children in order to foster social interaction.					
Uses guidance techniques that help children become increasingly responsible for their own behavior.					
Anticipates problems and plans to prevent their occurrence.					
Utilizes non-punitive ways of dealing with out-of-bounds behavior, and can exert authority without requiring submission or undermining the child's sense of self.					
Assists in developing flexible guidance strategies.					
Guides children to work out increasingly effective ways of making social contacts and settling disputes.					
Does not avoid problem situations; can generate alternative ideas and can implement and evaluate solutions.					

Leader's Resource 6–3

PARENT FEEDBACK SURVEY

Dear Parents,

    This questionnaire is designed to find out how we are meeting the needs of families in our program. Your candid and honest responses will enable us to improve communication and services for you and your child. It is not necessary to put your name on this form. Circle the numeral from 1 (strongly disagree) to 5 (strongly agree) that best represents your feelings regarding each of the statements below.

	strongly disagree			strongly agree	
1. I have received adequate information about program policies and procedures.	1	2	3	4	5
2. My child received a warm introduction into the program.	1	2	3	4	5
3. Teachers encourage me to be actively involved in my child's learning.	1	2	3	4	5
4. I am regularly informed about my child's development.	1	2	3	4	5
5. Classroom newsletters and teachers' written notes keep me well-informed.	1	2	3	4	5
6. I have had sufficient opportunity for informal conversations with the teaching and administrative staff.	1	2	3	4	5
7. My parent-teacher conferences have provided me with useful insights about my child.	1	2	3	4	5
8. I have been invited to participate in classroom activities and field trips.	1	2	3	4	5

How has your child benefitted from his/her experience at this center?

In what ways could we improve the program to better meet your child's needs?

From Bloom, P. J., Sheerer, M., & Britz, J. (1991). *Blueprint for Action: Achieving Center-Based Change Through Staff Development,* New Horizons, P.O. Box 863, Lake Forest, IL. 60045 Reprinted with permission.

Leader's Resource 6–4

PEER OBSERVATION

Name of colleague observed _____ Date _____

As you observe, please note comments about the following aspects of the classroom environment: interactions between the teacher and children; interactions between the teacher and other co-teachers or volunteers; interactions between the teacher and parents; the physical arrangement of space; the curriculum; and health, nutrition, and safety aspects of the program.

Aspects of this classroom I was impressed with include:

1. _____

    _____

2. _____

    _____

3. _____

    _____

Aspects of this classroom that might be improved include:

1. _____

    _____

2. _____

    _____

3. _____

    _____

Signed _____

Adapted from Bloom, P. J., Sheerer, M., & Britz, J., (1991). *Blueprint for Action: Achieving Center-Based Change Through Staff Development,* New Horizons, P.O. Box 863, Lake Forest, IL., 60045. Reprinted with permission.

Leader's Resource 6–5

SAMPLE PERFORMANCE APPRAISAL

Performance Appraisal—Lead Teacher

Name: ___Linda Smith___

Date: ___2/15/01___

	seldom	sometimes	frequently	always	Comments
To establish and maintain a safe and healthy learning environment					
1. Establishes and maintains an environment for children, which is clean, safe, stimulating and appropriate for each child's developmental level.				√	
2. Responsible for the appearance, décor, and learning environment of the classroom.			√		
3. Assumes an equal share of the joint housekeeping responsibilities.			√		
4. Promotes healthy eating practices.			√		
To advance physical and intellectual competence					
1. Supports emerging literacy and language development in response to each child's interests through whole language experiences.			√		
2. Implements a curriculum that fosters the construction of mathematical knowledge through hands on activities.			√		
3. Provides an integrated curriculum that meets the needs of individual children.			√		
4. Uses equipment and materials for indoor and outdoor play that promote children's fine and gross motor development.			√		
5. Designs and implements activities that foster the development of physical knowledge.			√		

Adapted From Bloom, P. J., Sheerer, M., & Britz, J. (1991). *Blueprint for Action: Achieving Center-Based Change Through Staff Development*. New Horizons, P.O. Box 863, Lake Forest, IL., 60045. Reprinted with permission.

Performance Appraisal—Lead Teacher

Name: _____Linda Smith_____

Date: _____2/15/01_____

	seldom	sometimes	frequently	always	Comments

To support social and emotional development and provide positive guidance

1. Gears program to the needs of the individual child and pace of learning. — — — ✓

2. Considers the individual child in relationship to his/her culture and socio-economic background. — — — ✓

3. Treats each child, co-worker, and parent with dignity and respect. — — — ✓

4. Helps each child to become aware of his/her role as an integral member of the group. — — — ✓

5. Plans and implements a curriculum that reflects the culture diversity of the group. — — — ✓

6. Provides an environment that fosters the development of self-esteem. — — — ✓

To establish positive and productive relationships with families

1. Views parent-teacher relationship as a partnership, focusing on each families' individual strengths and abilities. — — — ✓

2. Plans and implements hands-on activities that develop self-esteem. — — — ✓

3. Uses and promotes positive guidance techniques and a variety of creative and expressive activities. — — — ✓

4. Coordinates with the Associate and Assistant Teacher. — — — ✓ — —   *goal #3 to develop a plan*

5. Gathers information from team members for feedback to families. — — — ✓ —   *to meet w/Asst. and get feedback*

6. Parent concerns are directed and handled by the Lead Teacher. — — — ✓

Adapted From Bloom, P. J., Sheerer, M., & Britz, J. (1991). *Blueprint for Action: Achieving Center-Based Change Through Staff Development*. New Horizons, P.O. Box 863, Lake Forest, IL., 60045. Reprinted with permission.

Performance Appraisal—Lead Teacher

Name: _Linda Smith_

Date: _2/15/01_

To ensure a well-run, purposeful program responsive to participants needs.	seldom	sometimes	frequently	always	Comments
1. Plans, supervises, and implements the curriculum in accordance with the policies and philosophy of the program.				✓	
2. Uses support services and resources relating to the individual needs of the families and children.			✓		
3. Maintains daily, weekly, and monthly written plans that reflect the individual interest and abilities of the children.			✓		
4. Observations and documentation of individual progress through anecdotal notes, development checklist, portfolio assessments and other designated screenings.			✓		
5. Documentation is completed with agency guidelines and time limits.			✓		
6. Paperwork for local, state, and federal agencies completed.		✓			goal #1 to complete HS paperwork
7. Effectively supervises the Associate, Assistant Teachers, and volunteers in the classroom.		✓			goal #2 development of supervisor skill
8. Effectively assists the director in evaluating classroom staff.			✓		
9. Facilitates weekly staff meetings to address children's development and makes necessary adaptations to the environment.			✓		
10. Punctual in meeting daily work schedule.				✓	
11. Follows attendance and punctuality policy of the center as stated in the employee handbook.				✓	
12. Maintains professional appearance at all times as stated in the employee handbook.				✓	

Adapted From Bloom, P. J., Sheerer, M., & Britz, J. (1991). *Blueprint for Action: Achieving Center-Based Change Through Staff Development.* New Horizons, P.O. Box 863, Lake Forest, IL., 60045. Reprinted with permission.

Additional Comments:

Name of Supervisor _____

Adapted From Bloom, P. J., Sheerer, M., & Britz, J. (1991). *Blueprint for Action: Achieving Center-Based Change Through Staff Development.* New Horizons, P.O. Box 863, Lake Forest, IL., 60045. Reprinted with permission.

Goal Blueprint

Name **Linda Smith**

Supervisor **Renée Daniel**

Date **3-29-00**

Areas in need of growth

1. **To complete Head Start paperwork in a timely manner.**

activities	time needed	resources needed
1. develop a checklist/ tracking form 2.	1 month	assistance from Barb Smith.

2. **To develop supervisor skills**

activities	time needed	resources needed
1. To attend scheduled trainings 2.	5 months	time off to attend.

3. _____

activities	time needed	resources needed
1. Develop Agenda and format 2.	6 months	teacher to provide coverage for nap time

Linda Smith — Teacher

Renée Y. Daniel — Supervisor

Adapted from Bloom, P. J., Sheerer, M. & Britz, J. (1991). *Blueprint for Action: Achieving Center-Based Change Through Staff Development.* New Horizons, P.O. Box 863, Lake Forest, IL., 60045. Reprinted with permission.

Employee Name   Linda Smith
Date of Hire   3/10/89   Date of Last Increase   3/20/90
Level   4   Education   BA Early Childhood
Experience   51 years

Current Salary   26,000.00
Total Amount of Increase   3,000.00

Salary Goal Breakdown   1000.00 per goal

Goal 1
Date to Accomplish Goal   5/30/01
Hourly _____
Monthly _____
Yearly   27,000.00
Notes: ____Linda did complete all Head Start paperwork. Enjoyed doing the home visit. Need to____
_____have her do training for other staff._____

Goal 2
Date to Accomplish Goal   7/21/01
Hourly _____
Monthly _____
Yearly   28,000.00
Notes   ____Linda has attended classes. My observations of her in the classroom; She is direct, she has set up guidelines and processes that____
_____each teacher understands. Assistant and Assoc. are aware of roles._____

Goal 3
Date to Accomplish Goal   10/22/01
Hourly _____
Monthly _____
Yearly   29,000.00
Notes: ____Linda is now meeting monthly with her assistant teachers, she is providing feedback to them as well as support on classroom proj-____
_____ects. The classroom team is discussing children, and their growth and development. Will share with other directors at meeting____
_____about the classroom._____

Adapted from Bloom, P. J., Sheerer, M. & Britz, J. (1991). *Blueprint for Action: Achieving Center-Based Change Through Staff Development.* New Horizons, P.O. Box 863, Lake Forest, IL., 60045. Reprinted with permission.

Leader's Resource 6–6

STAFF DEVELOPMENT ACTION PLAN

Goal	Objectives	Action Steps	Timeline	Evaluation
Exhibit professional knowledge	Plan and implement DAP activities	Create DAP activities list. At least 5 activities per curriculum area.	Complete by December 10	Discuss activities with co-teachers and Heather
		Use list. Conduct 2 activities per week	Start week of December 13	Discussion and feedback by co-teachers
		Create weekly "lesson plan" with co-teachers	Start week of December 13	Discussion and feedback by co-teachers. Submit to Heather
	Use environment as teaching tool	Create room arrangement plan with co-teachers		
		Rotate toys according to needs of children	Start week of December 6	Discussion and feedback by co-teachers
Develop parental relations skills	Assist in communication	Read contents of daily reports	Start week of November 22	Ask questions if needed
		Complete daily reports	Start week of December 13	Give to current staff for feedback
Develop teamwork skills	Take an active role in operation of room	Create and implement rotating schedule for diaper changes	List complete by December 3	Ongoing communication about effectiveness. Submit copy to Heather
		Create and implement rotating schedule for meal clean-up	List complete by December 3	Ongoing communication about effectiveness. Submit copy to Heather
		Create rotating schedule for toy rotation	List complete by December 3	Ongoing communication about effectiveness. Submit copy to Heather
		Use naptime to gather materials for activities, find pictures, read articles, create games.	Begin immediately	Informal and formal observations by co-teachers and supervisors.
		BE ACTIVE. Move around with the children.	Begin immediately	Informal and formal observations by co-teachers and supervisors.

From Children's for Children, Children's Hospital Medical Center Cincinnati, OH. Reprinted with Permission.

Leader's Resource 6–7—

STAFF DEVELOPMENT ACTION PLAN

Name Shelly   Date October 2000-May 2001

Objective #1   To improve the physical arrangement of the classroom learning environment

Activities	Time Needed	Resources Needed
1. Read Greenman, J. *Caring Spaces* -View Dodge, D. T. *Room Arrangement as a Teaching Strategy* -View High/Scope video on space	1. approx. 10 hours reading/viewing time	1. Borrow book and videotapes from community college
2. Experiment: restructure space, observe behavior, assess and refine	2. Weekly planning time with mentor- 1hr.	2. coverage for classroom 1 hr. per week

Evaluation (how/when)   weekly meetings with mentor. Use assessment tool #15 as pre & posttest

Objective #2   To improve classroom management strategies

Activities	Time Needed	Resources Needed
1. Observe Georgia's preschool class during freeplay period	1. 2 hrs/week for 3 weeks	1. coverage for classroom 6 hrs × $8/hr = $48
2. Experiment with different strategies: prevention, redirection, and intervention. Keep journal to reflect on progress	2. ongoing-one entry per week	2. Notebook

Evaluation (how/when)   Weekly meetings with mentor to discuss progress

Objective #3   To monitor classroom interactions through anecdotal notes

Activities	Time Needed	Resources Needed
1. Keep note card for each child Note examples of positive interactions	1. ongoing in classroom	1. notecards
2. Read Lay-Dopyera, M. *Becoming a Teacher of Young Children* for observation guidelines	2. approximately 8 hrs. total	2. borrow book from staff library

Evaluation (how/when)   weekly meeting with mentor to go over entries

Adapted from Bloom, P. J., Sheerer, M. & Britz, J., *Blueprint for Action: Achieving Center-Based Change Through Staff Development* (1991), New Horizons, P.O. Box 863, Lake Forest, IL 60045. Reprinted with permission.

Leader's Resource 6–8

RESIGNATION/TERMINATION OF
EMPLOYMENT CHECKLIST

Name: _____　Date: _____

Position: _____　Status: _____

Last day of Employment: _____

_____ If termination, a meeting with the employee was held with
_____; _____ was a witness.

_____ If resignation, the letter of resignation was received and filed.

Final paycheck will include (this information is sent to payroll):

Salary for the period from _____ to _____.

Severance pay from _____ to _____.

Deduct _____ paid days taken in advance. Add _____ unused, accrued vacation days.

Confirmed address and phone to which last paycheck will be sent:

The following steps were completed by the last day of employment listed above:

_____ Returned to employee any personal property brought to the center.

_____ Notified staff.

_____ Notified other _____.

_____ Notified parents (_____ by phone on _____ or _____ by attached memo).

_____ Collected the following items:

　　_____ ID　　　　　　　　　_____ personnel policies

　　_____ key　　　　　　　　_____ staff handbooks

　　_____ other center or sponsoring company property

Comments:

Signed _____　Date _____

(This completed form should be filed in the employee's personnel file at the center.)

© 1996 *Prime Times: A Handbook for Excellence in Infant and Toddler Care;* Redleaf Press, 450 North Syndicate, St. Paul, MN 55104. 800-423-8309.

Reproduced by permission, © *Prime Times,* J. Greenman, 1996, Redleaf Press, St. Paul, Minnesota.

Leader's Resource 6–9

ISSUES TO ADDRESS IN EXIT INTERVIEWS

Lead Teacher

- **Reason for leaving**
- **Relationship with the children** *(Was it a teacher/child relationship? Friends relationship? Authoritative? Were they in control of the classroom?)*
- **Responsibilities in the classroom** *(Were they overwhelmed? Did they want more to do? Were they frustrated with certain responsibilities?)*
- **Communication with co-workers** *(Open communication? Did they have certain issues with their co-workers? Did they feel assistance or did they feel alone in the classroom?)*
- **Communication with Director** *(Open door policy? Intimidated? Did they feel like they were being heard?)*
- **Opinion of management** *(Did they know who "management" was? Had they ever approached management about concerns? If not, why not?)*
- **Views on philosophy** *(Were they in line with RLC's philosophy? If not, this could be what led them to leave.)*
- **Describe a positive experience you had in the classroom.**
- **Describe what you perceived as a negative experience in the classroom.**
- **What will you remember most about your employment with RLC?**
- **What changes would you recommend to the agency to better help them retain employees?**
- **What will you look for in your next job?**
- **What are your long-term goals?**

Associate Teacher

- **Same as above, except I will address their relationship with their Lead Teacher also.**

Assistant Teacher

Interview will be briefer. I will focus more on issues such as:

- **Reason for leaving**
- **Amount of contact you had with the children**
- **Relationship with co-workers**
- **Eventual career goals**
- **Recommendation to the agency on how to better serve our part time employees**
- **Describe positive/perceived negative experience you had with the agency**
- **First impression of agency**

Reprinted by Permission from Roark Learning Centers, Inc., Cincinnati, OH.

Leader's Resource 6–10 ————————

SUPERVISORY BEHAVIOR QUESTIONNAIRE

The purpose of this questionnaire is to give you an opportunity to provide feedback about the supervisory and evaluation processes at this center. In answering the questions that refer to a specific person, please provide feedback regarding the individual noted at the beginning of the section. When you have completed all three parts of this questionnaire, please put it in the envelope provided and give it to your staff representative. The results of this survey will be tabulated and a written summary will be given to your supervisor and center director.

Name of supervisor ————————————————

PART I. Check (√) all those statements with which you agree.

_____ At this center, I have many opportunities to learn new things.
_____ Evaluation of my teaching is used to help me improve.
_____ The standards by which my teaching is evaluated are clear and well specified.
_____ The methods used in evaluating my teaching are objective and fair.
_____ I know what I'm being evaluated on at this center.

My supervisor . . .

_____ provides suggestions to help me become the best possible teacher.
_____ encourages me to try out new ideas.
_____ encourages me to be independent and self-reliant.
_____ spends enough time in my classroom observing my teaching.
_____ sets high but realistic expectations.
_____ takes a strong interest in my professional development.
_____ displays a strong interest in improving the quality of our program.
_____ helps me understand the sources of important problems I face.
_____ provides the resources I need to help me improve my performance.
_____ provides constructive suggestions that help me deal with problems I encounter.
_____ uses praise appropriately.
_____ communicates effectively.
_____ is dependable and reliable.
_____ is friendly and sociable.
_____ is ethical, honest, and trustworthy.
_____ is patient and supportive.
_____ is knowledgeable about early childhood education.
_____ uses time wisely.
_____ is available when I need him/her.
_____ stays calm in difficult situations.

PART II. Check (√) the following statements that reflect your appraisal of your supervisor's listening behavior.

When you and I are talking together . . .

1. _____ you make me feel as if this is the most important thing you could be doing right now.

2. _____ your attention is often divided; you interrupt our conversation by answering the phone or addressing the needs of others.

3. _____ you sometimes begin shaking your head or saying "no" before I finish my thought.

4. _____ you refer to our previous conversations; there is a history to our communication.

5. _____ you fidget and squirm and look at the clock as though you can't wait to get on to other more important projects and conversations.

6. _____ you begin asking questions before I finish my message.

7. _____ you look me in the eye and really focus attention on me.

8. _____ you ask thoughtful questions that let me know you were really listening.

9. _____ you finish my sentences for me as though nothing I have to say could be new to you.

10. _____ you change the agenda by taking over and changing the content of the conversation.

11. _____ you follow up on what we discussed and keep me posted on what is happening.

12. _____ you are sensitive to the tone of what I have to say and respond respectfully.

13. _____ you give me credit for ideas and projects that grow out of our communications.

14. _____ you try to speed things up and leap ahead with conclusions as though we're in a rush.

15. _____ you smile at me and make me feel comfortable and valued.

16. _____ you make jokes about things that are serious to me and thereby belittle my concerns.

17. _____ you get defensive and argue before I can fully explain my point.

18. _____ you often make me feel I have nothing worthwhile to say.

19. _____ you ask questions which demonstrate your efforts to understand what I have to say.

20. _____ whether or not you agree with me, you make me feel my opinions and feelings are respected.

Part II adapted from Neugebauer, B. (1990, September/October). Are you listening? *Child Care Information Exchange*, p. 62. Reprinted with permission.

Reprinted with permission from Child Care Information Exchange, P.O. Box 3249, Redmond, WA 98037, (800) 221-2864; childcareexchange.com.

Leader's Resourse 6–11

STAFF SELF-EVALUATION FORM

Dear Staff,

To prepare for a staff conference, please briefly answer the following questions related to your experiences as a staff member in the child care center. Your answers should serve as a springboard for a meaningful discussion. Within one week, please complete this form and set a 30-60 minute appointment with me so we can talk privately.

1. What did you do that you are most proud of this past year?

2. What was the biggest challenge? How did you meet it?

3. What was your biggest disappointment? How did you handle it?

4. If you had to do it over again, what would you do differently?

5. What did you find to be most stimulating and caused you to grow the most?

6. What are you looking forward to in the new year?

7. What worries you the most about the coming year?

8. What would you like to say about your performance one year from now?

9. How can I help you?

Reprinted with permission from *Child Care Information Exchange,* P.O. Box 3249, Redmond, WA 98037, (800) 221-2864; childcareexchange.com.

References

Bloom, P. J., Sheerer, M., & Britz, J. (1991). *Blueprint for action.* New Horizons. Distributed by Gryphon House.

Caruso, J. J., & Fawcett, M. T. (1999). *Supervision in early childhood education: A developmental perspective.* (2nd Ed.). New York: Teachers College Press.

Katz, L., & Chard, S. C. (2000). *Engaging children's minds: The project approach* (2nd Ed.). Stamford, CT: Ablex.

Khanagov, D. S. (1999). Healing staff after a termination. *Child Care Information Exchange,* Nov/Dec, 35-38.

Peters, T. (1994). *The pursuit of WOW.* New York: Vintage.

Read, K., Gardner, P., & Mahler, B. (1993). *Early childhood programs: Human relationships and learning.* Harcourt, Brace, Javanovich.

Sciarra, D. J., & Dorsey, A. G. (1998). *Developing and administering a child care center* (4th Ed.). New York: Delmar.

The Leader in Action

CHAPTER 7

The Leader as a Change Agent

Juanita Wallace is the director of an urban center, Hopewell Child Development Center. The center serves 100 children from six months through kindergarten. Members of the local school board have approached the Hopewell board to request that a before- and after-school program be held at the center. Many children attending the local school arrive early and wait outside the school with no supervision. After school there is no safe place available for them. The school gym and cafeteria have been converted to classrooms due to overcrowding. Therefore, children eat lunch in their classrooms. The situation is pretty dismal.

Ms. Wallace knows the community well. She has been director at Hopewell for five years and has made a point of becoming familiar with the area and the people who live and work here. Because of the school-age children had attended Hopewell through kindergarten, she knows them and their families. She has advocated for them in a variety of situations. She has watched the children as they transitioned to elementary school. When they pass the center on the way to school, it is not uncommon for them to stop by "to see how the little kids are doing," but they always get a hug from Ms. Wallace, too. In fact, many of the school-agers are responsible for escorting younger siblings to the center. Juanita knows that some of them are also responsible for getting those same youngsters ready for child care each day—faces cleaned, hair combed, clothes buttoned almost correctly. "These school-agers are growing up early," she mused.

Ms. Wallace snapped her attention back to the problem at hand. The center board president had just phoned. He had told her he knew she would work something out. He'd be available if she needed help, he had said. Ms. Wallace wondered if he really understood that every square inch at the center was already being used from morning until evening.

She thought how hard she had worked with the board to get NAEYC staff-child ratios. Several board members had been adamant that, because the state felt more children per teacher was good enough, why should these children be in smaller classes. Ms. Wallace and the staff know how important the lower ratios have been in terms of child development and teacher morale.

Nonetheless, the only recourse seemed to be creating larger classes again. That would free up one classroom for school-age care. How would the teachers feel about that? What about the parents? How did she *feel about it? The faces of all those first, second, and third graders who stopped by every morning swirled through her head—eager children, fun-loving, serious, friendly, frightened, cheerful, sad—she saw them all in her mind's eye.*

What to do? How to decide? Should this change to Hopewell Center be made? Were there other options? For five years she had managed the center exactly the way Mr. Terrell, the previous director, had managed it. She hadn't even considered changing. Everything ran smoothly. Everyone was content. Children were thriving. Who could help her figure this out? What should she do?

REFLECTION

You have just read an example of one kind of change a director might face. What would you do if you were Juanita Wallace?

As you read this chapter, consider the dilemma Ms. Wallace faces. Think about how each section of the chapter might apply to her situation. After you read the chapter, decide what you would do if you were Ms. Wallace. Compare your response with your initial response.

Change occurs in everyone's lifetime. The study of child development is a study of change. When one examines history, geography, science, education, medicine, manners, clothing, technology, and almost every other aspect of our lives, we can easily find examples of change. While some of us may wish we could go back to the good old days, be they the 1950s or the 1990s, that kind of change is unlikely to happen. Even if that return to an earlier era did occur, we might be surprised at how quickly we would ask to return to the present.

Many of the changes we experience in our lives are affected by leaders in various fields. Leaders in medicine create new pharmaceuticals that contribute to the quality of life by easing pain and curing illness. Leaders in engineering find ways to build bridges and roads to better withstand various weather conditions. Leaders in technology formulate hardware and software that connect us around the world in ways not even dreamed of a hundred years ago.

On the other hand, change can also be debilitating to an organization if it is unnecessary or poorly planned and implemented. Keep in mind that for some leaders the status quo is boring and uncomfortable. They want to be change agents and risk takers. They are eager to make something different happen, whether or not change is needed. Change for the sake of change can be costly in terms of dollars and detrimental effects on staff and clients.

The change Juanita Wallace is considering in the opening scenario presents a difficult choice. She seems to be weighing the good that could be done for school-agers against the probable lessening of quality programs for preschoolers and staff. Because this dilemma involves choices that presumably must be made between two "goods" or appropriate choices, Ms. Wallace faces an ethical dilemma. You will read more about using a code of ethics in Chapter 8.

Using Change to Move an Organization Forward

The knowledgeable, informed leader has learned the skills associated with change and innovation and uses these to move the organization forward (Chapman & O'Neil, 2000). The skills needed to implement change are:

- Envisioning: the ability to develop, articulate and communicate a clear vision of what the future will look like if change is successful.
- Energizing: the ability to motivate large groups of people and infuse them with the leader's own sense of enthusiasm, excitement, and confidence.
- Enabling: the ability to figure out how to provide people with the necessary support structures, processes, resources, and rewards—and how to remove the obstacles standing in their way. (Conger, Spreitzer, & Lawler, 1999, p. 23)

In early childhood programs, a leader who envisions may think about how the program will look when all staff are fully trained and knowledgeable about the principles of their profession. Such a leader will then work to energize the board of directors, funders, legislators, trainers, and staff to develop and be enthusiastic about the education and training of staff. Finally, the director will enable the program by working to bring together the stakeholders. A second part of enabling will be the process of helping staff members address the roadblocks, which might impede their success in completing the plan. In one county in which training was provided to Head Start staff at no cost to the staff, one of the roadblocks encountered on the way to obtaining an associate degree in early childhood education was weak academic skills, which necessitated providing pre-English and pre-mathematics courses. Another challenge was getting to the university campus, which led to providing classes at one of the centrally located centers. For the second group of trainees, distance learning classes were developed. Students could view videos in their own centers or make copies of them for home viewing. They then communicated with an instructor by e-mail to ask questions, submit assignments, and make suggestions.

Using Principles to Guide Change

A good leader is also one who recognizes that "The shared obligation of all who serve in any leadership capacity is the engagement in interdependent, cooperative and dynamic action on behalf of the good that is held in common. Such creative engagement calls for a spirit of courageous imagination in considering what might be, along with a spirit of humble relinquishment in letting what has been" (Markham, 1999, p. viii). An effective change agent is principle-centered. *Principle-centered* refers to leaders who have the following traits.

- They are continually learning.
- They are service-oriented.
- They radiate positive energy.
- They believe in other people.
- They lead balanced lives.
- They see life as an adventure.
- They are synergistic.
- They exercise for self-renewal. (Covey, 1992)

In his book, *Principle Centered Leadership,* (1992), Stephen Covey describes principle-centered people as change catalysts. "They improve almost any situation they get into. They work as smart as they work hard. They are amazingly productive, but in new and creative ways" (p. 37).

Recently, a major change in a huge consumer goods corporation led to a change in management of the company. "After a second straight quarter of disappointing results, Mr. Pepper was lured out of retirement to replace (the chairman of the board)." A company veteran became president and chief executive officer. He "will do the hard day-to-day work. But Mr. Pepper . . . was called back to fill perhaps P. & G.'s most pressing need: restoring the credibility of a company that has shown solid profits on which people have depended for more than 150 years" (Peale, 2000, p. 1). Not surprisingly, this knowledgeable leader is a strong advocate for children. He was instrumental in establishing an effective mentoring program while supporting many related initiatives.

Although child care may seem to be very different from the complexity of the example that you have just read, leaders in child care are also responsible for a wide range of changes, some of which may be quite extensive. The leader of a large corporation has a whole raft of managers and support staff. Although some centers operate as parts of large corporate structures, many directors find themselves to be leaders as well as being involved in day-to-day decisions and even actions. For example, a director may have to decide the format for the parent handbook and may even have to type it, assemble it, and arrange to have it distributed to parents.

A more far-reaching change might involve plans to move the center to a new location. That director might be involved in working with realtors to find a site, working with an accountant to establish a financial plan, and working with a licensing specialist to ensure that all requirements are being met.

Leaders in early childhood education must be well-prepared for recognizing the need for change. These leaders must also be able to plan for change, guide the change process, and support staff, families, and children through the change. The principles that the leader of any group must follow are pretty basic: "gather information, assess the situation, figure out what has to be done, decide what role you can play to add the most value, and lay out a sequence of steps to get started. Obviously, the hard part is doing it-and doing it in a way appropriate to the situation at hand" (Conger, Spreitzer, & Lawler, 1999, p. 12).

LEADER'S CORNER

As a child care center director faced with a state licensing mandate to provide staff with fifteen clock hours of training and a very limited budget, I had to find a way to provide the training for eight new staff members. I agreed to work with a nearby university that is piloting a web-based program. They have made available fifteen-minute training segments with built in assessments. Staff members can use their break time or can log on at home or at the public library.

The program allows each staff member to key in a password and to complete the assessment on line. Once they have completed module one, they click on module two and work on that. A print-out of scores for each module is available only to the staff member who must give it to the director to be placed in her employee file.

Trainees can repeat modules. I think an added advantage is that they can work together and are building relationships with other staff members. The program has been a lifesaver for me.

Director, urban child care center

Determining the Need for Change

The leader's first step in determining the need for change is development of a sound understanding of the current situation. This step is particularly important when a new leader takes the helm, even when that person has been promoted from within and is relatively familiar with the organization.

A key starting point is review of the legal limitations involved in operating a particular type of program. Leaders must be familiar with laws related to hiring and firing staff, paying staff, enrolling children, withholding and paying taxes, and a range of other legal issues. In addition to laws, rules have been promulgated, such as licensing rules. Funders understandably usually impose their own requirements as to how the money they provide is to be spent. Making changes in conflict with legal limitations is almost certain to cause problems for the organization. Not knowing the requirements is rarely accepted as an excuse.

The leader must also review the program's mission, vision, and current goals. The leader must understand when these documents were prepared and by whom. Have any major circumstances changed since then? For example, when an early childhood program had as its mission "Provision of excellent quality half-day programs for children in low income neighborhoods," that mission may have become relatively meaningless when families receiving public assistance were required to develop job skills and enter the work force. Those parents then needed full-day care. In fact, many of them needed care at atypical hours, such as weekends and second shift. The organization's mission will probably need to be changed. Furthermore, programs, facilities, staffing, and policies and procedures must also be reviewed.

Another example would be full-day programs that served children from infancy through kindergarten. As more and more public schools began to offer full-day kindergarten and after-school programs, some child care centers found that the kindergarten programs were not well enrolled. On the other hand, other centers might find that full-day kindergarten at the center became *more* valued by families with kindergartners and younger siblings who wanted to keep the children together. A third example relates to demographics of the surrounding neighborhood. When large portions of a community's land and housing are taken over by a governmental body in order to build a highway, a neighborhood may be bisected, making it difficult for families to reach the center and creating a new neighborhood configuration. In this case, a major review of the center's plans is essential.

REFLECTION

Think about your own reaction to change. Are you generally comfortable with change? What kind of changes do you find disturbing?

Changes Affected by the Community Culture

The leader must also be cognizant of trends in the community. Two trends that could potentially affect child care programs are the trend toward home schooling and the trend toward working from the home. In addition, job sharing may become even more prevalent. Therefore, the leader will consider the effects on child care. Will as many families need child care? Will they need daily, full-day child care? Anyone who has faced the logistics of planning around part-time enrollment knows what a financial and staffing nightmare this situation can create. What about center staff? Will they want to participate in job-sharing? What effect might that have on young children? If two full-time teachers agree to share one full-time job with your approval, will the center be able to provide benefits for each of them? If not, will those teachers decide to work elsewhere?

Another kind of change is reported by Neugebauer (2000): "The continuing expansion of the economy, coupled with parents' increasing awareness of the developmental importance of the early years is spurring the sustained growth of the for-profit child care sector" (p. 18). As a result, a major shortage of staff-managers, teachers, cooks, and bus drivers has occurred. Another change reported by Neugebauer is the increased appropriation of tax dollars by states for public school preschool. When salaries and wages are high, and when the employment rate is also high, the state and federal governments collect more tax dollars and thus have more to spend.

Changes in Day-to-Day Operations

Many potential changes faced by an early childhood leader may not be as momentous as changes in the major purposes of the program or as significant as basic staffing reorganization. Rather they may involve the day-to-day operation of the organization at a more detailed level. To ascertain this type of potential change, the director then reviews the policies and procedures manual, minutes of meetings, and financial reports for the past several years, and any other available documentation, such as brochures, marketing plans, and public relations pieces. Do the available materials seem to be effective? What is the evidence? What additional information is needed? New directors may decide to meet with each staff member individually to develop an understanding of staff perspectives and to gain some possible answers to these questions.

Armed with an understanding of the mission, vision, and goals as well as of current circumstances that impact the center, the director must decide whether change seems to be needed and how to proceed. Later in this chapter, you will read about others who may be involved in the planning and decision-making. For the moment, we will continue to focus on the leader.

Many changes faced by the leader will be of limited magnitude in terms of the big picture, but will probably seem huge at the time. For example, the sudden resignation of a key staff member can throw the director and the rest of the staff into turmoil and cannot be specifically planned for. Other changes may seem significant to particular staff members but may have less serious impact on the director or the program as a whole. Examples would be opening the center one hour earlier each day or allowing young school-aged children to use the activity room after school, thus curtailing use of that space by preschoolers during those hours.

In the case of earlier opening, the staff members who open the center may have to re-arrange their own child care plans, find alternate transportation, and adjust their daily living patterns. In the situation involving after-school care, staff members who close the center may have to adjust curriculum to accommodate the fact that their children no longer have access to the activity room after rest time. Alternatively, they may have to learn to negotiate with the school-age caregiver to devise some options for use of the space. Wise directors provide opportunities for staff input during the planning of the changes. However, note that it is imperative that directors clearly state what the role of staff will be. Will the majority rule or will their comments be used as input for the director's decision only.

Another kind of change relates to the curriculum and provides an example of how a change may be implemented on the surface, but not become part of the organization's real culture. Assume that the director has read a number of articles and attended a conference at which the importance of early literacy is discussed. She provides the information to the staff and schedules a speaker to address the topic at a required staff meeting. The teachers learn how to implement the literacy program and they do, in fact, implement it. Most of them disagree with the program and believe that it will not help their children become literate. Structurally the change has taken place. However, a normative change has not occurred. Teachers have not changed their attitudes toward the literacy program. They are going through the motions of doing what they have been told, but they are not committed to it. Directors must be aware of these two kinds of change. Telling staff what to do and how to do it in every aspect of their jobs may result in structural change only.

REFLECTION

Think about your relationship with friends and family. When you have a great idea that you know would really help them, how do you react when they seem disinterested?

Early childhood leaders recognize that their organizations have business purposes as well as program or educational purposes; thus, the leader must be aware of both types of purpose in planning for change. The forces that are likely to affect change in the business aspect of the program are bureaucratic, personal, and market forces. For example, if a governmental body increases the number of square feet required per child, then logistics and finances will probably be involved. Professional, cultural, and democratic forces generally affect the program component. For example, research that supports a new approach to early literacy may suggest changes in professional development of staff, program materials, and scheduling.

No matter what type of change is being considered, leaders must do their homework before proposing change. They must also be knowledgeable about and follow basic planning procedures.

Planning for the Change Process

In planning for change, the leader must consider the importance of the organization's culture. When collegiality is a hallmark of the culture, change will be easier because there is a high level of collaboration among staff members. "Collegiality as a professional virtue is comprised of three dimensions: a conception of the good person who values colleagueship for its own sake, connectedness to a community that provides one with the right to be treated collegially and the obligation to treat others collegially, and interpersonal relationships characterized by mutual respect" (Sergiovanni & Starratt, 1998, p. 200-201). Colleagues share work values. They cooperate with one another, and they converse about specific job-related issues.

Another key aspect in planning change is avoiding focus on the leader. The leader controls the change process but must be careful to focus instead on the involvement of everyone rather than attempting to draw attention to herself. When a charismatic leader dominates an organization, the contributions of others are seriously limited. This leader-domination is especially damaging during times of change. Employees value being able to communicate with leaders and knowing that their ideas are being heard. They want to be involved, to share ownership. They want to have their roles recognized as meaningful in the overall purpose of the organization.

> "While authority and leadership are essential to the functioning of any group, rigidly structured hierarchic authority lines that promote stability and order will doom any group. This will happen because synergistic, highly creative imagining and decision-making are thwarted by limited communication, limited access to information and a lack of openness and respect for the contributions of each member. Consequently, the group suffers from loss of morale and attrition of personnel. Arrogant self-sufficiency has taken its toll." (Markham, 1999, pp. 8–9)

It is easy for directors, even in small centers, to place themselves far above the rest of the staff. Leaders who act in this manner may receive minimal cooperation from staff during the change process.

When change occurs, staff members begin to think about themselves and their colleagues in different ways. Assuring that these ways of thinking are positive is an outcome that can be facilitated by the leader.

Organizing the Change Teams

When the probable need for change has been identified, the leader calls together appropriate people to help with the decision. Who should be involved must be based on the type of decision to be made and the particular expertise needed to make a good decision in the case at hand. Whether or not to increase tuition would surely involve someone with financial expertise as well as someone with an understanding of the current marketplace. It would, of course, include whoever is responsible for the program's accounting. In some circumstances, parents may be particularly helpful. Once they see the financial need of the center, they may be able to smooth the way among other parents who, understandably, may question the need for additional funds. In other cases, such as not-for-profit organizations, funders may be brought into the discussion so that they can recognize the true cost of child care. The Department of Human Services or the Community Action Agency may not be as aware as directors are of the competition for child care staff among centers and from businesses within the community. This situation is particularly critical in time of high employment.

When a board governs an organization, that group determines some types of changes. For example, they will have the final say on tuition increases or major changes in the budget. However, the board should not micromanage the organization. Therefore, the director will lead much of the decision-making, while keeping board members fully informed. Some programs plan occasional joint board/staff meetings or events to facilitate communication and foster the change process.

Directors must develop a shared vision and a shared commitment with the staff. In the case of a one-site center, probably every staff member will be involved. When there are dozens of sites across the country under one president or CEO, that person will engage selected members of the leadership team to assist in planning and guiding the change.

Building Team and Leaders' Strengths

Keep in mind that to become a team, generally members must participate in some sort of team-building opportunity. If at all possible, go off-site to a pleasant, reasonably secluded spot so that the group will not be distracted from the task at hand. Give people plenty of opportunities to share their thinking and to ask questions. Make sure everyone has a chance to speak. If the culture of the organization includes reasonable acceptance of mistakes, then members should feel free to speak. But if, in the past, everyone has been expected to mimic the leader's thinking, many people will be afraid to say what they really believe. This type of climate can lead to failed change or to serious resistance.

Major businesses recognize the importance of helping their leaders strengthen areas of weakness so that they will be as effective as possible. The ultimate goal, of course, is to benefit the company. Today a corporation may spend up to $25,000 per week to send up-and-coming leaders to training sessions. At these sessions, psychologists meet individually with each participant and then hold group sessions. The group may be given opportunities to provide honest feedback to each participant that can help the individual modify her way of working with others.

For example, one person may approach the group with a proposal but lack the assertiveness necessary to manage the team. Another person may be deemed too harsh during group participation. As individuals in the situation learn about their own leadership styles and shortcomings, they are able to focus on change. A receptive leader training session participant summed it up this way: "One of the most difficult things to do is to try to affect change, change within yourself" (Glater, 2000, p. 1, 6).

Although it is beyond imagination to consider sending a rising early childhood education leader to a $25,000-per-week leadership school, finding appropriate funding is not beyond the realm of possibility. Just as there is a serious shortage of well-qualified managers in major businesses, so too is there a serious shortage of well-qualified leaders in our profession.

Prospective and current leaders must seek out the training they need. For example, the NAEYC has begun offering management and leadership programs and more attention is being given to this topic in the professional literature and at conferences. Board members, university faculty, and professional organizations may be able to provide leads. State departments of education, departments of human services, and foundations which support early childhood education initiatives may be supportive of efforts to improve leadership. Regardless of the sponsorship of such an initiative, it is important that the components include:

1. basic information about management and leadership
2. approaches to helping individual leaders recognize their own strengths and weaknesses and find ways to develop their abilities

The first component can be obtained in part by listening to speakers, reading, and participating in discussions. The second component involves serious self-reflection, willingness to change, and sustained effort.

REFLECTION

Have you ever participated in a team-building activity? If so, what did you find out about your personal strengths and weaknesses? If you have not participated in team building, reflect now on your strengths and weaknesses and decide what you would like to change. How will you make these changes?

Wise directors build on their strengths and work toward shared leadership by identifying strengths in others, which complement their own abilities and balance their weaknesses. They find people from throughout their organization to work on the change process and they do not limit the group to teachers, but may include assistants, the cook, or the bus driver.

When team members work together, they too build on their strengths and look for ways to find members who can compensate for their weaknesses. They learn to depend on each other's abilities and to recognize that others excel in some areas where they do not. If the culture of the organization is one of acceptance, then recognition that others are better at something is nonthreatening (Covey, 1992). Following the model set by the leader, team members speak freely, but specifically avoid personally embarrassing a co-worker. They support one another and expect the best work from each colleague.

Making Decisions Independently

The director may decide to make changes that involve policy without consulting others. This is appropriate when, in that person's judgment, the change is needed for the effective management and operation of the program. The policy might involve the requirement for an orientation program or it may relate to the type of continuing education required by the organization. Although involving the staff is often a wise procedure, directors must understand when to take the initiative and make independent decisions. The key is balancing staff involvement and director decision-making. The challenge is understanding when each is appropriate.

Changes may affect in-house elements of the operation primarily. For example, the staff may be reorganized or the procedures for calculating pay, benefits, and vacation time may be modified. Usually, this type of change will not directly affect clients. Other changes, however, such as number of days the program will be closed for inservice training, holidays, professional conferences, parent meetings, and so forth, will be of interest and perhaps concern to the broader community, particularly parents. In the latter case, it is essential that the staff understand the proposed changes well and can speak effectively and accurately about them. They can listen to parents' questions and concerns and take those to the broader group as necessary. In some cases, it may be appropriate and expected to involve families in decision-making.

Directors must be sure that, no matter who is consulted, they must be told whether their input is sought as a vote. In such cases, directors listen to them and follow the guidance of the majority. More often directors will ask for the thinking of individuals on a topic and use those ideas to support decision-making. When this is the plan, it is essential that everyone understands that their ideas may or may not be used but that they will be taken into consideration. Finally, among the many decisions directors make, some will be of such little consequence that spending time on them would be quite inappropriate.

For example, no time would be wasted on deciding between red and blue tricycles, but directors must consider tricycle safety factors as well as durability and may consult other directors and check reviews of items published in reliable sources such as *Child Care Information Exchange*. When faced with a decision whether to install air conditioning in the center or not, directors are usually required to prepare specifications and get bids. Such a purchase involves consultation with several heating, ventilating, and air conditioning specialists, as well as background reading. Locating a specialist in that field who would not be competing for the sale would also be worthwhile when the director has little personal understanding of what is involved. The decision to make such a major commitment cannot be taken lightly, nor can the comfort and well-being of children and staff.

Dissemination of Plans for Change

Large corporations carefully orchestrate announcements of major changes. They prepare their public and work to keep their allegiance. Although the plans of leaders in early childhood education will not be nearly as extensive or expensive, they must still be given careful thought. Announcements of new programs may be made in local papers, for example. When the change affects current clients primarily, each should receive written information with an explanation for the change and an opportunity to ask questions or discuss related issues. This opportunity may consist of a phone number to call or a meeting to be held by the director or board chairperson. The goal is to keep the change process as smooth as possible by ensuring that staff and clients are reasonably satisfied with the process and outcomes.

One successful corporate leader saw his role in the change implementation stage as regularly employing four teaching techniques.

- First, he constantly made a point of putting issues in context, rather than just diving in.
- Second, when he made a decision or took action, he always explained the rationale.

- Third, he regularly engaged in reflection; in other words, he would make his people step back and consider why something had worked or why it hadn't so they could learn from experience.
- Finally, he engaged in constant repetition-repetition that could occasionally seem maddening to his subordinates, who occasionally complained about it. But his repetition was conscious and purposeful, intended to drive home important lessons (Conger et al, 1999).

Addressing Resistance to Change

The director depends on trust and trustworthiness as a major factor in gaining the support of staff. These conditions are not automatic; they grow out of demonstration of personal integrity and competence. ". . . (I)f trust is present, you have an empowerment approach as an administrator. You also have a larger circle of influence that can begin to have some impact on the design and structure of the system" (Covey, 1992, p. 305). However, if trust is not part of the agency's culture, then resistance to legitimately made decisions is likely.

Because each staff member brings a set of basic assumptions about the culture, breaking old assumptions will often be necessary in time of change. ". . . (T)hese assumptions can only be challenged and broken within the context of trust, relationships, and self-discovery" (Lambert et al, 1995, p. 62).

A staff member's concerns may be based on the following questions.

- How will the proposed change affect me?
- How will the proposed change affect my relationships with others?
- How will the proposed change affect my work?

However, although these questions and concerns are real, they may not be the actual reasons behind the resistance to change (Sergiovanni & Starratt, 1998, p. 192). For example, a teacher may be concerned if the proposal involves creating observation booths for the classrooms. She may feel that some observers may discuss her teaching in a negative way without giving her any feedback. She may be concerned about never knowing what people are saying. Instead, she argues that it is an invasion of the children's privacy and that parents will bring younger children to the booth, creating a disturbance when those toddlers want to come in to the classroom rather than stay in the booth.

To counter these staff issues, Sergiovanni and Starratt propose a "concerns-based adoption model," which "charts the changing feelings of teachers as they learn about a proposed change, prepare to use it, then use it, and finally make it a part of their everyday repertoire" (1998, p. 197). Their model proposes seven states of concern:

1. awareness
2. informational
3. personal
4. management
5. consequence
6. collaboration
7. refocusing

By focusing on where in the list each employee seems to be, the leader can adjust approaches to helping that individual move forward toward change (adapted from Sergiovanni & Starratt, 1998, p. 197).

Although there will always be old assumptions based on the previous culture, the leader can use the following approaches to help staff break away from those assumptions toward the new model.

- Try to understand the staff member's point of view.
- Use creativity and imagination. Involve staff in designing new ways of addressing old problems.
- Share a new experience together (Lambert et al, 1995, pp. 62–63).

As staff members work together in supportive groups, they look for ways to expand the possibilities. Although some may favor a clean break, insisting that the old ways be eliminated, forgotten, or no longer discussed, those old ways are shared ways and the group may move beyond them but will not necessarily discard them. The knowledgeable leader understands the contributions the past has made to who these people are and what the organization is today. Such a leader is able to help the staff move forward without negating the past.

Employee-Instigated Change

In some instances, employees recognize that change is essential. Their morale is low, leading to low performance. Perhaps staff are working in a cluttered, dark, drab environment with little interaction with one another. Children, too, may begin to sense the rather depressed state of affairs and behave accordingly, leading to further discouragement on the part of the staff. In a similar vein, parents respond by leaving hurriedly, with little or no comment to the staff, and the leader may feel that the situation is hopeless. However, it is the leader's responsibility to take charge and make changes. In some cases, a staff member may call for change. Such a courageous and thoughtful staff member is to be commended and supported although the challenge may be immense. If the group can begin to have honest dialogues about the dismal situation, the driving force of their combined efforts can lead to change (Sergiovanni & Starratt, 1998).

Meeting Continued Resistance

Despite the leader's best efforts, one or more staff members may continue to resist change. The leader must deal with this resistance quickly and firmly. The first step would be to find out what the problem is from the employee's perspective. There may be a misunderstanding; for instance, the employee may be afraid of being let go. Or perhaps the person likes to disagree no matter what the situation. Be sure to consider this employee's perspective carefully. It may represent points of view that others are unwilling to express. Perhaps some valuable ideas are included in this employee's thinking— ideas that you had not considered. Could it be a question of your power-play? Might someone who does not have the best interests of the organization at heart have influenced you? Consider that it takes courage to confront a leader or authority figure. Therefore, give serious consideration to this new perspective.

When basic needs are threatened, common needs of teachers are:

1. clear expectations.

2. future certainty.

3. social interaction.

4. control over the work environment and work event. (adapted from Sergiovanni & Starratt, 1998, p. 198)

Directors can handle each of these needs by paying attention to signals from staff members relative to which need each is experiencing. Clear expectations of the staff can be presented during staff meetings, giving staff plenty of time to ask questions and seek clarification. Expectations should also be put in writing and included in the staff handbook. Let's suppose the change in question involves providing a general storeroom for equipment and supplies. If a vague procedure is developed, such as "All staff shall cooperate to keep the storeroom orderly," then little information is provided. If the director expects each staff member to be responsible for an area of the room, for ordering new equipment or supplies when needed, and for ensuring that the items are properly inventoried, then those requirements should be spelled out. On the other hand, when procedures are overly detailed, staff members spend more time attempting to determine exactly what to do. In such instances, expect frustration.

If staff seem to feel uncertain about the future, they may be wondering what other new jobs and responsibilities the director will be assigning to them. Or if the two teachers who were recently hired have a bachelor's degree, a teacher with a CDA may wonder whether she will soon be replaced by a degreed teacher. To alleviate uncertainty, the director can explain and create written policies regarding requirements for teaching positions. These should state whether or not current nondegreed teachers will be required to complete a degree and, if so, whether any financial assistance will be available from the center. If a decision is taken to change expectations, then directors must first make sure the new requirement is legal. If a decision requires employees to meet new requirements, current staff often will be allowed to continue. Otherwise they should be given ample time to meet the requirement.

Providing for Ongoing Staff Needs

In an agency that does not meet ongoing staff needs, change may be especially difficult. Sometimes employees may appear to be resisting change when the crux of the situation is that they are actually seeking change. Employees may be looking for opportunities to create their own culture within the agency's culture. When staff members seem to feel the need for social interaction, for example, directors can take a proactive approach by discussing with staff ways to allow this to happen. Providing a break room would be one option. Another idea would be to plan for a brief time at the beginning of each staff meeting for refreshments and conversation. Directors may also post news items about staff and their families. A "Did You Know . . ." bulletin board could be used to include events such as "Stacey's daughter, Cassie, will be in her first dance recital on Saturday. Watch this space for pictures," or "Congratulations to Franklin, DeWanda's husband. He'll receive his degree in computer science from Jefferson University this weekend."

Staff may also want to plan outings together after hours or on weekends, possibly including their families. Some employees may want to organize teams or leagues related to sports such as bowling, softball, or soccer. Care should be taken to allow ideas to come from the staff. When the director becomes overly involved in planning, events may seem like activities at which attendance is expected, thus defeating the purpose.

When staff members express a need for control over their work and their work environment, directors should recognize several possible causes. One obvious cause is that a director may be micromanaging the work process. Policies and procedures are important, but when workers have little or no opportunity to make decisions, they feel controlled and dis-respected. A controlled job is often a monotonous job. For example, directors who repeatedly enter classrooms to tell teachers what to do in given situations are responsible for ensuring that they have provided proper preparation and guidance for the teachers. After that, they should be able to assume that teachers are competent to make decisions.

REFLECTION

In your experience as a student or an employee, have you had a teacher or supervisor who provided vague directions? Have you encountered someone in charge of your work who had elaborately detailed expectations? How did you feel in such instances? What did you do?

When a director has a concern about a teacher's ability to make judgments regarding children's activities, it is time for the two of them to have a conference. Perhaps the teacher and director have differing philosophies regarding curriculum. Possibly the director's expectations are limited to experiences from work in a classroom many years ago. It may be that the teacher has become lax about meeting her responsibilities. In any event, discussions should help clarify the situation. The director may need to provide more freedom, exercise more control, or even dismiss the teacher. The teacher may need to meet the center's expectations, demonstrate her capabilities, obtain additional education, or consider working in another place.

Controlling one's own work environment is one benefit early childhood educators should expect to have even when fiscal benefits are minimal. Very few teachers have offices, but all should have some personal storage space, storage for teaching materials, and adequate space in which to conduct a worthwhile program. The space must be well-maintained and reasonably comfortable and attractive. Teachers should be permitted and encouraged to decorate the space to their liking while keeping children's perspectives in mind.

Setting Limits

When you are faced with someone who is ready to cause trouble within the organization, you must firmly and fairly require that this person and all employees follow the new plan. One person with "an axe to grind" can cause dissension among employees, detracting from focus on the group's real purpose. When you do take a final stand, take into consideration which employee is likely to leave, particularly if the job market is fairly open. If the employee is otherwise highly valued, your priority may be to work particularly hard to resolve the disagreement.

When teachers and other staff members recognize that both they and their work are valued and valuable, sustained resistance to change is less likely to occur. Some resistance is to be expected and provides an indication that the staff have developed a culture and become acclimated to it. Some resistance indicates that staff members are interested in the organization and its welfare. Nonetheless, extensive resistance to change requires that the leader take action, minimize areas that may be problematic for staff, clarify misconceptions, and then take a stand and lead.

Summary

Being a leader is challenging and demanding, but being a leader in time of change is even more so. Leaders have to recognize the need for change, know the organization well enough to be able to design an appropriate change plan and determine how best to implement that plan. They have to be able to understand whom to involve and when to involve various stakeholders. Although there are many parallels between leaders in business and industry, there are also a number of expectations in the field of early childhood and child care that differ from those in the major corporate world. Sensitive early childhood leaders understand and address those differences.

Class Assignments

1. Interview a community, education, or business leader. Ask about any changes that have taken place in his or her organization. Find out how those changes were implemented and what the outcomes were. Write a report on your interview on Working Paper 7–2.
2. Check your local newspaper for items related to change. Explain what the proposed change is and why it is being proposed. If the change has not yet been made, indicate what you think will happen and why. Prepare a brief oral report for your class on this topic.
3. Look for websites that address concerns of early childhood leaders. Make a list of sites that might be helpful for directors. Write this information on Working Paper 7–3.

Class Exercises

1. Discuss the dilemma faced by Ms. Wallace described at the beginning of this chapter. Include ideas from this chapter as you consider how she could handle the situation. Work with your classmates to reach a decision about how the case should be handled.
2. Think of examples of change in your community. Change may be occurring in a corporation, school, or church. You may think of other situations. Discuss how these changes are being handled and whether or not the approaches to change appear to be reasonable.
3. Discuss the effect of technology on change in our profession. Share any examples that you have found of internet use by leaders, particularly in early childhood education.

Working Paper 7–1

Write your reaction to the Juanita Wallace case after reading Chapter 7:

Working Paper 7–2

Name of leader whom you interviewed: _____

Leader's organization: _____

Changes in that organization:

How changes were implemented:

Outcomes of changes:

Working Paper 7–3

List Web sites that address concerns of early childhood leaders:

Leader's Resource 7–1————————

THINKING THROUGH THE CHANGE PROCESS

1. What change do I think is needed?

2. Why is this change needed?

3. Who should be involved in planning for this change?

4. What should my role as a leader be?

5. How will I inform those who need to know?

6. Who will implement this plan?

7. When will the change go into effect?

8. What will be the impact on staff, children, and families?

9. What will be the impact on budget, facilities, and program?

References

Chapman E., & O'Neil, S. L. (2000). *Leadership: essential steps every manager needs to know, 3rd ed.* Upper Saddle River, NJ: Prentice Hall.

Conger, J. A., Spreitzer, G. M., & Lawler, E. E., III., Eds. (1999). *The leader's change handbook: An essential guide to setting direction and taking actions.* San Francisco: Jossey-Bass.

Covey, S. (1992). *Principle centered leadership.* New York: Simon & Schuster (Fireside).

Glater, J. D. (November 22, 2000). Shape up to ship up: Boot camps for executives on the fast track. *New York Times,* C1, 6.

Lambert, L., Walker, D., Zimmerman, D. P., Cooper, J. E., Lambert, M. D., Gardner, M. E., & Slack, P. J. F. (1995). *The constructivist leader.* New York: Teachers College.

Markham, D. (1999). *Spiritlinking leadership: Working through resistance to organizational change.* New York: Paulist Press.

Neugebauer, R. (January/February, 2000). Booming economy fuels continued expansion of for-profit child care: Annual status report #13. *Child Care Information Exchange,* 131, 18–20.

Peale, C. (June 17, 2000). 'Nice guy' Pepper begins to right P. & G. Cincinnati, OH: *The Cincinnati Enquirer.*

Sergiovanni, T. J., & Starratt, R. J. (1998). *Supervision: A redefinition, 6th ed.* Boston: McGraw-Hill.

CHAPTER 8

The Leader As a Professional

Jaime and another director, LaTicia, were having lunch together, a real treat for both of them. They had agreed to meet to discuss a possible joint conference for teachers to be held locally.

Usually, leaving their child care centers during the day was quite difficult. But for the past year, Jaime and LaTicia had belonged to a directors' support group. Each member had chosen a goal for herself. Both Jaime and LaTicia had decided to begin to train a staff member in the duties of directing. They realized the difficult position their center staff members and families would be in if no one were available in case of emergency.

For the past six months, each of these women had been training one of the lead teachers. They had been able to convince their boards that assigning the title, Assistant Director, along with a small salary increase was just good business. The contacts these directors had made in the support group had been quite helpful. There they had ob-tained the impetus to make necessary changes and to begin to think in the future, rather than focusing solely on the day-to-day minor crises that beset child care programs.

"Having a conference for teachers is a great idea," said LaTicia, "but what about us? How can we learn things when we are so busy trying to lead? I say it can't be done." Jaime seemed a little overworked too. "I haven't read anything professional since I be-came a director. I guess we're just expected to find out everything by magic. Anyway, if I did subscribe to a journal, I'd probably stack up the back issues and never even open them."

With this lament, the two again turned their attention to the conference they had come to discuss.

Directors are expected to assume responsibility for keeping current. They must constantly be aware of new developments and they must consider changes based on these developments. Although all staff members must be responsible for keeping cur-rent relative to the positions they hold, ultimately directors will be held accountable.

REFLECTION

Think about what you read. During the past year, what have you read re-lated to your current or planned profession? (Do not include textbooks or assigned readings.)

Why Leaders Should Keep Current

Leaders of organizations are charged with the task of providing the best service possible to their clients. Their role is to ensure that clients' needs are met. At the same time, the organization must remain fiscally solvent. Of course, in for-profit companies, a major goal is to provide a return on owners' money, that is, a profit.

The clients of an early childhood program, broadly defined, are the children, fami-lies, community, and staff. Directors who provide the best conditions for their clients offer them the most current, appropriate ways to meet their needs. For example, when we consider children as clients, directors must have current information about child de-velopment and programming. When they have accurate, reliable information, they can help children learn and enjoy coming to child care or preschool.

In the opening scenario, notice that Jaime and LaTicia were able to understand the importance of training an assistant. They even convinced their boards to support their idea. Yet neither of them has developed plans for keeping current.

Parents expect directors to have current information. Families look for programs that provide up-to-date services. Although in many cases, old ways are workable and serviceable, many parents prefer programs whose facilities look relatively new. For ex-ample, a child care center may have large, sturdy boxes and boards for children to use in creating play spaces. Although they may not look up-to-date, they provide excellent op-portunities for children to create interesting play scenarios, as well as to develop large muscle skills. Parents may prefer a playground with colorful, contemporary structures for children to use as they climb, jump, and slide. Other parents may be attracted to a center that offers opportunities to view children online from a distance. In this way, par-ents can check on their own children throughout the day, assuring themselves that their children are in good hands. Directors must decide whether the old or the new is more appropriate for each situation. Because new is not always better and often is costly, directors must obtain enough current information to make good decisions about equipment, communications, and every other aspect of their program.

Even the community at-large provides reasons for directors' maintaining currency. An early childhood leader who brings new ideas to a community may help that community by providing the kind of program that attracts business and helps the community grow. Families are usually concerned about opportunities for their children when they select places to live and work. Furthermore, center staff can take the lead in keeping a community informed about issues relating to children's safe development. They may bring to everyone's attention the latest thinking about what is needed when providing a play space free of hazards for children. What types of surfaces help reduce accidents? How has learning to wear helmets while riding tricycles reduced head injuries? What are some examples of nontoxic art supplies that children can enjoy using? More far-reaching currency, however, involves understanding the needs of children in groups and of individual children. Equally important is current knowledge of leadership principles, coupled with the ability to apply those principles on the job.

When directors keep current, they influence staff. Directors may provide new insights into children's development. They may gather information on successful and appropriate ways to document children's learning. They may also work out modern health care plans for staff. These are but a few of the ways in which directors keep staff alert and interested in their jobs. When directors exhibit current methods of running an organization, staff will benefit, but the organization, too, will share in those benefits.

Legal Issues Related to Keeping Current

Whether or not new information seems to benefit children, families, communities, and staff will probably be the leader's first concern. However, an essential reason for keeping current is to ensure that the organization stays within legal bounds. When new laws or rules regulating what is to happen in early childhood education situations are promulgated, they must be followed. Ignorance of their existence is unlikely to be an accepted excuse for noncompliance. Thus, it behooves leaders to know and follow legal changes. If, for example, there is a change in medical requirements for children, then directors must keep up-to-date on that topic. They need to know who will be affected by the new requirement, when it will go into effect, and what accommodations, if any, are made for children who are already enrolled. Directors must also communicate that information to staff and families and set up procedures to document that the new requirement is followed.

Some changes are broader, extending well beyond the field of children's programs. Perhaps a change is created in the tax structure. For example, if the state income tax is increased, the leader must make plans to revise the payroll computations so that each employee continues to receive the correct pay at the correct time. Simultaneously, the required amount must be provided to the state treasurer. What about the use of e-signatures signed into law in mid-2000? How will that affect your program? Will you consider changing to a system of e-signatures from parents and others, rather than requiring paper files? Directors must determine what accurate information is available, whether it applies to their programs, and what, if anything, will be done to change the center's policies.

Leaders should periodically ask themselves, "How current is my knowledge of teacher certification, program licensure, regulations regarding persons with special needs. Is my information about employment practices current? How accurate is the information I have about use of chemicals in settings occupied by young children? Are there new requirements for child nutrition?"

LEADER'S CORNER

When I took the job as executive director, I knew almost nothing about using a computer. I could send e-mail to my friends and I had ordered a few items online, but business usage was beyond me. Apparently, the previous director had felt the same way.

At the first board meeting, the president said to me, "You agreed when you were hired to bring our program into the twenty-first century. We are particularly concerned with the business aspects including fiscal reports. They should be computer generated as should children's and staff records."

I was embarrassed to say that in my two weeks on the job, I hadn't looked in to this issue. Board members graciously gave me several contacts for consultants and recommendations for software. It took me a while to get used to the system, but it works so well that I have volunteered to help other directors get started.

Director, multi-service children's agency

REFLECTION

Think about a situation in which you were responsible for keeping track of changes. Perhaps it involved changes in a course syllabus or course readings schedule. Perhaps there were frequent procedural changes where you worked. What were the approaches you used to accommodate to these unexpected changes? Were you able to employ any form of technology to make the changes easier?

Updating Understanding of the Leaders' Role

Leaders must also be cognizant of changes in the field of leadership. They must continue to learn about new research findings as they study the art and science of leadership. Evidence about effects of leadership styles continues to unfold. Examples include factors that motivate staff, more meaningful ways to work with adult learners, and components of team building. Continuing to function using one approach for years may be counterproductive as the work force changes. Consider newly developing ideas about team building. Learning about them and considering whether to use them should be high on the to-do list of every leader.

Leaders are responsible for ideas and information related specifically to the early childhood education profession. Leaders in this field should know what it takes to become accredited by the NAEYC. They should know or find out what is occurring with NAEYC's Accreditation Reinvention Project and how it will affect their centers. They should also be informed about other accreditation options. Early childhood leaders should be able to explain accepted practices in the field and why those are supported. In addition, they should be well-versed in approaches to modifying those practices based on the child's culture, individual needs, and individual interests. For example, with continued emphasis on literacy development, what does research tell us about how children learn to read? What is the role of the parent, of the teacher, and of the child? How does the burgeoning body of brain research relate to day-to-day classroom activities? Is there a connection?

REFLECTION

Think about possible sources of information you could access to determine what a well-versed early childhood leader would be expected to know. How will you go about finding these sources?

The breadth and depth of information with which early childhood education leaders are expected to be familiar can seem overwhelming. Nonetheless, knowledge in this field, as in most other fields, continues to grow at an exponential rate. Although this wealth of ideas is encouraging, it can also be intimidating. How can a leader cope with this abundance? When leaders look for current information, they face two dilemmas.

1. where to look for the information
2. how to judge its accuracy

In the next two sections, we will consider each of the dilemmas in turn.

Sources of Information

You are probably familiar with a wide range of sources of information that you use in your daily life. For example, if you wanted to plan a vacation, where would you find resources? How did you decide which college to attend and which courses to take? You may know where to get the best pizza in town or which clothing store has the best sales. You may also know how to get a loan with the lowest interest rate. Professional information may be found using similar types of sources. The sources described in this section are examples to get you started as you develop your own list of tools you will use to keep yourself current professionally.

REFLECTION

Think about a challenge you have encountered. What were the sources of information you sought to in order to meet the challenge? Was it necessary or helpful to seek more than one source? If you located widely differing information, how did you decide which was more sound?

Local Professional Groups

Leaders can join or form a group of people who are involved in the same field or who are concerned with the same issue. A good example is a group of child care center directors. They may choose to meet regularly to discuss whatever issues each of them wants to learn about, or they may organize around a specific issue, such as welfare reform and its effect on child care programs. No matter what the impetus for forming the group, maintaining it will allow members to give and receive support as they navigate their way through challenging responsibilities. Such a group will also present a united front as they address issues before legislators and other government officials. Some groups also arrange occasional social events, providing an opportunity to relax with people who have a clear understanding of the stresses under which each of them operates.

State and National Professional Organizations

The most widely recognized organization for early childhood leaders is the NAEYC. Its more than 100,000 members include many directors, supervisors, coordinators, center owners, teacher educators, and consultants. A large portion of the NAEYC's members works in classrooms. The NAEYC sponsors conferences, publications, position statements, and the journals *Young Children* and *Early Childhood Research Quarterly*. The NAEYC has many state and regional affiliates. The Association for Childhood Education International publishes *Childhood Education* and the *Journal for Reseach in Childhood Education*. Other professional organizations that help leaders keep current are found in Leaders' Resources.

Publications

Most of the major educational organizations publish journals. Some of these journals are oriented toward practitioners, that is, those people who are actually working directly in the field with clients (e.g., children, families, staff). Some organizations also provide research journals. These publications provide recent studies that describe and explain findings on relevant topics. Although practitioner journals are often *refereed,* research journals are always refereed. To referee a journal article means that the editor has sent each manuscript to several professionals who are knowledgeable about that topic. They respond by evaluating the manuscript and stating whether it should be printed, rejected, or revised. Reviewers also provide reasons for their decisions and usually give the author some guidance in terms of improving the manuscript. Almost all reviews are *blind reviews,* that is, the reviewer does not know the name of the author. Usually, the author will not know which reviewers were chosen to review a particular manuscript. That may be revealed when the article is being published. Using blind reviews helps ensure that materials that are published are worthwhile.

Additional magazines or journals not associated with a professional organization may also be of interest to leaders and staff members. For example, *Teacher* and *Pre-K to 8* include items that provide ideas and background information for staff at a range of levels. *Child Care Information Exchange* (CCIE) has for many years provided specific data and ideas for directors. Drawing on the work of a variety of experts, CCIE offers cutting edge information on child health, center environment, business practices, and classroom operation, among others. *Early Childhood Research and Practice* (ECRP) is a relative newcomer and appears on the internet only. It provides the added feature of video clips which enhance the articles and furnish immediate descriptions of points being made in the text. Watch for additional online journals.

Leaders should determine which journals are most helpful and subscribe to and read at least one regularly. Others may be obtained from libraries and, in some cases, online. Leaders should also provide subscriptions to one or more pertinent journals to be placed in the break room for staff use. Occasionally mentioning to a particular staff member or to the whole staff that a particular article is especially interesting will encourage them to keep up to date, too.

Not to be overlooked are local daily and weekly newspapers. These publications often contain items that alert leaders to local and national trends and issues. For example, concern about passing proficiency tests at the high school level in order to graduate has already pushed the emphasis on testing to earlier and earlier grades. Work is being done to determine appropriate curriculum for preschoolers and toddlers. Leaders must keep abreast with local and national activities on such issues. More important, they must become involved at whatever level they can sustain.

REFLECTION

Have you seen any articles about testing young children? Have you encountered instances of testing during the early years, perhaps in a practicum situation or while you were working in a center. How do you feel about this issue? What information can you obtain to help you analyze the situation? What would you tell staff and parents about testing? Be sure to go beyond your personal opinion.

Internet

Most of you are probably quite comfortable using the internet. However, if you are not, it is essential that, as a leader, you learn to use this tool. A skilled, disciplined user can obtain a wealth of valuable data fairly quickly. An undisciplined user can fritter away hours, becoming side-tracked with the wide variety of sites that are easily accessed.

Much of the information available in journals and at conference presentations is becoming available via computer. It can be down-loaded or printed if you find that format easier to read and study. When the full text is not available, you may be able to find references with call numbers so that you can locate a particular book or article quickly at main libraries. You may also be able to borrow them via interlibrary loan.

The internet also allows you to communicate quickly with others interested in the same topics. If you become involved in this sort of exchange, look for information and data. Opinions of others are interesting and may be valuable, but you'll definitely need factual information.

LEADER'S CORNER

I'm ashamed to say that I don't have a regular plan for keeping up with important information. But I do carry a folder in my briefcase. Then whenever I have a few minutes or longer, I take advantage of the time for reading. Last week, for example, I had a meeting with a potential funder at her office. She was unavoidably delayed about twenty minutes. Instead of being stressed, I pulled out a journal from my briefcase and read quite a bit.

Leader of a community agency

Conferences

Both the national associations and their affiliates sponsor conferences that provide excellent opportunities for keeping current. Regional and local organizations, colleges, and commercial groups also organize conferences. Speakers include practitioners, many of whom are experts at what they do. Most conferences highlight speakers whose wide reputation, knowledge, and communication skills provide valuable learning opportunities. Starting by attending a local or affiliate conference is a good idea and is often less costly. Leaders may find this choice especially important for newer staff who could be overwhelmed by 25,000+ people who gather at national conferences.

Leaders can help their staff members have good conference experiences by preparing them in advance for the fact that sessions often fill up quickly. Making a second and third choice in advance for each time period smooths the way. Then, if the desired session has reached capacity before you arrive, you can go to your next choice. The rather hectic pace of obtaining parking, food and beverages, and even a spot in the restroom line may be challenging for inexperienced conference goers. Arranging for a buddy to accompany a new conferee may enhance the experience. When they return to the center, they can share what they have learned with the rest of the staff. Perhaps they could also prepare an article for the parent newsletter or give a brief report at a board meeting.

A major attraction at conferences is the opportunity to see and often try out a huge range of classroom equipment and supplies and a wide variety of books for children and educators. Keep in mind that the exhibits are screened minimally, if at all. Thus, some products may be quite inappropriate, at least for your center. Staff members may need to be alerted in advance to that fact.

Do you remember the opening scenario in which LaTicia and Jaime were discussing planning a conference? Often, leaders in an area will be the driving force behind planning and implementing local conferences. In this way, they provide a service to staff members who cannot afford to travel or who cannot be absent from their center for several days. Although Jaime and LaTicia have a great idea, perhaps they will also think about including some sessions for leaders.

Continuing Education

Although you are probably currently immersed in education, whether you are taking one class or a whole program, your learning certainly should not stop when that work is completed. No matter how knowledgeable you are, it is essential that you engage in continuing your education in some organized manner. Perhaps you will take one course at a nearby college or via distance learning every year or two. Or you may attend a weeklong symposium on a topic of interest, such as how to develop an appropriate infant care program or working with children who have been abused. You may choose to attend a weekly series in your community, perhaps on working with families in time of divorce, writing successful grant proposals, or new child care center regulations. You may also decide to work toward an advanced degree in your particular field or one that is related. The point is that you will be moving forward, recognizing that the body of knowledge in this field and in almost every field changes rapidly. Each time you participate in a new learning experience, you will bring more knowledge to that experience and will take away new perspectives. During the learning situation, you will have much to share with colleagues and to learn from them as well as from the presenter or instructor.

When you have decided which of the many opportunities for continuing education you will choose, be sure to find out who sponsors the session or program. Also check on who the instructor will be and what qualifications that person has. Will the information be presented at a basic, beginning level, or will it be more advanced? Certainly, you will want to match your own needs relative to level. If you have been using a computer for years and have produced a wide range of types of documents, you will obviously want a very advanced computer course, probably on a specific kind of software or usage. If you know little or nothing about brain research as it might apply to the classroom, you will need a beginning course.

Check on the cost of the options you are interested in. Does the cost of a symposium cover materials? Lodging? Meals? Will you be able to obtain college credit? If so, to what will it apply? Will there be an additional charge? Will there be additional expectations from you? Is there a price break if two or more people from one organization sign up? Will your organization provide funding? If not, will you be able to deduct your expenses on your income tax return?

Personal Contacts

Right now, you can probably think of many people whom you know who could provide you with information. Perhaps the person who sits next to you in class takes great notes and could help you when you can't decode yours. Perhaps there is a woman in your dorm who can tell you where to shop for just about anything at the best price and best quality, too. And what about the friend who told you what was wrong with your car when it kept making that grinding noise? It's a good thing you found out that you had to take it to the mechanic right away. Being stuck on the highway is no fun.

The kinds of contacts you have now may or may not be the same ones you will need when you assume the role of leader. But the fact that you have and use contacts can demonstrate to you the importance of this type of association. For example, what does the director of a center do when she cannot find a teacher to replace the one who has just resigned? Contacts in the field may be a big help. Let's suppose you are a director who needs to purchase several new cribs for the infant room. Where can you find the best price, the best quality, and speedy delivery? Checking with a couple of your peers may give you some good answers.

Sometimes your contacts may be individuals who provide the great service of friendly and professional listening. When you are in the leadership role, although you have very positive relations with your staff, you also are operating at a different level. There will often be topics which you cannot and should not discuss with them. Many times these are thoughts that you would just like to "get off your chest." Having someone who understands your role can be a stress reliever. Perhaps you have a staff member who does a great job in the classroom but is consistently late to work. You are working on this, but you are losing patience. Just talking about it with a peer can help.

Keep in mind that when you discuss issues relating to your center, no matter how stressed you are, you must maintain confidentiality. You are not free to name names or provide descriptions that would make an identity clear. To do so would be unethical and possibly illegal.

REFLECTION

Have you ever been in a situation in which someone told you something about another person? Perhaps you thought afterwards that it really was not appropriate to pass that information on to you. What will you do if that happens again? You may also be in situations in which you are asked for confidential information. How will you handle a parent's question such as, "What's wrong with that Hendricks child?"

As you seek out contacts to support you, others will also view you as part of their support system. Think about the kinds of support you can offer. If you have learned about active listening in terms of working with children, families, and staff, then you will certainly be able to use that same valuable tool in listening to a fellow director or supervisor. As the listener, you too must maintain confidentiality. If you feel that your colleague is going out of bounds in telling you about a person or situation, you must be responsible to tactfully point that out. In fact, as you participate in classes and in practicum or perhaps student teaching and as you work in centers, now is the time to check yourself to see that you are following the important principle of maintaining confidentiality.

Consider that board members can be important sources of current information. Sometimes you may obtain new ways of thinking by paying close attention at board meetings. Some of the ideas that may seem relatively minor at the time may help you manage your work in the future. Perhaps a board member describes changes in the way her company is handling employee benefits. Although that may not be a current issue at your center, the concepts involved may be applicable at a future date. During pre-meeting informal conversation, a board member may describe a parent activity at his child's elementary school. It could be something for you to make note of for future reference.

Your own staff members are also valuable sources of knowledge. Each of us brings a particular background to the workplace. We each have had and continue to have a range of experiences and understandings. Listening to staff provides a wealth of creative ideas. Asking staff for their thinking on a matter not only provides the ideas, but also empowers them as they recognize how valuable they are to the organization.

Do not forget about parents as sources of information. Most people in early childhood understand that parents know their own children better than anyone else does. But do we realize that parents know far more than their children? They have experiences, interests, jobs, and connections-all wonderful sources of information for alert leaders. Parents are also usually strong supporters of their children's center and are willing to share ideas, time, and energy.

Evaluating Information

Although you will generally welcome the fact that so much information is readily available on a wide range of topics, you will also be stymied at times. Some of what you uncover may directly conflict with other reports or ideas. How do you know which to follow?

In evaluating information, first consider the source. What are the qualifications of the person with whom you spoke or the author of the article? Although the individual may be well-versed in elementary education, does that person also have a strong background in early childhood education? In the area of finance, your consultant may know a lot about for-profit companies and large corporations. Is that consultant's knowledge equally strong when it comes to not-for-profit agencies or agencies with very small budgets? Some authorities are not particularly interested in what they perceive to be small problems. Others are deeply committed to assisting such groups. Do not be afraid to ask about the background of the person with whom you are speaking or to check on the author of a book, paper, or website.

In some cases, you will be provided with minimal information that may be misleading. How often have you read a headline and very short article stating that a particular food has been found to be beneficial to health? Perhaps a month later, you read about the same food and find that it is detrimental to one's health. It may be that the circumstances in the two studies varied widely. Perhaps the subjects in one study were men only, whereas the other study examined a range of people. It is usually smart to avoid very brief articles—Delve further into the details. Who is presenting the ideas? What is the basis for the findings? Try to check with more than one source.

Because the internet is still relatively new, some users tend to believe that if they found it on the internet, it must be valid. Here, too, it is essential to check the source. Virtually anyone can post ideas and comments on the internet. The speed of accessing the internet and distributing information to perhaps thousands of people means that you must be extra cautious. It might not be too difficult to believe that a Congressperson has proposed a five-cent tax on every e-mail and to forward that message to everyone you know. If that happened to you, did you retract it with e-mails to everyone when you were told it was a hoax? Keeping a list of reliable websites can help you determine the validity of what you might find.

Although none of us can be expected to know all the people who are writing and speaking on issues related to early childhood education, knowing where the work has been published often provides some credibility. Generally, major organizations select main speakers carefully. Nonetheless, no one can control what a speaker will say. Each of us still has the responsibility for checking information we receive as much as is reasonably possible. The more we work to maintain our own professional currency, the better the chance that we will not be misled.

Making Time to Keep Current

Leaders must set aside a particular time weekly to address current information. Every leader is constantly in demand, with staff and other constituents needing frequent communication. Despite this fact, leaders must plan their time. It is accepted practice that a center director will have specific times during each day or week when the "Do not disturb except in an emergency" sign is posted either literally or figuratively. This procedure allows the director to accomplish paperwork, planning, conferences, and so forth. Directors can add a weekly half-hour to that secluded time and allocate it for learning about current information in the field. Many leaders will rightly point out that thirty minutes is inadequate. Perhaps many more directors will assume that this period would be impossible in their schedules. However, failure to learn about current information and issues may prove to be quite costly in terms of both time and money.

Directors must also help staff members find time to acquire current information that impacts their work. Again, the cry may go up, "There simply isn't time." But helping the staff update their thinking and understanding will bring them an increased sense of being a professional early childhood educator who is respected for both knowledge and skills. Keeping current in one's profession provides the realization that the work that early childhood educators do is based on theory and research, rather than on merely following procedural steps. Providing staff with growth opportunities will also demonstrate to families that the people caring for their children are doing so as professionals. As in most professions, early childhood educators continue to grow and learn.

Using Ethics Codes to Make Professional Decisions

Even when directors have access to excellent resources and have kept current with what is happening in the field, there will still be challenges. One such challenge is an ethical dilemma. In such a situation, it is not clear what action one should take. Covey sees ethics as "ultimately grounded in commitment to doing right things" (1992, p. 105). To help leaders and staff members in most professions cope with these situations, many professional organizations have created codes of ethics. These codes can guide decision-makers, but they do not provide a recipe for what to do. Some of the codes that may help early childhood education professionals are:

- The NAEYC Code of Ethical Conduct
- The Code of Ethics of the Division of Early Childhood Council for Exceptional Children
- The Code of Ethics of the Education Profession (National Education Association, NEA)

Leaders and most staff members in early childhood education need a code of ethics because they have a fair amount of autonomy in decision-making, rather than detailed prescribed behaviors.

The NAEYC code is divided into four sections, addressing our ethical responsibilities to children, families, colleagues, and community and society. Each of the four areas contains ideals and principles. "The ideals reflect the aspirations of practitioners. The principles are intended to guide conduct and assist practitioners in resolving ethical dilemmas encountered in the field" (NAEYC, 1998).

Although leaders must uphold the entire NAEYC code, of particular interest is the section on colleagues regarding responsibility to employees. The ideas in this section revolve around respect for employees, creation of a climate of trust, and attempts "to secure equitable compensation" (NAEYC, 1998). In the principles section, the code addresses working conditions, personnel policies, and staff evaluations, among others.

It is the leader's responsibility to be familiar with the code and how to use it and to use it in addressing ethical dilemmas. Providing copies for every staff member and making them available to parents will solidify understanding that this is a professional organization and that its staff know and follow a professional code of ethics. Leaders must provide training for staff members so that they understand how and when to use the code.

The Leader As an Advocate

Although leaders in child care programs are generally quite busy tending to the work of their agencies, more attention must be devoted to moving beyond the centers to the community and particularly to grass roots politics. Once leaders recognize the influence that government and business have on their day-to-day lives, it may be easier for them to become involved.

One of the first steps is to form alliances with others in the early childhood field. Influential people are more likely to listen to a cohesive group representing a number of programs and a large number of employees, families, and children. Leaders who are well-established in the profession have an obligation to move into this arena.

The next step is to determine what the field needs and to develop a plan to work together to meet those needs. Such a plan entails identifying the people in power and what they are interested in. It involves understanding how decisions are made in a particular community and governmental body. If legislation is likely to be needed, then advocates must understand the process of creating such legislation. They must also be aware of the history of the issue for which they are working. Have bills been presented within the last few years? If so, why were they defeated and by whom? Who is likely to support such legislation now? Who would be the best representatives to send to meet with those who can influence the decision? Of course, sending representatives does not preclude involving as many advocates as possible in letter writing and so forth. Carefully assessing the climate will help early childhood leaders determine whether demonstrations of strength on the state capitol lawn are called for or whether additional preparatory work is needed. Enlisting the support of key community leaders who have the ear of the decision-makers often moves an agenda quickly.

Leaders often find strength and support from major professional organizations. These organizations may have staff members who have researched issues and can provide background information. Note that leaders, who themselves conduct research, are also contributing to the advocacy role. Decision-makers value data and are more likely to listen to arguments backed by research. Other advocates may focus on the media, providing information that will help the public understand and ask for the kinds of services for children and families that are needed.

Some advocacy initiatives take a long time to come to fruition. Advocates must understand how to balance assertiveness and patience. Demanding to be heard is not always the best route to take, nor is waiting until someone else brings up a position. In the face of a defeat, advocates must support one another and return to the important work of reaching a goal with a renewed sense of purpose and self-confidence (Rodd, 1994; VanderVen, 2000).

A well-known child care advocate, Helen Blank (1997) explains the politics of deciding which issues to focus on, when to relinquish parts of the plan, and how to form a coalition. Blank describes the strategies used in a number of successful advocacy attempts. Bowman and Kagan (1997) call for a broadened understanding "of what leadership is and how it is best produced. . . . Leaders should be understood to include those individuals who contribute to the field through research, teaching, scholarship, and advocacy and those who work at local, state, and national levels, as well as those who provide direct services to children and families" (p. 158).

Summary

Resources surround each of us. Some of them may seem to be hidden or disguised, whereas others are more obvious. In some locations, a greater variety of resources are available, but with the combination of the knowledge explosion and the communications breakthroughs that continue to mount, no leader has reason to lag behind. Leaders must find and use these resources in the service of leading.

To lead effectively, leaders must be familiar with and use the code of ethics to which their profession has committed. They must ensure that their colleagues are familiar with the code and encourage support of its principles.

Finally, a broader definition of leadership is needed in order to move the field forward. Such a definition encompasses the many facets of advocacy. This broadened definition makes eminently clear the need for support and training for leaders interested in the well-being of children and their families.

Class Assignments

1. Choose a topic related to advocacy. Research your topic using at least three types of resources. Write your findings on Working Paper 8–1. Examples of advocacy topics include licensure for preschool teachers, food programs for children, standardized testing, and many others

2. Working with a partner, interview a leader. Find out how this leader keeps current. Write the results of your interview on Working Paper 8–2.

Class Exercises

1. Discuss in class the sources you used for Class Assignment 1. What difficulties did you have as you attempted to use various resources? Which sources were relatively easy to access?

2. Work in small groups. Share experiences, interests, and knowledge you have which might help others in early childhood. Although some of you may feel uncomfortable about doing this and may feel that what you say would be seen as bragging, remember the goal is to help fellow professionals. If you are aware of a skill or knowledge that another group member has, you may share that, too. For example, perhaps you know that the person sitting next to you was responsible for locating and ordering all the supplies needed for "Clean-up Our Neighborhood Schools Day." Those skills could certainly apply to a child care center director's work in locating and ordering supplies.

Working Paper 8–1

The topic I have chosen to research is:

_____

The three resources I used were:

1. _____

2. _____

3. _____

Summary of what I learned:

Working Paper 8–2

The leader who I interviewed was _____

During the interview I learned:

Leader's Resource 8–1

NAMES AND ADDRESSES OF PROFESSIONAL ORGANIZATIONS AND SOURCES FOR LEADERSHIP EDUCATION

Association for Childhood Education International
The Olney Professional Building
17904 Georgia Ave, Ste 215
Olney, MD 20832
http://www.acei.org

Association for Supervision and Curriculum Development
1703 N. Beauregard St.
Alexandria, VA 22311-1714

Center for Career Development in Early Care and Education
Wheelock College
200 The Riverway
Boston, MA 02215
http://ericps.crc.uiuc.edu/ccdece/ccdece.html

The Center for Early Childhood Leadership
National Louis University
1000 Capitol Dr
Wheeling, IL 60090-7201
www.nl.edu/cecl

Council for Early Childhood Professional Recognition
2460 16th St NW
Washington, DC 20009
http://www.cdacouncil.org

ERIC Clearinghouse on Elementary and Early Childhood Education
University of Illinois
51 Gerty Dr
Champaign, IL 61820-7469
http://ericeece.org

ERIC National Library of Education
Office of Educational Research and Improvement
U.S. Department of Education
http://www.accesseric.org

The Forum for Early Childhood Organization and Leadership Development
Henry W. Bloch School of Business and Public Administration
University of Missouri—Kansas City
5100 Rockhill Rd
Kansas City, MO 64110-2499
http://cctr.umkc.edu/user/mcnl/

Head Start—Johnson and Johnson Management Fellows Program
University of California, Los Angeles
110 Westwood Plaza
Box 951481
Los Angeles, CA 90095
http://www.anderson.ucla.edu/

Leadership Development Program
Bank St. College of Education
210 W 112th St
New York, NY 10025
www.bnkst.edu

National Association of Child Care Resource and Referral Agencies (NACCRRA)
1319 F St, NW
Washington, DC 20004-1106
http://www.naccrra.net

National Association for the Education of Young Children (NAEYC)
1509 16th St NW
Washington, DC 20036-1426
http://www.naeyc.org

National Association of Early Childhood Specialists in State Departments of
    Education
http://ericps.crc.uiuc.edu/naecs/

National Child Care Information Center (NCCIC)
http://nccic.org

World Organization for Early Childhood Education
U.S. National Committee
http://omep-us.crc.uicu.edu/

References

Blank, H. (1997). Advocacy Leadership, In Kagan, S. L., and Bowman, B. T. (Eds.), *Leadership in early care and education.* Washington, DC: ASYC.

Bowman, B. T., and Kagan, S. L. (1997). Moving the leadership agenda, In Kagan, S. L., and Bowman, B. T., (Eds.) *Leadership in early care and education.* Washington, DC.: AEYC.

Covey, S. (1992). *Principle-centered leadership*. New York: Simon & Schuster (Fireside Edition).

National Association for the Education of Young Children. (1998). *Code of ethical conduct and statement of commitment*. Washington, DC: NAEYC.

Rodd, J. (1994). *Leadership in early childhood: The pathway to professionalism.* New York: Teachers College.

VanderVen, K. (2000). Capturing the breadth and depth of the job: The administrator as influential leader in a complex world, In Culkin, M. L., (Ed.) *Managing quality in young children's programs*. New York: Teachers College.

Leader's Resource

Culture

Schein, E. H., (1992) *Organizational culture and Leadership,* 2nd ed., San Francisco, CA: Jossey-Bass. This book contains a wealth of information about organizational cultures and is useful for leaders and managers as well as students who are trying to understand organization. The reader will find detailed discussions of the dimensions of organizational culture, the role of the leader interpreting and building the culture, and helpful insights into how organizational culture changes and evolves.

Leadership

The Art of Leadership: Managing Early Childhood Organizations (Vol. 1 & 2), (1998), Neugebauer B. and Neugebauer R., (Eds), Redmond, WA: Child Care Information Exchange. This two-volume work is a compilation of articles by numerous authors. The articles deal with various aspects of leadership, including what it means to be a leader and the responsibilities of those in leadership positions. There are articles in Volume 1 on advocacy for children and families, organizational management, and legal issues and questions. The articles in Volume 2 cover various aspects of working with staff, including staff selection, supervision, staff development, and evaluation. The final article in Volume 2 covers working with parents and community relations, including marketing and community outreach. There is also a comprehensive list of references at the end of Volume 2.

Begley, P. T. (Ed.), (1999) *Values and Educational leadership,* Albany, NY: State University of New York. An examination of how personal and professional values come into play in educational settings. One chapter is devoted to the issue of moral education.

Bennis, W. (1994). *On Becoming a Leader,* (1994) Reading MA: Addison-Wesley. The author has written a number of books on the topic of leadership, has researched his topic well, and is a frequent speaker on the national circuit. He identifies what one must do to become a successful leader.

Bloom, P. J., Shearer, M., and Britz, J. (1991). *Blueprint for Action,* Lake Forest, IL: New Horizons. Blueprint for Action offers leaders helpful information on staff development and center improvement. This book has sections on organizational culture and the director's role in change, assessing needs and climate, performance appraisal and staff development. There are numerous forms, questionnaires, assessment tools and checklists related to the areas covered in this book.

Bloom, P. J., (2000). *Circle of Influence: Implementing Shared Decision Making and Participative Management,* Lake Forest, IL: New Horizons. This book serves as a guide to leaders who wish to have teaching staff actively involved in decision-making. Bloom point out that participative management is based on trust. It requires time, persistence, and patience to reach the high-quality program functioning that is attainable through participative management. Some of the important questions addressed here are: How do you perceive power? Who are the stakeholders? Who should be involved in making decisions?

Culkin, M. L., (Ed.), (2000). *Managing Quality in Young Children's Programs,* New York: Teachers College Press. This compilation of informative articles by many outstanding leaders in the field of early childhood includes information on roles, duties and responsibilities of program directors, plus a good overview of the issues, concerns, and future plans for credentialling program directors.

Covey, S. R., (1992). *Principle-Centered Leadership.* New York: Simon & Shuster. So many people live by Covey's earlier work, *The 7 Habits of Highly Effective People,* that it is not surprising that this newer book is also widely read. As before, Covey emphasizes achieving balance in life.

Conger, J. A., Lawler, M., and Lawler, E. E., III, (Eds.), (1999). *The Leader's Change Handbook: An Essential Guide to Setting Direction and Taking Action,* San Francisco: Jossey-Bass. As more and more of leader's time is spent planning and implementing change, this book provides insightful commentary on how to make change happen as smoothly as possible.

Dunklee, D. L., (2000). *If You Want to Lead, Not Just Manage: A Primer for Principals.* Thousand Oaks, CA: Corwin Press. Although the author addresses school principals specifically, the contrast between leadership and management provides valuable insights for all would-be leaders.

Kagan, S. L. & Bowman, B. (Eds.), (1997). *Leadership in Early Care and Education.* Washington, DC: National Association for the Education of Young Children. Two prominent women, each of whom has earned a stellar leadership reputation, have brought together a broad spectrum of authors who present equally broad group of leadership issues.

Kouzes, J. M. & Posner, B. Z., (1999). *Encouraging the Heart: A Leader's Guide to Rewarding and Recognizing Others.* San Francisco: Jossey-Bass, 1999. Recognizing the importance of the influence leaders have over their followers, Kouzes and Posner encourage readers to take a very psychosocial approach to the workplace. They present a picture of a positive, well-organized plan.

Pellicer, L. O. & Anderson, L. W. (1995). *A Handbook for Teacher Leaders,* Thousand Oaks, CA: Corwin Press. Although intended for teachers who assume leadership roles in public schools, sections of this book are useful for educational leaders in other settings. The information on creating helping relationships and helping teachers make decisions and grow professionally are well done and apply to leaders/supervisors in early childhood settings.

Yukl, G. A. (1989). *Leadership in Organizations,* 2nd ed., Englewood Cliffs, NJ: Prentice-Hall. If you are new to the field of leadership or if you are moving on to a more complex leadership situation, you will benefit from the very clear presentation of what the leader's role entails. The author also provides a thorough grounding in the research in the field, giving credence to the principles he espouses.

Staffing

Whitebrook, M., and Bellm, D., (1999). *Taking on Turnover: An Action Guide for Child Care Teachers and Directors,* Washington, DC: Center for the Child Care Workforce. Starting with a startling statistic that at least one-third of the child care workforce leaves the job each year, this book examines the turnover problem. It not only examines this current problem, but also reviews the effect of turnover on children and families. An action plan to reduce turnover includes ideas about how to focus attention on the three things that can contribute to stabilizing your workforce: (1) work environment, (2) hiring practices, and (3) compensation.

Supervision

Caruso, J. J. and Fawcett, T., (1999). *Supervision in Early Childhood Education: A Developmental Perspective* (2nd ed.), New York: Teachers College. Directors, educational coordinators, and consultants will find this book helpful. It is a practical guide to supervision covering supervisors' roles and responsibilities and aspects of supervision and staff development.

Sergiovanni, T. J. and Starratt, R. J. (1998). *Supervision: A Redefinition,* 6th ed., Boston: McGraw Hill. Although rather public school-oriented, the authors provide readers with a welcome guide to use when their role calls for staff supervision. Both large and small issues are addressed.

Index

68005796R00146

Made in the USA
San Bernardino, CA
29 January 2018